Other Books by Jack and Marcia Kelly

Sanctuaries: A Guide to Lodgings in Monasteries, Abbeys, and Retreats of the United States

   The Northeast

   The West Coast and Southwest

One Hundred Graces: Mealtime Blessings
   (editors)

The Whole Heaven Catalog: A Resource Guide to Products, Services, Arts, Crafts, and Festivals of Religious, Spiritual, and Cooperative Communities

by Marcia Kelly

Heavenly Feasts: Memorable Meals from Monasteries, Abbeys, and Retreats

Sanctuaries

The Complete United States
Updated Edition

A Guide to Lodgings in Monasteries, Abbeys, and Retreats

Jack and Marcia Kelly

AN AUTHORS GUILD BACKINPRINT.COM EDITION

iUNIVERSE, INC.
NEW YORK   BLOOMINGTON

Sanctuaries, The Complete United States
A Guide to Lodgings in Monasteries, Abbeys, and Retreats

iUniverse books may be ordered through booksellers or by contacting:

iUniverse
1663 Liberty Drive
Bloomington, IN 47403
www.iuniverse.com
1-800-Authors (1-800-288-4677)

Because of the dynamic nature of the Internet, any Web addresses or links contained in this book may have changed since publication and may no longer be valid.

ISBN: 978-1-4401-8160-3 (sc)

Printed in the United States of America

iUniverse rev. date: 12/18/2009

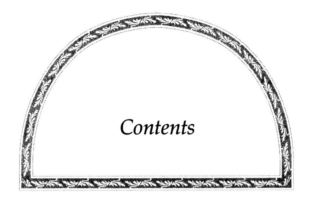

Contents

CONTENTS

CONTENTS

CONTENTS

Special thanks to these friends and all the others whose generous help, encouragement, hospitality, interest, and advice were essential to the successful completion of our *Sanctuaries* U.S.A. series: Jennie and Jack Blumenthal, Liz Conners, Sister Donald Corcoran and the Transfiguration Monastery community, Maggie Eidem, Judith Emery, Millie and Jim Harford, Carole Kraus, Katherine Latour, Robert Lax, Toinette Lippe, Geordie and Tom Miller, Kathleen Norris, Ram Dass, and Judith Stanton.

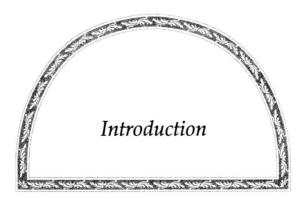

Introduction

This book reflects our travels to monasteries, abbeys, and retreats throughout the United States. We've found each region to be unique: the Northeast with its forests and meadows, and views of the Atlantic; the West and Southwest with awe-inspiring mountains and deserts; the South with palm trees and lush vegetation; the Midwest prairies and miles of fertile farmland. We found much similarity: an open door, welcoming smiles, a quiet chapel, a secluded path, or a lakeside bench—inviting one to take time to reflect, away from busy lives.

Many of you have written us with thanks for the lovely experiences you've had visiting the monasteries, abbeys, and retreats in our first two *Sanctuaries* covering the Northeast and the West Coast and Southwest. Most of these letters also asked when we planned to do books that would include the rest of the country. This volume is the response to those questions. We've chosen representative places from the first two volumes, and added our visits to the Southeast, the Deep South, Texas, Oklahoma, Utah, Missouri, and across the Midwest as far as North Dakota. Although we haven't visited every state, we've included listings from all of them, and added a list of Jewish retreats along with our "Other Places" section at the end of the book. Someday we hope to visit that exotic-sounding list from Hawaii, and make the journey north to Alaska, but until then we'll have to rely on you to report back to us with your impressions, or with places we've missed altogether. You'll notice that we've included more places from some states than others and this is because those states *have* more retreats.

Many people thought that there were no accommodations for couples, others that you could visit only if you were of the same religion as the monastery, and many didn't realize that you could stay overnight. The following basics will help to clarify some of these points.

Philosophy An essay on silence and hospitality by the abbess of St. Walburga's in Colorado says, "Who are visitors but friends we haven't met yet . . . guests who enter our property for a moment, perhaps in need of a blessing, a prayer, a welcoming thought?" The places that have chosen a ministry of hospitality do so with a spirit of openness and warmth, and unless noted in the text, welcome people of all faiths, with no requirement to attend any services or participate in any activities. You are free to join the community in prayer or just enjoy the surroundings, and no attempt will be made to urge you to do anything other than what you choose. We came as casual guests, for short visits, and our observations reflect this experience, not what it might be like as long-term residents.

A few of the places worry that travelers will come with the intention of using their centers as a motel during sightseeing and vacation trips, and will find themselves in conflict with the spirit of quiet and the early hours. Most places are contemplative communities which invite people to share their life and prayer. So do let them know when you call to make your reservation that you are looking for a sanctuary, a respite, a place of quiet retreat, and that their place seemed just right for you.

Purpose Monasteries and abbeys are usually functioning religious communities that have some rooms for visitors, while the purpose of retreat houses is to provide a setting for groups to hold meetings or retreats. There are often rooms available for individuals (private retreatants) even when a group retreat is going on. Individuals can sometimes participate in the group sessions, and can almost always join in prayer services. It is important to remember that the people who live in these places are not prepared to do psychological counseling, so don't make a retreat if that is your expectation or need.

Settings and accommodations We stayed in everything from a riverside plantation once owned by Clare Boothe Luce to seaside estates with tropical gardens to simple cabins in the woods, reached only by a swaying suspension bridge. We visited a Mennonite farm with a beautifully refurbished barn where retreatants stay, and a Marcel Breuer–designed monastery in the middle of the Great Plains.

Some places have hermitages, usually for one person who would like to be alone, sometimes for two. Although many of the buildings were once houses of the very rich, the accommodations are usually simple, though comfortable and clean. Most places welcome men, women, and children. Any variations are noted in the text. Where dormitory space is provided, it is separate for men and women in most cases. Though most have double rooms that can be shared by couples, a few places have only singles, and men and women are in different sections.

You should not bring pets with you, but you will encounter resident cats and dogs from time to time. On the western trip we also met resident llamas, peacocks, emus, and even a bobcat!

Costs   There is an effort to keep the fees moderate, although in many cases they do not cover all the expenses, so supplemental donations are gratefully accepted. If the fee is a burden, special arrangements can be discussed. Many places have work/study programs, some have work/exchange available for a period of time. Prices for 1995 ranged from $25 to $175 a night, often with reduced rates for longer stays. Fees usually include three meals a day, but it's important to confirm meal arrangements when making reservations. Some places have cooks only when a group is coming, so you may have to bring your own food or dine in the area.

Customs, comportment, attire   It is a custom in this world to "turn the bed," or make the bed with fresh sheets for the next guest. One monastery asks you to say a little blessing for the next guest as you prepare the bed. Occasionally you may have to bring your own linens or sleeping bag, something you should ask about when making reservations. In some places, guests are expected to pitch in and help with chores (this is noted in the text); in others, the staff prefer no help at all. Work on the property, with the community, is usually available on request.

Courtesy and sensitivity to others is the general rule. Guests and community are there for quiet and contemplation, so radios, typewriters, and chatting in the hallways or chapel will only be disturbing. Following the lead of the community will easily carry you through any local customs.

Attire can be casual, though it should be respectful in those places that are religious communities. We've included some hot springs and other nonreligious retreats that are extremely informal in every way. Many in the religious communities wear work shirts and jeans except when in chapel, though guests may dress casually even there. We certainly didn't immediately identify the man in overalls and a baseball cap who waved at us from his bicycle as a monk!

INTRODUCTION

Reservations   Reservations are essential. Some places are booked weeks or months ahead on weekends, particularly for groups. Individuals can often get a bed with less notice, and weekdays are easier for all. In any case, do not appear without having called ahead. If you can't come, be sure to give as much notice as possible, or if it's at the last minute, offer to forfeit the fee, since these communities depend on the income to survive. If you request a brochure with details about a particular place, one will be mailed to you.

Transportation   To help orient you geographically, we have included driving directions, but some places are very hard to find, so be prepared for wrong turns. In snowy areas, chains and sand are a good added precaution. Most places have directions in their brochures for arrival by car or public transportation. Many can arrange to meet you at the airport or station.

What to bring   It's a good idea to bring a flashlight to find your way at night, on walks, down the hall to the bathroom, or along the path to the outhouse! We stayed in one place that had not only flashlights but umbrellas in every room, but that is rare. Be prepared with extra sweaters in cold weather and cool clothes in the summer; often there's a place to swim on the property or nearby, so pack bathing suits for those places that require them. Be sure to ask if you need to bring any food or linens.

Day visits   Many of the places are available to individuals or groups for day use.

Access for the disabled   Be sure to inquire ahead. Some places are equipped, and others are still in the process of making everything completely accessible.

Other places   In the first two books, at the end of every state we had a list of additional places that were recommended to us but which we had not visited. In this volume, we have put the "Other Places" all together at the end of the book, alphabetically by state and then by city. This edition includes featured places listed in the two regional guides.

Conclusion   This book is the result of our visits to more than 250 monasteries, abbeys, and retreats, and the experience has been enriching beyond words. What a blessing to have had the opportunity to be welcomed into such places, reminding us of the many faces and manifestations of God. Though we visited many spiritual paths, we found that loving kindness was a language all had in common, reason enough for continued visits with these special people.

C A N A

Seattle

WA 242

248
240

246

ND

194   192

Portland

202

206

204
200

OR

SD

48

ID

WY

NE

16

228

26
36
50   44
54

20   34

NV

UT

60

CO

KS

San Francisco

56
30
52
32

CA

58

148

146 • Santa Fe

150

144

10

6

14

AZ

152

OK

18

NM

Santa Barbara

22
24
28   Los Angeles

42

38
46

40

8

Tucson •

12

TX

Gulf of
California

226

M E X I C O

The numbers on the map correspond to the page

numbers on which the Sanctuaries are described.

Hinduism
"In the effulgent lotus of the heart dwells Brahman, the Light of lights."—*Mundaka Upanishad*

Judaism
"The Lord is my Light; whom shall I fear?"—*Psalms*

Shinto
"The light of Divine Amaterasu shines forever."—*Kurozumi Munetada*

Taoism
"Following the Light, the sage takes care of all."—Lao Tsu

Buddhism
"The radiance of Buddha shines ceaselessly."—*Dhammapada*

Christianity
"I have come into the world as Light."—*Holy Bible*

Islam
"Allah is the Light of the heavens and the earth."—*Holy Koran*

Sikhism
"God, being Truth, is the one Light of all."—*Adi Granth*

African Faiths
"God is the sun beaming light everywhere."—Tribal African

Native American Faiths
"The light of Wakan-Tanka is upon my people."—Song of Kablaya

Other Known Faiths
"Truth is one, paths are many."

Faiths Still Unknown

Quotes taken from the Light of Truth Universal Shrine (LOTUS), Satchidananda Ashram—Yogaville, Buckingham, Virginia

Sanctuaries

The Complete United States

Benedictine Spirituality and Conference Center of Sacred Heart Monastery
Cullman, AL

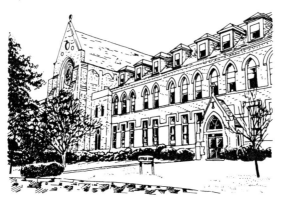

Sacred Heart Monastery was formed by the union of two branches of the same Benedictine motherhouse in Elk County, Pennsylvania. Sisters from Covington, Kentucky, and St. Leo, Florida, came together to northern Alabama to found a school for German immigrants during the late 1800s. In 1902, they bought 200 acres and built the main monastery to house the community and students. As one sister explained: "We were always building at the wrong time. In 1902 when we had no money, in 1929 at the beginning of the Depression, then in the 1940s during World War II."

This is a splendid complex and it is a pleasure to walk the halls with 15-foot ceilings and visit the chapel where the community gathers to pray four times a day. Mass is celebrated daily at different times to accommodate the schedules of this warm community, which includes an amazing array of talents: administrators, teachers, chaplains, nurses, a lawyer, and a legal secretary. They have a variety of ministries according to the gifts of the members and the needs of the church, including apartments for the elderly. Their mission statement says that they are a channel through which the monastic community shares with the people of God its particular charism, which includes praying the liturgy, celebrating the Eucharist in a monastic setting, and witnessing the value of community living.

The sisters present programs throughout the year on spiritual topics: the Gospels, Assessing and Developing the Skills in Love, the Enneagram, Centering Prayer, and Women's Spirituality. They host

Elderhostels and retreats for Lent, Advent, and Holy Week. There are rooms in former dormitories with shared baths. Delicious food is served buffet-style with the community.

Down the road and across the creek is St. Bernard's Benedictine Abbey, which also has a retreat program and guesthouse. The grotto there, miniature scenes in stone—a labor of many years by one of the monks—is well worth a visit.

Benedictine Spirituality and Conference Center
Sacred Heart Monastery
916 Convent Road
Cullman, AL 35055
(216) 734-8302
www.shmon@shmon.org

Visitation Monastery
Mobile, AL

This monastery traces its beginning to 1832 when five sisters arrived by ship from Georgetown in Washington, D.C., to establish a school at the request of the first bishop of Mobile. There were 40 pupils that year, and through the trust and generosity of many southern families, the number of students grew. The history of the community reads like a southern adventure novel. A tornado swept through on the evening of March 24, 1840, and in seven minutes the little monastery school of seven years was demolished. An eyewitness wrote: "No ray save the lightning's vivid flash shone upon this scene of terror," leaving "no roof above save the vault of an angry sky." Fortunately no lives were lost, and rebuilding began soon thereafter. Then in 1854, the monastery and chapel burned to the ground. Neighbors responded to help and a Jewish man, one Dr. Mordecai, rushed through smoke and flame to save an exquisitely carved crucifix which still hangs in the community room. During the Civil War, Mobile was blockaded and supplies were short. Two of the sisters took a boat to New Orleans, where they were arrested by Union forces, then allowed to return to Mobile with a full supply of provisions and clothing.

After the Civil War, benefactors made substantial building possible. In 1895 the present chapel was dedicated, and in 1896 the eastern annex was erected. The convent and grounds have played a significant part in the life of Mobile, and the Historic Preservation Society has made awards recognizing the efforts to preserve and maintain the integrity of the charming buildings.

There is an eight-foot wall surrounding almost two acres of lawn with stately old trees and bushes. This offers a sense of privacy and solitude. A gazebo and chairs and benches are suitably placed. The dining room is entered from a covered walkway. The rooms, former dormitories, are on the second floor and open onto a porch that overlooks the lawn.

Retreat programs began in the 1950s for women, and in 1964 the refurbished monastery added retreats for men. There is a schedule of retreats throughout the year for cursillos, engaged and marriage encounters, and separate weekends for men and women. Individuals can be accommodated by appointment. It is also possible for women to experience the routines of the cloistered community for a few days or longer. The sisters gather in the chapel five times a day for community prayer, with morning mass at 6:30. Guests are welcome.

Visitation Monastery
2300 Spring Hill Avenue
Mobile, AL 36607
(251) 473-2321
www.visitationmonasterymobile.org

Arcosanti
Mayer, AZ

About 65 miles north of the population sprawl of Phoenix, an 860-acre cattle ranch has been transformed into an urban vision of the future. There is a development that will eventually house 6,000 people on only 17 acres. By eliminating the automobile, which needs streets and garages, individual living space of 2,000 square feet is only a short walk from anything. One can find cultural enrichment in a series of inter-locking units, and the surrounding land is used for agriculture, ranch-ing, and recreation.

Arcosanti (from *arcology*, an amalgam of *architecture* and *ecology*) is the concept of Paolo Soleri, an Italian-born architect who came to the United States to apprentice himself to Frank Lloyd Wright. In the early 1970s, the brilliant and controversial Soleri, described by some as a day-dreaming utopian and by others as the most important architect of our time, believed the time had come to make his dream a reality. Committed to keeping Arcosanti mortgage-free, Soleri decided to charge helpers a modest fee for the experience of building the future. More than 3,000 workshop participants have lived here for periods of four to six weeks in spartan concrete cubes, taking meals in the café, which bakes bread daily. Concerts and other cultural events are brought in, and helpers enjoy the interaction of fellow workers and the regular staff of 50.

Once a month, the entire community gathers for "Frugal Soup," a plain meal of soup and bread, water and juice, to focus thoughts on world hunger, reminding themselves during this 1½-hour event that even this simple fare would be a feast to some people. "We are," one speaker said, "like fleas on the back of the tiger, living in a flea world on the frightening tiger of reality."

The buildings of Arcosanti are on a mesa above the Agua Fria River valley, a few miles from Interstate 17—the major road between Flagstaff and Phoenix. The building outlines can be seen from the highway. It appears like a space village on the planet desert. There are ten guest rooms for 17 people. Visitors are welcome to retreat here to view the future.

More than $3 million has been spent so far, with funds earned from the sale of bronze and ceramic wind bells. Slowly but surely the vision grows to reality through the dedicated efforts of staff and workshop members. In the main office, there is a model of the completed Arcosanti. Soleri was once asked how much it would cost to complete the entire project. Reportedly, he smiled and answered: "About the price of one attack bomber."

Arcosanti
HC74, Box 4136
Mayer, AZ 86333
(928) 632-7135
www.info@arcosanti.org

Desert House of Prayer
Tucson, AZ

The Desert House of Prayer in the Sonoran Desert is a place where "in a climate of quiet and solitude, with the support of a small community of people committed to the contemplative life, one might come for a time to renew and deepen one's relationship with God . . . where one can get more deeply rooted and centered in God through prayer." This is the mission statement of Father John Kane and two sisters who began in a building at Picture Rocks Retreat (see page 257 in "Other Places"), and eventually acquired 31 acres just across the road, where they established this haven for solitude and quiet prayer. They welcome serious retreatants.

The current staff of five has 12 rooms with private baths available for retreatants. Three meals a day are provided in the dining room; breakfast and lunch are picked up there and eaten in silence. At the evening meal, which is taken with the community, talking is permitted. There are two self-contained hermitages nearby, well thought out and beautifully crafted. The mighty saguaro cacti, some standing 40 feet high, seem to guard against intrusion.

In the chapel, a separate building with a picture window at one end framing a magnificent desert scene, the community meets three times a day for mass, a prayer service, and 1½ hours of meditation that is similar to Zen sitting and is broken by walking meditation at 25-minute intervals; each person sits forward in the chair, spine erect, synchronizing the repetition of a mantra with the breath.

There is a library with 6,000 volumes and hundreds of tapes, including a complete set of Thomas Merton's discussions and addresses, many of which he made when he was novice master at Gethsemani.

The outdoor stations of the cross were donated by Dr. Richard Chun of Honolulu. The scenes on wooden crosses are complemented by the desert chaparral and the rugged mountain background. As one retreatant remarked: "The grace of the place is its silence."

Desert House of Prayer
7350 W. Picture Rocks Road
Tucson, AZ 85743
(520) 744-3825
www.deserthouseofprayer.org

The Healing Center of Arizona
Sedona, AZ

South of Flagstaff, where the red rock buttes of Arizona flow into canyons, the town of Sedona sits in the rugged foothills of the Rocky Mountains. Native Americans have been coming here for centuries to be refreshed and healed, for this place is said to be the site of an energy vortex. This has long been recognized by people with psychic powers, who have settled here and given the town the reputation, though it has no TV station, of being the home of 400 channels.

Native Sedonan John Paul Weber returned after ten years in San Francisco to found the Healing Center of Arizona. Choosing a site in Wilson Canyon, where juniper trees grow in abundance, he meditated on a rocky outcrop as to what kind of building to construct. His meditations inspired him to build a large geodesic dome surrounded by four smaller ones. With the help of clients and friends, construction began in 1981 and was completed five years later. When the structure had been framed, before the doors and windows were installed, John Paul was working inside one day when he heard a loud crash. He discovered that the boulder on which he had spent so much time meditating had broken loose from the cliff, rolled through a door opening, and come to rest in the corner of a room. As big as a table, it remains there still, obviously wanting not to be left out.

There are 4,200 square feet in the five domes, shaped like a large daisy, where up to 20 people can be accommodated, some in private rooms. Glorious flowering plants thrive in the light, airy space, which is tastefully furnished. The bathrooms are tiled and gleaming, and there is a hot tub, a sauna, and a flotation tank; one of the smaller domes is a meditation chamber, where energy seems amplified and awareness increased. Delicious food—usually vegetarian—is served in the main living-dining space. There are superb views across the canyon where the magnificent rocks are outlined in the normally blue sky.

The center offers personalized retreats tailored to the needs of individuals. Some involve massage and acupressure, along with the use of heat and water. There are hiking trails into the canyon, and the awesome beauty and clear air of the Arizona landscape help one relax and let go of any illness. This place seems to be a major step toward what John Paul describes as "the need for centers of light and love of all humanity that are nondenominational and open to all to give grounding and remembrance of the divine presence."

The Healing Center of Arizona
25 Wilson Canyon Road
Sedona, AZ 86366
www.arizonahealingcenter.com

Holy Trinity Monastery
St. David, AZ

Deep in Apache territory, about 14 miles north of Tombstone and 17 miles from Cochise Stronghold, this Benedictine monastery was founded serendipitously. Formerly the Wilderness Ranch for Boys, the 93 acres was run by an ecumenical group to help young men in trouble. While giving a retreat in Tucson, Father Louis Hassenfus of the Pecos Benedictine Monastery (see page 152) was asked to take over the ranch in order to provide a spiritual renewal center for the whole area. Wary of committing himself to such a venture and concerned about what would happen to his oblate outreach program, he agreed on condition that the Pecos group gave consensus approval. Knowing that they could never reach consensus on anything, he felt certain that his ministerial direction would not change. Much to his surprise, there was a unanimous vote that it should be done, and in September 1974, accompanied by two helpers, he founded Holy Trinity Monastery.

Following the liberal tradition of Pecos, and the evolving growth and modifications to monastic traditions, Holy Trinity is a community composed of priests and brothers, sisters, laypeople, and married couples. The monastic community of 12 monks, 6 sisters, and 2 laypeople work at separate responsibilities such as tending the orchards, cooking and cleaning for the regular visitors and retreatants, running the gift shop and art gallery, and maintaining the grounds and caring for the variety of farm animals and the peacocks.

Thousands of people have come here to experience the monastic space. Some couples come regularly, for months at a time, hook up their homes on wheels to power and water in a back section, and join the community in work and prayer. "It's uncanny," one monk said, "how people come along with skills to help solve some problem or help with building, as needed."

The monastery gets its income from varied sources, including the sale of pecans from the 150-tree orchard and the spring and autumn festivals, which grow each year in popularity and participation. In 1995, there were 85 booths rented to craftspeople who sold to the large crowds attracted by the great food and music provided by friends and oblates.

Visitors are expected to observe the monastic disciplines of silence, solitude, and prayer. There are eight private rooms with shared baths for guests in the Casa de Bernardo, which has a comfortable lounge with coffee, tea, and snacks. Meals are taken family-style with the community in the main dining room a short distance across the courtyard. Prayer services are held daily in the beautiful adobe chapel, with mass celebrated at noon. A nearby pond is home to many ducks. The striking outdoor stations of the cross, behind the chapel, are made from weathered wood and old ranch implements.

Unnecessary talk should be avoided, remembering, as one monk said: "The Lord has a sense of humor, and the Holy Spirit's got this ground, so just be still and you'll get the answers."

Holy Trinity Monastery
1605 S. Saint Mary's Way
St. David, AZ 85630
(520) 720-4642
www.holytrinitymonastery.org

Our Lady of Solitude House of Prayer
Black Canyon City, AZ

Up a long, steep drive to a mesa in the Sonoran Desert, this house of prayer complex sits alone and quiet. It's hard to imagine a more fitting place for solitude and contemplative prayer. The road to Phoenix can be seen to the north, but traffic noise is nonexistent and views to Black Canyon City and the mountains beyond accentuate the separation.

Through a joint effort of a layman seeking spiritual fulfillment and the Catholic bishop of Phoenix, who sought to establish a contemplative group in the diocese, benefactors funded a house of prayer in 1980. Four years later a donation made it possible for the prayer community to buy these 20 acres surrounded by state and federal land. At the end of the drive, the main house sits on a high point with sweeping desert views to the south and west. It has a spacious reading room stocked with more than 1,500 books.

On a separate knoll is the Dwelling Place, a chapel dedicated in 1988. The circular stucco building has a picture window looking out over the valley below; a window-cross of stained glass depicting Christ in a collage of color is the only decoration in the subdued interior.

Near the chapel are three sturdy and comfortable hermitages set apart from one another. Each hermitage has a kitchenette, a single bedroom, a private bath, and cooling and heating units. The absolute privacy enables retreatants to appreciate the silence and sweetness of the surrounding desert air.

Signs on the property advise NO HUNTING EXCEPT FOR PEACE AND GOD and NO SMOKING EXCEPT FOR THE FIRE OF PRAYER.

Our Lady of Solitude Monastery
19950 St. Joseph Road
P.O. Box 92
Black Canyon City, AZ 85324
(623) 374-9204
www.desertnuns.com
(Religious only for moment.)

Abbey of New Clairvaux
Vina, CA

In 1955 in the orchard belt of Tehama County, part of the rich farming region in the northern Sacramento Valley, Trappist monks from Gethsemani, Kentucky, acquired about 600 fertile acres. Over the years, they have transformed much of the land into prune and walnut orchards. The trees grow in long, orderly rows as far as the eye can see. The prunes are sold to Sunsweet, the walnuts to Diamond, and the income from the harvest supports the monastery.

Named after the Abbey of Clairvaux in France, where St. Bernard founded the Cistercian order in 1115, New Clairvaux ("clear valley" or "valley of light") was the largest winery in the country when Leland Stanford owned the property. The winery, the large brick building to the right of the monastic enclosure, is now used for equipment storage.

More than 30 monks live here and are summoned by bells to the chapel to sing the canonical hours. Guests and visitors are welcome at all services. After Compline at 7:30 P.M., Grand Silence is observed until morning. There are single and double rooms with private baths for guests in an unobtrusive motel-like building and in two other buildings. The rooms are comfortable and well maintained. A guest refectory is in a separate building; good meals are brought from the monastery kitchen and served family-style. There is a separate room off the main dining area for those who are observing silence. Guests clean up after the meals. Coffee, tea, and snacks are always available here.

There are no formal retreats but, as one monk observed, "True hospitality is giving someone the space to breathe. If you want to talk to a monk, you'll have to ask." There is a separate chapel for prayer and meditation just behind the main entrance reception area. A pleasant building with a fountain in front, it has a timeless look and recalls the words of Thomas Merton: "Actually, what matters about the monastery is precisely that it is radically different from the world. The apparent 'pointlessness' of the monastery in the eyes of the world is exactly what gives it a real reason for existing. In a world of noise, confusion, and conflict it is necessary that there be a place of silence, inner discipline, and peace."

Deer Creek winds around the property and flows into the Sacramento River. There is fine walking along the creek and, during the evening, on the service roads through the orchards. "It gets so quiet here at night," one guest observed, "you can hear a prune drop."

Abbey of New Clairvaux
Seventh and C Streets
Vina, CA 96092
(530) 839-2434
www.newclairvaux.org

Dhamma Dena
Joshua Tree, CA

On Copper Mountain Mesa, in the California high desert just north of Joshua Tree National Monument, Buddhist teacher Ruth Denison purchased 12½ acres of land in 1978. Having camped in the area for years, she loved the isolation and quiet where she and her family and friends could get away for rest and repair. Ruth initially intended to use the spot as a private sanctuary but she often invited her students to spend time there and eventually began to hold retreats. In the 1980s, a community began to form and facilities were added. A meditation hall, big enough for 50 people or more, was built a short distance from the main house. Here the community gathers for Vipassana (insight) meditation with helpful comments from Ruth voiced to the meditators during the sittings: "Watch your breathing . . . become your breathing . . . sink into the silence of your breathing."

Formal retreats in Vipassana are held periodically; private retreatants can usually be accommodated any time. Men and women stay in separate housing. The accommodations are spartan and visitors should bring sleeping bags and be prepared to use an outhouse. Light vegetarian meals are served in the main house. Water is trucked in and is treated as precious; every drop is saved to water plants. The runoff from the shower house is captured and used to refresh the oleanders and pampa grass.

A youthful and vigorous ambience permeates this isolated desert setting where creosote bushes grow in abundance. The tall, spindly plants survive by joining their roots, a marvel of adaptation, suggesting the analogy of like-minded people surviving and growing by joining their spiritual roots. Awareness is heightened in the desert, which is conducive to contemplation. Vipassana meditation, a simple and direct practice, helps the individual to examine the mind-body process through focused awareness. It helps us to accept all aspects of living with equanimity and balance, which leads to wisdom and compassion.

The austere setting seems to magnify the rugged beauty of the distant mountains and the color of the sky at sunrise and sunset. The black, star-filled night sky is awesome.

Dhamma Dena Monastery &
Desert Vipassana Center
HC1, Box 250
Joshua Tree, CA 92252
www.dhammadena@gmail.com

Green Gulch Farm Zen Center
Muir Beach, CA

In the early 1970s, the San Francisco Zen Center was looking for a country location where its members could live, work, and practice meditation. During the same period, the Nature Conservancy was looking for a group to maintain a farm, part of 535 upland acres deeded to it by George Wheelright III, whose intent was to preserve the property in its unspoiled and natural condition and maintain the plant and animal life.

This superb land is only 25 minutes by car from San Francisco and is located between Mill Valley and Muir Beach. Made up of low hills and ridges, the property has half a mile of ocean frontage. Surrounded by the Golden Gate National Recreation Area, Green Gulch is an exquisite example of California's coastland, accessible by the two-lane winding Route 1, where slow, cautious driving is not only intelligent but necessary. An arrangement was made for the Zen Center to buy 115 acres on the condition that it would be farmed in perpetuity and remain open to the public.

As part of its practice, the Zen community demonstrates that Buddhist attention to detail in land stewardship produces good crops, a spiritual reward in itself. Green Gulch Farm has become a showcase, growing superb-quality produce, herbs, and flowers that are prized in the Bay Area. The 15 acres of carefully tended fields with rainbow rows of lettuce—more than a dozen kinds—are a source of fresh supply to area restaurants, including the affiliated and famous Greens Restaurant in San Francisco.

The resident community of 50 adults and 8 children keep the farm going and also have an active schedule of retreat programs, classes, and gardening workshops. There are two daily zazen periods, one in the morning and the other in late afternoon. Part of a former barn is used as the sitting room; the rustic wooden building with polished wooden floors, dimly lighted by small windows, is quiet and appropriate. Statues of the Buddha are graced by flowers, candles, and artifacts.

The handcrafted Oriental-style Lindisfarne Guesthouse, which also serves as a conference center, has nails only in the sheetrock under the plaster walls. All the wood was hand-planed, some of it oak from a tree that fell at Tassajara (the mountain retreat center), some of it Port Orford cedar, often used in Japanese buildings. The two-story structure's rooms flow together toward the 30-foot atrium in the center where guests can sit around the woodstove on chairs and sofas. The rooms are elegant and comfortable. Each guest room shares a modern bathroom.

Green Gulch Farm Zen Center
1601 Shoreline Highway
Muir Beach, CA 94965
(415) 383-3134
www.sfzc.org

Immaculate Heart Community
Center for Spiritual Renewal
Santa Barbara, CA

The center is located in a large stone manor house and shares 26 acres of beautiful grounds with La Casa de Maria (see page 24) in the Montecito neighborhood just below San Ysidro Ranch. A small group of Immaculate Heart Community women live here; the headquarters of the 189-member community is in Los Angeles.

In response to the call for renewal from Vatican II in the late 1960s, the Immaculate Heart Community tried to adapt to a new form of religious life integrating the richness of past history with contemporary circumstances and understanding. The modifications from past traditions included a choice of work, a modified dress code, and active involvement in social justice. The Cardinal of Los Angeles reacted by issuing a decree to the community requiring uniform dress and set scheduled prayer. The sisters were shocked and hurt by the authoritarian mandate. In 1969, a majority of the sisters declared independence, announcing they would become "a noncanonical community of religious persons." The gentle strength of the community is evident as its members look forward to an ever-changing future. As one said, "It is true to say the Immaculate Heart Community is something it always was, and it is also becoming something it never was."

The center has rooms with private baths for six guests on retreat. The resident community makes every effort to provide warm hospitality in an atmosphere of gentle silence. Community members are available for conversation but otherwise visitors structure their own time. A nondenominational evening prayer meeting is scheduled after dinner and guests are welcome. There is a large selection of tapes and books available. Breakfast and lunch may be picked up from the well-stocked kitchen; the evening meal is served family-style with everyone sitting down together at the large dining table.

The manor house has an elegant wood interior and is comfortably furnished and carefully maintained. The serene atmosphere is easy to adjust to and difficult to leave. As one guest wrote: "This is the only place where I can give in to myself—one of the most valuable gifts of my life." Another wrote: "Home away from home, like Grandmother's, where everything is homemade."

Immaculate Heart Community
Center for Spiritual Renewal
888 San Ysidro Lane
Santa Barbara, CA 93108
(805) 969-2474
www.immaculateheartcenter.org

La Casa de Maria
Santa Barbara, CA

The entrance of this 26-acre retreat winds through the wooded neighborhood of Montecito, past orange and lemon trees and one of the largest eucalyptus trees in the county. The abundance of outstanding and unusual trees and bushes on the grounds includes a monkey puzzle tree and a star pine. Along a gently curving road, the buildings resemble haciendas with white walls and tiled roofs. A strumming guitar at siesta time would complete the picture.

This tranquil setting is where an energetic director and staff organize and run a full program of spiritually oriented single-day and weekend retreats. The topics range from AA to prayer and dance workshops and a "work weekend" when guests help to maintain the facilities by painting, gardening, and cooking while laughing and praying together. This is a popular place for people to gather together in a neutral environment to seek solutions to personal and global problems. There are rooms for more than 150 people in motel-like wings and most have private baths. The dining room with adjoining terrace serves meals buffet-style. By all accounts, the food gets high marks.

The Casa's history goes back to 1780, when the king of Spain granted the land to the Franciscan missions and the padres built a way station for traveling missionaries. The land came under private ownership in the 1800s, when citrus groves were planted. La Casa was a grand estate for the Wack family, who raised horses here in the early 1900s. The Sisters of the Immaculate Heart purchased the property and took possession on Easter Monday, 1943. A large donation in 1955 made it possible to build a 24-room unit where married couples could come for retreats, the first in the western United States for that specific purpose. The chapel was also built at that time, and has a window looking out on a huge gnarled oak with a life-size crucifixion in front of it.

During the 1970s, an independent board of trustees was founded, with a mandate from the Immaculate Heart Community to keep the Casa in perpetuity as a retreat center. Every year a donation is received from a Swiss visitor who on his initial retreat here was asked neither if he could pay nor his religious affiliation. The money is used for scholarships for those who cannot afford to pay.

This is a place of healing and conciliation. One of the staff commented, "We urge those in conflict always to listen to the other side; don't allow rigid idealism to become brutalization, like the Crusades and the conflict in the Middle East."

La Casa de Maria
800 El Bosque Road
Santa Barbara, CA 93108
(805) 969-5031
www.lacasademaria.org

Monastery of Mount Tabor
Redwood Valley, CA

This Eastern rite contemplative community of a dozen monks has lived on these 200 sloping, hilltop acres in the coastal range of Northern California since the mid 1970s. Mount Tabor, named after the mountain where tradition says Christ was transfigured, is a Byzantine monastery of the Ukrainian Catholic church. Their exceptional liturgy with all its fervor, beauty, and grace is the focal point of each day. The three services last about five hours in all. The experience is very powerful: beautifully sung prayers, some prostrations, clouds of incense, candles lighted and extinguished, bearded monks moving about the altar dressed in magnificent vestments, rich full voices filling the small church. There are no distractions; everything, including the elegant icons on the walls, focuses one's attention on the reason for being here: profound divine worship.

There are rooms for 16 guests in a guesthouse up the hill from the church. The simple, spare rooms have a single bed, desk, chair, and sink and share baths. There is a kitchen for making hot drinks or snacks, which guests should bring. Regular meals are taken with the monks in the dining room just below the church, and in cool weather there is a roaring fire in the fireplace. The windows look out on the gardens below and the hills beyond. During the noon meal one of the monks reads aloud from a spiritual text. The food is hearty and nutritious. Twice a week fasting is observed and only bread is available. Every Friday the monks pick up leftovers from local food stores, and some neighbors send food regularly.

Guests are expected to attend all services and meals and to help with some of the work. A monk can be available for spiritual guidance but this should be prearranged. Hiking on the mountain property is rigorous. The views down the valley are exceptionally peaceful from this mountain of spirituality.

Monastery of Mount Tabor
P.O. Box 217
17001 Tomki Road
Redwood Valley, CA 95470
(707) 485-8959
www.byzantines.net

Mount Calvary Monastery and Retreat House
Santa Barbara, CA

On a rocky ledge in the foothills of the Santa Ynez Mountains, 1,250 feet above Santa Barbara, Mount Calvary offers breathtaking views of the Pacific Coast. On a clear day you can see north 40 miles to Point Magoo and south 25 miles to the Channel Islands. The natural cliffs on one side go down to Rattlesnake Canyon, on the other to the switchback road that winds up through an affluent neighborhood.

The monks are of the Order of the Holy Cross, an Episcopalian monastic community in the Benedictine tradition founded in New York City in 1884. They acquired this property in 1947 after searching up and down the coast. The building was little more than a shell when Father Karl Tiedemann found it, but he succeeded in raising the money to buy it. Known for his fund-raising ability, he wanted as his epitaph "And the beggar died." Father Tiedemann rests peacefully; a fellow monk noted he even got a free funeral.

The monastery is superbly constructed, with white stucco walls and a red-tile roof. The main entrance, through a large foyer with polished wood floors, has Spanish colonial antique furnishings under beamed ceilings. The room and central corridor are decorated with outstanding religious art and artifacts, including a carved wooden altar trimmed in gold leaf.

The monks sing the canonical hours in a separate chapel room and guests are welcome. A charming inner courtyard is dominated by a large sculpted iron cross. Fruit trees and flowering bushes grow in this protected area and some of the guest rooms open out onto it. Picture windows have glorious views of the Pacific. At night, the lights of Santa Barbara reach to the ocean's edge.

The monastery was founded as a retreat house and as a seat of spirituality from which the monks could go out to preach. They regularly descend from their mountain to Trinity Church in downtown Santa Barbara to prepare and serve meals for the homeless.

There are 11 double rooms and 8 singles for retreatants. From time to time a "working retreat" is offered when individuals and groups donate time and skill to improving the facility. People of every religious denomination are welcome.

The Great Silence is observed from Compline, the last prayer service of the day, until breakfast. This quiet period enhances the experience of the location, an ocean of limitless space.

Mount Calvary Monastery
and Retreat House
P.O. Box 1296
Santa Barbara, CA 93102
(805) 962-9855
www.mount-calvary.org
(Burned in wildfire 11/14/08)

Mount Madonna Center
Watsonville, CA

On a sloping hilltop with a sweeping, panoramic view of Monterey Bay, the Mount Madonna Center sits on 355 acres of meadows and forests. Situated equidistant between Watsonville and Gilroy, this is an international community of 70 adults and 30 children. Followers of the yogi Baba Hari Dass acquired the former cattle ranch in the 1970s and established a spiritual community with education as its primary focus and spiritual growth and character development as underlying themes. The core component is the study and practice of yoga, which they believe is not a religion but a spiritual path. "Yoga's basic disciplines are essentially the same as Catholicism, Buddhism, or any other great spiritual path," a spokesperson said. "Each has its own shadings or variations. We here are concerned with what is basic, true, and timeless; we're not concerned with separating ourselves from others or saying we are different than others."

The center's 38 buildings were financed as they were built. The redwood community building, facing the majestic western view, is the heart of the complex, with the kitchen and dining room, classrooms for the 100-plus students from kindergarten through high school, and administrative offices. It can accommodate 300 people. Nearby is the seminar building, which is big enough for groups of 60. The well-stocked and inviting library is in a separate building. Along the winding roadways are staff housing and guest facilities interspersed with gardens.

People here are friendly, cheerful, and happy to meet visitors. The excellent vegetarian food is served cafeteria-style and is carefully prepared with nutrition in mind. There is a variety of guest accommodations in many of the buildings as well as a cottage and a guesthouse, or you may use your own tent or van. The property has acres of open meadows and redwood forests for hiking. The center also features a lake and volleyball and basketball courts.

Programs during 1995 included Jack Kornfield and many other internationally known presenters. The center staff organizes retreats with its spiritual leader, Baba Hari Dass, who has observed a vow of silence for 40 years and communicates by writing on a slate. It seems fitting that this outstanding community has a leader vowed to silence—what a pleasure to see how clearly silence speaks.

Mount Madonna Center
445 Summit Road
Watsonville, CA 95076
(408) 847-0406
www.mountmadonna.org

New Camaldoli Hermitage
Big Sur, CA

The hermitage is located 1,300 feet above the sea in a remote area of the Santa Lucia Mountains overlooking Highway 1, the two-lane scenic road that traces the California coastline. This 800-acre monastery affords inspirational views of the ribbons of surf below. The ever-changing weather of the Big Sur region is more pronounced here. On those glorious days when the sky is clear, the sea is a startling blue.

In 1958 three Benedictine monks came from Camaldoli in Italy, found the property, and built a monastery based on the contemplative and eremitical lifestyle espoused by their founder, St. Romuald: "Sit in your cell as in paradise. Put the whole world behind you and forget it. Watch your thoughts like a good fisherman watching for fish."

The Camaldolese monks live here as a community of hermits and have their own cells in a private enclosure. They congregate in the chapel four times a day to sing the liturgy (5:45 A.M. Vigils, 7 A.M. Lauds, mass at 11 or 11:30 A.M., and Vespers at 5 or 6 P.M.). Guests are always welcome. There is a powerful silent meditation period following Vespers in the church rotunda.

There are nine single rooms in a guest building at the end of the monastery road. Each room has a bed, table, and chair, a bathroom, and a garden with a view west to the sea. Food is brought to a separate pantry at mealtimes. Guests help themselves to the simple, hearty soups and salads accompanied by freshly made bread. Retreatants eat alone in their rooms and are responsible for keeping plates and utensils clean. Individuals structure their own time, but a monk is available on request.

There are also five trailers on the hillside overlooking Highway 1, each with full bath, half-kitchen, and sundeck. These are for stays of one week to one month.

The monks are known for their Hermitage Cakes, which they sell by mail order. The fruitcake and date-nut cakes are dipped in brandy and have a very distinctive flavor. There is an excellent bookstore, which also carries a selection of chalcedony art pieces, pottery, and art in oil and watercolor created by the monks.

The outstanding setting of this remote spiritual outpost attracts many. The rooms are usually booked, so plan far ahead.

New Camaldoli Hermitage
Big Sur, CA 93920
(831) 667-2456/2341
www.bigsurhermitage.com

Nyingma Institute
Berkeley, CA

Almost at the crest of "Holy Hill," at the northern edge of the University of California at Berkeley campus, where every religious persuasion seems to have a building or an office, Tibetan Buddhist Tarthang Tulku was able to purchase an old fraternity house in 1973. The large but compact house has 25 residential rooms and space for up to 20 guests. Private retreats are available for those who have already attended a weekend workshop. From the entrance porch and the front windows, San Francisco Bay appears like a mirage on the horizon.

The great walls of the building protect the meditation-sitting room on the lower level against any outside noise or distraction. Seven prayer wheels spin here continuously, as do those on the front porch and a seven-ton prayer wheel in the backyard. These revolving copper drums are etched with mantras and filled with prayers and mantras written on paper; as the drums spin, the prayers are sent forth into the world. These are the only electric prayer wheels known—an American version of this ancient tradition.

Tarthang Tulku was one of the first Tibetans to arrive in this country in the late 1960s. A brilliant scholar and teacher of the Nyingma, or "Old Ones," school of Tibetan Buddhism, he engaged many Western psychologists in discussion and exploration of Tibetan Buddhist meditation and other practices.

There are classes (some for college credit), programs, workshops, and retreats given throughout the year on Buddhist teachings, Tibetan language, meditation, and psychology. There is a demanding nine-month work/study program during which the student is involved six days a week, 12 hours a day, plus some evenings and weekends. The work includes creating sacred art, maintaining institute facilities, and producing Dharma Publishing books and reproductions. Tarthang Tulku's teaching emphasizes directing energy to contribute something of value, developing skills to improve the quality of life, and recognizing limiting patterns in action and learning to break them.

Dharma Publishing, a major publisher of books on Tibetan Buddhism, was conceived when thousands of Tibetans fled their homeland and brought with them precious texts of their lineage. Tarthang Tulku found the means and ways to preserve the ancient texts by translating them for the West. There is an outstanding four-color catalog that lists these high-quality publications and reproductions of sacred art.

Nyingma Institute
1815 Highland Place
Berkeley, CA 94709
(510) 843-6812
www.nyingmainstitute.com

Orr Hot Springs
Ukiah, CA

This remote retreat is named after Samuel Orr, who brought his family to the West in a covered wagon in 1850 so he could prospect for gold. Eventually he acquired considerable land and settled in the mountains west of Ukiah to raise cattle and sheep. To utilize the hot springs found on his property, he built a bathhouse and a hotel with rooms for a dozen people, and opened for business in the late 1850s. The modest resort remained in the Orr family until the early 1970s. It is now run by people who maintain it in a delightful way.

The winding two-lane road to the retreat is an adventure in California mountain driving, over the historic low gap road, which was built from Ukiah along an old Indian trail. Pomo Indians passed through the hot springs on annual trading expeditions and all tribes agreed to coexist peacefully while stopping here. It was a rest stop for the Ukiah-Mendocino stagecoach line and a popular resort for those seeking health and relaxation. A story from a 1906 publication claimed the waters made "the skin feel like velvet . . . the hair soft and glossy, and the joints lose their stiffness like magic."

The guest rooms and cottages around the grounds, constructed in the 1940s from locally milled redwood, are in remarkably good condition. The bathhouse built in 1863 still stands near the hot springs where four porcelain Victorian tubs in private rooms are filled with mineral water at body temperature, then drained after use and refilled for the next person. A large wooden tub, filled with hot mineral water, can be used by five or six people at the same time. There is a large swimming pool built into the hillside, with cool mineral water, that is easy to plunge into after a hot bath or sauna.

Guests can choose from a private redwood room or cottage, a group sleeping loft, or tent sites for camping. Except for the private rooms and cottages, guests bring their own sleeping bags. All visitors should bring their own food, which can be prepared in the large community kitchen complete with cooking utensils and tableware, and eaten in the adjacent dining room. Refrigerator space and dry storage space are assigned.

The extraordinary care taken with the property demonstrates the resident community's great love for the place. The pathways have colorful borders of flowers and utility boxes are painted with elegant murals. There is no religious affiliation, but anyone who wants to observe silence can wear a necklace of red beads, obtained at the main desk.

The sign near the entrance reads CLOTHING OPTIONAL ESTABLISHMENT . . . YOU MAY ENCOUNTER NUDITY BEYOND THIS POINT (in summer months, clothing is rarely seen); but you'll also encounter a respect for nature and for quiet.

Orr Hot Springs
13201 Orr Springs Road
Ukiah, CA 75482
(707) 462-6277
www.orrhotsprings.tribe.net

Prince of Peace Abbey
Oceanside, CA

As we waited in the dining room at Prince of Peace Abbey, the 83-year-old abbot scurried by us with a nod and disappeared through the kitchen door. Minutes later he reappeared pushing a cart laden with boxes of food, bread and bananas protruding from them. He swept by us into the lounge. We could see him deliver the cart to a man who had been sitting, hat in hand, on a sofa. His face brightened as the abbot approached. The man took the cart and wheeled it away. The abbot then turned and came back to us. He sat down and apologized for keeping us waiting, explaining that the man was out of work and had a family to feed. "Now," he said, "what can I do for you?"

This compassionate spirit is a hallmark of the abbey. For many years, Brother Benno, one of the monks, took a truck out to gather food and served meals to the hungry at what came to be called Brother Benno's Kitchen in Oceanside. Every week, the monks baked 500 loaves of bread for those meals. In 1991, they opened the Brother Benno Center, where, in addition to providing food and clothing as the kitchen had done, there is space for shower facilities, a mail and message center, an employment office, a counseling program, and literacy classes. "People see the abbey trying to do good things," one monk explained, "so they contribute. The more we help, the more help we get."

The abbey was conceived in 1958 when a small group of Benedictine monks were invited by the local bishop to come west from St. Meinrad's Archabbey in Indiana. The bishop was eager to have the benefit of monastic prayers in his diocese. The monks located a 100-acre ranch but were staggered by the asking price. Undeterred and resolute, the prior buried a St. Benedict medal on the grounds and left the problem in the hands of the Lord, who eventually delivered the ranch to the young community for some $55,000 less than the original asking price. The abbey grounds are on a hilltop looking west to Oceanside and the Pacific Ocean and south and east to the San Luis Valley. There is a local airport in the valley, and planes take off into the prevailing western wind and fly by at eye level, but far enough away so there is no intrusive noise.

At the monastery, there are single and double rooms available for retreatants in a large building with a lounge and dining room. Three meals a day are served cafeteria-style, and friends of the monastery often drop by to eat there. The magnificent chapel nearby, completed in 1987, has excellent acoustics, and the monks gather there six times a day to sing the liturgy; mass is celebrated daily at 11 A.M. and on Sunday mornings at 10:30. There are no formal retreats, but a monk can be available for discussion if needed.

Prince of Peace Abbey
650 Benet Hill Road
Oceanside, CA 92054
(760) 967-4200
www.princeofpeaceabbey.blogspot.com

Rancho La Puerta
Tecate, Baja California, Mexico

Near the southwesternmost corner of the United States, the Baja is an area just across the Mexican border. There, outside Tecate, Rancho La Puerta sits in a valley surrounded by rock-strewn mountains. The most prominent, Mount Cuchuma, is one of the 14 energy vortex points in the world. This valley has long been recognized as a sacred place, a pathway connecting ocean and desert, and a center of trade and spirituality for the Mexican Indians. To Ed and Deborah Szekely, it seemed a perfect place to start a health camp in 1940 for people interested in simple, nutritious, home-grown food and exercise in the fresh mountain air away from the stress and pressure of everyday life. Szekely had studied and written about the early Christian sect of Essenes, who advocated a life linked to the land. The Essene School of Life, which started modestly in an adobe hut with no running water or electricity, was eventually renamed Rancho La Puerta, Ranch of the (Open) Door, after live oaks that arched across the entrance to the property. In the early days, guests such as Aldous Huxley brought their own tents. Over the years luxurious villas have been built with private terraces for sunbathing and enjoying the fine views.

The guest rooms and villas are a few minutes' walk from the centrally located dining room, where first-rate chefs prepare a variety of colorful, healthy food at each meal. And adjacent to the various gyms (six in all), there is a separate lounge where on the first day of a weeklong stay guests may begin an optional fast of almond milk and juices.

No private vehicles are permitted on the grounds. The wide brick-paved paths are bordered with sage, rosemary, and parsley. Cactuses and palm trees thrive and add dimension to the local chaparral. More than 60 species of birds have been spotted in the winter season, and numerous hummingbirds dart in and about the flowering bushes.

The ranch has grown in physical size and reputation since its early days, when it attracted "health nuts" who explored the Essene philosophy of uniting body, mind, and spirit. This philosophy is still followed in many ways as guests exercise, eat properly, retire early, and awaken before sunrise to hike on sacred land. To what purpose? Perhaps to be better people overall, kinder to family, friends, and associates, more compassionate to those less fortunate, enjoying the blessings we have rather than grieving over not having more.

As one staff member said, "Many people come just to get away, not for the exercise programs but to get in touch with themselves." And it is a wonderful place for that, whether guests join a group or not, hike or not. It is a place of transformation. Here is a retreat devoted to health, a mecca for fitness where first mind and body find harmony, then the spirit comes alive, awareness increases, and the meaning of life is clarified.

Rancho La Puerta
Tecate, Baja California, Mexico
Mail: 3323 Carmel Mt. Road # 100
San Diego, CA 92121
(858) 764-5500
www.rancholapuerta.com

St. Andrew's Abbey
Valyermo, CA

In 1955, at the foothills of the San Gabriel Mountains on 710 acres in the Antelope Valley, a group of Benedictine monks who had been expelled from Communist China in 1952 settled. The community of 17 priests and brothers gathers daily in the chapel. They answer the call of the hand-rung bell to sing the canonical hours beginning with 6 A.M. Vigils and ending with Compline at 8:30 P.M. The low-slung, ranch-design chapel is made entirely of wood, and the roads and paths are bordered by meandering stone walls. Striking designs and architectural features can be found throughout the monastery, both inside the buildings and on the grounds. In the chapel, there are two altars: one is made of stone and wood and sits in the center; the other, to the side, is made of concrete and seems like a sculpture that focuses our concentration on a central eye. One section of the grounds is reminiscent of the Far East, with a Chinese pagoda and tea garden set around a pond; another section is a carefully tended lawn in a group of cottonwoods and pines.

Three meals a day are served in the dining room, two buffet-style; at the noon meal, the monks bring soup to guests at their tables. One wall in this room is completely glass (reinforced by angled struts), offering a view of palm trees and desert chaparral. The guest wing has 17 double rooms with private baths. These double-entry rooms have floor-length sliding glass doors out to the desert, and are available to groups or individual retreatants. The comfortable and spacious lounge, off the dining room, and the chapel are always open; coffee and tea are available at the snack area.

Mainly in the summer months, there is a series of workshops on themes such as the care of self and others, and sacred dance. An important part of the priory's year is the Fall Festival, a weekend celebration that attracts thousands of visitors to dance, drama, and musical events. Fresh farm produce and ethnic food are available.

In the ceramic studio, the monks produce beautiful works of art that can be purchased in the monastery gift shop and are available in many shops throughout the United States.

Outdoor stations of the cross follow a semicircular path through the desert. The monastery grounds offer fine walking with extended views of the valley and nearby mountains.

St. Andrew's Abbey
31001 N. Valyermo Road
Valyermo, CA 93563
(661) 944-2178
www.valyermo.com

Santa Sabina Center
San Rafael, CA

Occupying a quiet corner of the 100-acre campus of Dominican College, the elegant building that houses the Santa Sabina retreat and conference center has many European monastic touches. The arched doorway leads into a dark-wood interior, through one tastefully furnished room after another, to an inner courtyard of grass, flowers, and an orange tree—an inner sanctum where quiet and peace prevail; chairs invite the visitor to sit and reflect to the soft murmur of the fountain. The chapel has tall, narrow windows set in the stucco walls—another special place for quiet and contemplation.

There is a community of six nuns who live here coordinating thematic weekly retreats, monthly days of prayer, and evening studies of Scripture and the works of Thomas Merton. There are seasonal concerts on Sunday afternoons in the chapel. Private retreats are available by appointment. A community prayer meeting takes place each day at 6:30 A.M. and retreatants are welcome. Masses are available on the college campus at three different locations; there is also a mass in Spanish at the nearby San Rafael Mission.

There are 60 beds in 37 rooms with community baths for groups that come with a spiritual purpose or to attend a directed retreat. The conference room can accommodate 100 persons. Individual retreatants usually bring their own food or walk to the college dining room nearby. Though traditionally Roman Catholic, the center is ecumenical in its philosophy and outreach. Open to the influences of East and West, the sisters believe in the true essence of Thomas Merton's writings. They offer a chance for people to see the artist in everyone, the monk in everyone, and to appreciate the natural beauty of the place itself.

One can wander the entire college campus or hike up a fire trail to a lookout called the "rim of the world," which looks out over the entire San Francisco Bay, a panorama of city, bridges, and the ocean beyond.

Santa Sabina Center
25 Magnolia Avenue
San Rafael, CA 94901
(415) 457-7727
info@santasabinacenter.org

Self-Realization Fellowship Retreat
Encinitas, CA

The Hermitage House and its surrounding property were given to the Indian-born teacher Paramahansa Yogananda in 1937 as a surprise gift when he returned to the United States from travels abroad. The benefactor, who was a devotee, intended the place as a personal retreat for Yogananda. But a year later, the guru turned it into an open house so all could enjoy its beauty and serenity. The 17-acre property sits on a 400-foot bluff overlooking the Pacific. There are places for meditation along the bluff and there is a path down to the beach. To the side of the hermitage and above the main retreat building are the meditation gardens and ponds filled with colorful carp; the grounds of this tropical paradise are maintained with meticulous and loving care. At night, the lights of La Jolla can be seen ten miles south.

In the study of the hermitage, Yogananda wrote his classic *Autobiography of a Yogi*. His private rooms are preserved as a shrine where visitors are welcome Sundays from 2 to 5 P.M. The rest of the hermitage is now a residence for monastics of the Self-Realization Fellowship, who manage the property and run the regular retreat and education programs.

There are 20 rooms for retreatants and visitors in a building with a courtyard maintained with the same extraordinary care as the grounds. The food is vegetarian. The programs include structured meditation and classes on the teachings of Yogananda. Retreatants are expected to observe silence.

The rooms are usually filled by Self-Realization Fellowship members, one of whom said, "We all pass sooner or later between the beast and the saint, as different avatars come back. Here, we examine our attitudes and behavior and gently turn toward universal laws anchoring ourselves to that which is changeless—the Bhagavad Gita and the Bible."

Yogananda himself once said, "Every person needs a retreat, a dynamo of silence, where one can go for the exclusive purpose of being recharged by the Infinite."

Self-Realization Fellowship Retreat
215 K Street
Encinitas, CA 92024
(760) 753-1811
www.babaji.org/retreats

Shasta Abbey
Mount Shasta, CA

In the very northern reaches of California near the foot of Mount Shasta, where the huge mountain's visage is often shrouded in mist and fog, a group of Soto Zen Buddhists came in 1970 to found Shasta Abbey. The monastery occupies 20 acres of forested land a few miles from town. The first community members moved into the abandoned motel without any electricity, gas, or phone. One winter morning, they awoke to find that seven feet of snow had fallen and they were completely isolated. For two weeks they subsisted on carrot-and-onion soup—the only food they had —until outside help could reach them. Since those early days, an entire complex has been built among the tall pines where a thriving community of 35 monks live. Covered outdoor passageways lead from the dining room to the subdued meditation room, where there are magnificent Buddha statues and shrines. The community follows a rigorous schedule that begins at 5:55 A.M. with zazen, and continues with work and meals throughout the day till 10 P.M. Unlike any other Buddhist abbey, here the morning and evening office is sung in English in four-part harmony, like Gregorian chant, with organ accompaniment.

The abbey was founded by Reverend Master Jiyu-Kennett, an Englishwoman who studied Soto Zen Buddhism in Japan and came to the United States following her master's wish that she transmit the teachings to the West. She is the author of several well-known books on Buddhism, including *Zen's Eternal Life* and *The Wild, White Goose* in two volumes, diaries of her years in Japan.

Shasta Abbey is the headquarters of Buddhist Contemplatives in the

Soto Zen school and was founded as a seminary. Kennett-roshi describes the differences between Buddhism and Christianity thus: "There is no savior in Buddhism. You have to do it yourself. No one else will meditate for you. At the time of death you will judge yourself. . . . The ability to die in peace means the ability to live in peace. . . . We make our own hell. The only judging that is done is done by ourselves, thus hiding ourselves from the Cosmic Buddha. Everyone possesses Buddha nature— or, as Christians call it, the soul. It is hidden from our view because of our opinion of ourselves. The art of meditation removes that separation so we can return to our basic nature and truly know it. Meditation has nothing whatever to do with self-improvement. . . . Its purpose is to become one with the Cosmic Buddha, or have an experience of God."

There are guest rooms for 20 singles or 50 sharing. The rooms are clean and efficient. The food is vegetarian. There are retreats throughout the year from two days to two weeks, and many traditional Buddhist festival ceremonies are celebrated. This is a serious, sincere community, helpful and caring. Guests are expected to stay on the grounds during their visit. As a monk said, "There is always a schedule to follow. Be willing to stay where you are and concentrate on this specific approach while you're here."

Shasta Abbey
3724 Summit Drive
Mount Shasta, CA 96067
(530) 926-4208
www.shastaabbey.org

Sonoma Mountain Zen Center
Santa Rosa, CA

Set on 80 sloping, hilltop acres that look over the Valley of the Moon, where Jack London lived, the charming buildings of the Sonoma Mountain Zen Center sit unobtrusively in this quiet section of Sonoma County. The views across the valley are ever-changing in the mists that drift slowly in and out, then sharply clear on bright, sunny days—a natural metaphor for the condition of the mind during Zen practice.

In 1973–74, Jakusho Kwong-roshi with seven students formed the center to continue the Soto Zen lineage of his teacher, Shunryu Suzuki-roshi. Suzuki was one of the few Buddhist priests in Japan to publicly oppose the rise of militarism prior to World War II. He regularly published warnings against aggressive military action. In 1959, Suzuki came to San Francisco and brought the stability of his Zen practice into the chaos of the Beat Generation, a voice of integrity in a society searching for values. Many Americans had abandoned their religious heritage because they felt the spirit behind the form was dead. Zen was attractive, a new form, and it felt alive. "But," as Kwong-roshi points out, "if you only perfect the form without getting the spirit, Zen is just as dead. When the spirit is alive you can see changes in people's lives and this is experienced outside the zendo."

There is a community of ten who live here, and other regular practitioners live nearby. There is a program of retreats throughout the year from three to seven days, as well as one-day sitting sessions and introductory workshops. There is a year-long resident training program and a month-long Ango Practice in February and July. The rigorous daily schedule begins with 5:15 A.M. sitting meditation, balanced by walking meditation, where each mindful, slow step around the sitting room, following the person in front, helps one to be aware of every breath.

There are rustic cabins and rooms around the grounds for guests, who should bring their own sleeping bags. Heat is provided by woodstoves or electric heaters. There is a shared bathroom in the main building. Meals are taken with the community in the dining room.

The very available American-born Kwong-roshi encourages the friendliness and hospitality that are evident here. Kwong approaches Zen practice in a relaxed way: "The more you practice, you realize it's not for gain but for gratitude. Gratitude becomes the biggest treasure, and practice is the way." Suzuki-roshi had said to him: "We are the same." Kwong explained, "He was telling me that the student and the master are the same . . . we are both Buddha!"

Sonoma Mountain Zen Center
Genjo-Ji
6367 Sonoma Mountain Road
Santa Rosa, CA 95404
(707) 545-8105
www.smzc.net

Tassajara Zen Mountain Center
Carmel Valley, CA

Deep in the coastal mountain range of central California, in the middle of Los Padres National Forest east of Monterey and up a torturous 14-mile dirt road that ascends and descends more than 5,000 feet from Carmel Valley, the San Francisco Zen Center and its roshi, Shunryu Suzuki, established a monastic community in 1966. Closed to visitors during the winter for intensive Zen training periods, the remote retreat is open for guests from early May to September. During this period, visitors may join residents in sitting meditation, participate in programs and discussions, and attend lectures. The orientation is Zen Buddhist, which cultivates mindfulness to explore one's own nature and that of others, and awaken to and appreciate the natural beauty of life.

Formerly a resort where people came for the hot baths and seclusion, this area has changed little since the Esalen Indians used it for purification and healing. The baths are an integral part of community life. The hot spring area at the edge of a cold creek is divided so that men and women bathe separately; going from the hot tubs to the cold creek water is an invigorating experience. There are decks for sunning and relaxation. *Tassajara* is the Spanish word for "a place for drying meat."

The accommodations are spare but clean and comfortable. A new bathhouse was constructed in 1993. Rooms and pathways are lighted by kerosene lamps. Bring a flashlight and your own towel. Bedding is provided. The cuisine is vegetarian, abundant, and legendary. This is the home of Edward Brown's *Tassajara Bread Book* and *Tassajara Cooking*. If there is a sensual side to the austere regimen of Zen, it is in eating. The food itself is a lesson in mindfulness as one looks at it, prepares it, consumes it, and thinks of its benefit, thanking the plants for giving us their energy and dedicating it for the good of others.

There are programs through which participants can come for five days to two months and become fully integrated into the community through meditation, work, and study, or one can visit for just a few days.

The seclusion and peace, clean air, and magnificent views at Tassajara, the first mountain home of American Buddhist practice, have made it a popular refuge, so plan far in advance.

Tassajara Zen Mountain Center
39171 Tassajara Road
Carmel Valley, CA 93924
Mailing: 300 Page Street
San Francisco, CA 94102
(415) 865-1895
sfzc.org/tassajara

Vedanta Retreat
Olema, CA

The 2,000 acres of the Vedanta Retreat are surrounded by the 62,000-acre Point Reyes National Seashore, a part of the California coast set aside to remain forever in its natural state. The drive is bordered by huge eucalyptus trees and leads to a sanctuary of meadows and woods. The Vedanta Society of Northern California, located in San Francisco, acquired this property in the mid 1940s. There are a dozen rooms: four for men in the meticulously refurbished main house, built in 1867; and eight for women in a separate building in a nearby meadow. The rooms are comfortable and well furnished. Each guesthouse has its own meditation room. There is no formal retreat program. Visitors are asked to make sure that their personal practice does not interfere with others. Those who stay overnight should bring their own linens or a sleeping bag and bring and prepare their own food, cleaning up afterward.

Those interested in staying overnight or longer should arrange an interview with the swami in charge at the Vedanta Society headquarters in San Francisco. Day visitors are also welcome and can use the retreat from 10 A.M. to 6 P.M. with no reservations required. Spiritual seekers of any religious persuasion are welcome.

Vedanta means the end (*anta*) of the Vedas (ancient Sanskrit texts), or the culmination of spiritual knowledge. The basic teaching of Vedanta is that the essence of all beings and things, from grass to God, is spiritual, infinite and eternal, nonchanging and indivisible; that people in their true nature are divinely spiritual, one reality, one being. As is taught in the Upanishads, "Thou art That."

Swami Vivekananda, a chief disciple of Ramakrishna, brought Vedanta from India to the West in the 1890s. He taught that freedom can be attained "by work, or worship, or psychic control, or philosophy; by one or more or all of these." He emphasized three teachings as most appropriate and most needed by the modern world: A person's highest achievement and greatest happiness lie in fully manifesting one's own divinity; one's clearest vision lies in perceiving divinity everywhere; and one's truest worship is in selfless service to others, for they are in reality God.

Vedanta Retreat
P.O. Box 215
Oleama, CA 94950
(415) 663-1258
(415) 922-2323 1st time retreatants
www.sfvedanta.org

Villa Maria del Mar
Santa Cruz, CA

In 1891, the Catholic Ladies Aid Society of California accepted a gift of 20 acres of oceanfront land on Monterey Bay and built a three-story hotel where "women of limited means could spend a week recuperating from family cares, at little or no cost, and where sisters from teaching and nursing orders could afford to come in groups." Over the years, thousands have benefited from this altruistic attitude. The society rented half the rooms at prevailing resort rates to balance the costs of their charity. In 1963, the Sisters of the Holy Names purchased the property for a retreat center and committed themselves to keeping Villa Maria a place where hospitality prevails. There is an old-fashioned charm here as well as a sweeping view south to Carmel Point and north to Santa Cruz. The beach is easily accessible.

There are 20 rooms in the main house, and another 21 rooms in nearby Siena Hall and the Annex. The rooms are clean and comfortable, most with private baths. A large lobby with cozy places to read is next to the dining room, where the windows face the bay. The buffet-style meals are excellent.

Mass is said daily in Star of the Sea Chapel a few steps away. Built in 1906, the picturesque structure is a vestige of the past. Saturday evening mass is standing-room-only.

To maintain the spiritual mission of the villa, the community of sisters who live here host a regular schedule of retreats responding to the needs of today's Church. They are flexible to groups who have their own agendas. Private retreatants are also welcome. "Many who come are tired," one sister said. "They look out to the expanse of ocean, unwind, relax, and are healed."

Villa Maria del Mar
2-1918 E. Cliff Drive
Santa Cruz, CA 95062
(831) 475-1236
www.villamariadelmar.org

Nada Hermitage
Crestone, CO

This community of hermits chose its location for solitude and natural grandeur. It is situated on the gently sloping eastern edge of the San Juan Valley, which is the largest alpine valley in North America—the size of the state of Delaware. The site looks west to the San Juan Mountains some 50 miles away. The community moved here from Arizona in the early 1980s when the 180,000-acre Baca Ranch in southern Colorado was being divided into parcels that were donated to religious groups who would improve and live on the land. Nada is in the foothills of the Sangre de Cristos, where several mountains tower more than 14,000 feet. Visible to the south is Blanca Peak, the fourth highest peak in Colorado, one of four mountains sacred to the Hopi.

This youthful group of apostolic hermits, both men and women, was inspired by the teachings and writings of Father William McNamara, who had been deeply influenced by discussions with Thomas Merton in the 1950s. They live together, but each has an individual hermitage and lives a life of solitude, with personal duties and responsibilities to community life. The schedule is a simple one: Lauds at 6 A.M. and Vespers at 5 P.M. daily except on days of solitude. On Saturday night there is an all-night vigil before the Blessed Sacrament in the chapel, each person signing up to spend an hour during the night. On Sunday there is a sung mass at 9 A.M., followed by a community breakfast in Agape, the lovely main building, which houses a library, the dining room, the main kitchen, and food supplies. This is a happy, convivial occasion when guests and community members share social time and only one person speaks at a time, thus all are able to follow the discussion.

Retreatants come for a week from Thursday afternoon to the following Wednesday at noon. A monk is available for spiritual direction if requested. The artfully designed and constructed adobe hermitages are heated by passive solar energy and a backup woodstove. Each has electricity, kitchen facilities and utensils, and a bathroom. The hermitages are set apart from one another and face south with a view of the valley and distant mountains. Bedding and food are provided, but each person sleeps when tired and eats when ready—alone.

The chapel is always open for prayer and reflection; the high ceilings over the altar are balanced by tall windows looking out to the grand mountains. There is a significant sculpture of Christ crucified that seems to capture the essence of the suffering. Standing outside alone in the quiet of that desert, looking at the vast, clear sky filled with stars and the black outlines of the far-off mountains, one experiences the full power of solitude.

Nada Hermitage
Spiritual Life Institute
P.O. Box 219
Crestone, CO 81131
www.spirituallifeinstitute.org/nada

St. Benedict's Monastery
Snowmass, CO

In 1956 a group of Trappist monks from Spencer, Massachusetts, chose this place deep in the Rocky Mountains as the site for their new foundation. Seven miles from the nearest village, in a valley more than 8,000 feet above sea level, it is surrounded by the craggy peaks of the majestic mountains that run north and south through the state of Colorado. One monk mused, "A monastery should be in a place that is hard to get to and difficult to leave." Traversing mountain passes on the way from Denver, one realizes the courage and tenacity necessary to build and live here. The daily drama of nature is awesome: The wind moves the snow on the distant mountain peaks, coyotes utter their mournful cries, an owl hoots in the still night air beneath the star-filled sky.

All the more striking are the somberly attired monks who assemble seven times each day in the stark, timeless chapel to sing the canonical hours. Guests are invited to sit along the walls just behind the monks' chairs, much closer than usual. Hymnals and prayer books are available for those who wish to join in the liturgy. On Thursday evening, mass is celebrated at a table, like the Last Supper. After the main service, the monks assemble in the foyer and chat amiably with retreatants: "We're glad you're here; thanks for making the effort." They see this as an extension of the service. The goodwill these men bring to visitors is wonderful to behold.

This is the home of Father Thomas Keating, the noted writer and proponent of centering prayer. The guestmaster is Father Theophane, author of *Tales of a Magic Monastery*, a gem of parables that has helped many on their spiritual search. The guesthouses, one a former farm-house, have facilities for cooking, and visitors should bring and prepare their own food. The guest facilities are some distance from the chapel, along a road used only for the monastery, and it is a pleasant walk to services. The 4,000 acres of monastery property offer plenty of space for hiking. In the winter, one can cross-country-ski.

The monastery supports itself by ranching and by baking and selling the popular Snowmass Monastery Cookies. When the monks began their cookie business some years ago, they called on Bernard Tetsugen Glassman, a Zen master in New York, who founded and still runs the Greyston Bakery, and he helped them get started.

There is a once-a-month intensive retreat often run by Father Keating. From time to time, groups will meet here, using this quiet, out-of-the-way spot to concentrate on their own spiritual program. Private retreatants can usually be accommodated for a few days or longer. There is even a six-month program for those interested in living with the community and learning the discipline of St. Benedict through "the bells and the eyes of the brethren."

St. Benedict's Monastery
1012 Monastery Road
Snowmass, CO 81654
(970) 927-1162
www.snowmass.org

Abbey of Regina Laudis
Bethlehem, CT

The original land for this monastery was donated by an industrialist from Waterbury who felt that the hilltop was too beautiful for anything but the worship of God. In 1946, nuns of the Catholic Benedictines of Strict Observance arrived from the French abbey of Jouarre and settled in what is now St. Joseph's, the guesthouse for men.

The main monastery building, a former factory, has been remodeled to house the 50 nuns. Surrounded by wooden fences, the main building is off limits to all guests, except for the entrance, the guest refectory, and the wood-paneled chapel that is connected to the convent. Here the nuns gather seven times a day, between 6:45 A.M. and 8 P.M., and once at night, at 2 A.M., to sing the Hours of the Divine Office. Mass in Gregorian chant is sung every day at 7:45 A.M. The nuns sit behind a screen, the curtain parted for most services so the habited singers can be glimpsed through the latticework.

The guesthouses are austere—reminiscent of a working farm—but clean and sensible, with great attention to whatever is needed. St. Joseph's, with sparsely furnished (bed, writing table, and chair) single rooms for men only and community bath, is like a French farmhouse. The main living/dining area is dominated by a stone fireplace, with windows on either side that give balance and light to the dark wood walls.

St. Gregory's, the women's guesthouse (an authentic 1794 New England farmhouse), is decorated in soft, pale colors. Women take their meals in the monastery in a separate refectory from the nuns. Men's meals are brought to St. Joseph's and served by one of the nuns. The monastery is a working farm with dairy cows that provide fresh milk that the nuns make into butter and cheese. They also bake their own bread, and the food is excellent.

There are no organized retreats, but hospitality is a very important part of the life here. A nun is assigned to talk with each visitor as the need arises. The monastery makes no distinction as to race or creed, but those who come should be willing to observe the monastic lifestyle. The nuns are rooted in the ancient Benedictine monastic ways, but are still flexible to the future. "Come to find peace of mind," one suggested, "and the strength of a spiritual existence."

The monastery grounds comprise 300 acres, most of it used for farming. There is a separate building that houses an 18th-century Neapolitan crèche. The elegant figures depict individual attitudes toward the infant Jesus, from devotion and love to indifference. It is fitting that this nativity scene should be a major point of interest on the grounds of a monastery in a place called Bethlehem.

Abbey of Regina Laudis
Box 273
Flanders Road
Bethlehem, CT 06751
(203) 266-7727
www.abbeyofreginalaudis.com

Vikingsborg Guest House
Convent of St. Birgitta
Darien, CT

This spacious guesthouse is on a cove of Long Island Sound, in a quiet residential neighborhood. In 1957 the property was donated by Margaret Tjader Harris to the Birgittines, an order of nuns founded by Saint Birgitta of Sweden in the 14th century. Margaret's parents, a Swedish father and an American mother, were missionaries, deeply religious people who made their house available to people of all faiths except Catholics. Margaret, who was curious about all religions, often traveled to Sweden. There she became a friend and admirer of Mother Elisabeth, who was instrumental in the resurgence of the Birgittines in the 20th century. Margaret converted to Catholicism, and donated the beautiful waterfront property to the Catholic nuns who now live here. In her book on the life of Mother Elisabeth, Margaret wrote, "Change is the law of nature, the rhythm of history; the tumult, decline, resurgence, triumph and decline again—the wheel of human life."

The sisters, who still wear religious habits with distinctive white bands securing the veils to their heads like hot-cross buns, have 12 beds available for guests. The furnishings, gathered by the Tjaders during their mission travels, are outstanding, museum-quality pieces. Meals are served in the grand dining room by the nuns three times a day. One of the wings of the house, the former trophy room, has been converted to a chapel where the nuns gather daily to sing liturgy at 6 A.M., noon,

4 P.M., and 8 P.M. Mass is said Monday through Friday at 7 A.M. and at 8 on Saturday and Sunday. Guests are welcome.

There is a spacious porch, often used as a meeting room for local groups who come to worship in the chapel and have a meal. The nuns do not give retreats, but make their house available for group meetings and for individuals and couples seeking a quiet, restful place.

The nine-acre convent grounds, with tall pines and well-tended lawns, have a feeling of substance and continuity. The seawall has stairs where missionaries led their followers into the water to be baptized. There is a small stone chapel, set on a knoll, a former playhouse that has been converted to a place of prayer and contemplation. At night there is a wonderful view to the south, across the water, of the twinkling lights on Long Island.

Vikingsborg Guest House
Convent of St. Birgitta
4 Runkenhage Road
Darien, CT 06820
(203) 655-1068
www.birgittines-us.com

Camp Weed and the
Cerveny Conference Center
Live Oak, FL

Located in Suwannee County in north central Florida on 350 acres next to White Lake, the buildings of this Episcopal center were sited to respect live oaks of exceptional beauty. The natural wood structures have connecting walkways and decks that meander in a casual way yet work efficiently. There is a beautiful new chapel building constructed on log pilings out over the lake, with high beamed ceilings and windows that look out to the water and shoreline. Mandi's Chapel, completed in 1995, was donated by the Pettway family of Jacksonville in loving memory of their daughter. A full-time priest joined the center in 1995.

The first camp experience was held in this diocese on a public beach in 1924 through the influence of Bishop Weed. During the decades that followed, the summer experiences were repeated to ever-growing numbers in different locales. Realizing the benefits and importance of the gatherings, the Episcopal diocese acquired this property on White Lake in 1978, and Camp Weed found a permanent home under the guidance of Bishop Cerveny. In 1982, seven cabins were built near the lake, and a new dining room and kitchen were added in 1983. In 1985 the adult conference center was started, and by 1988 first-rate rooms were available. Now there are 40 motel-like rooms with double beds and private baths, cabins with 150 bunk beds, plus tent sites and RV hookups. The 350 acres of rolling woodlands and recreation fields offer ample space. The service roads that wind around the property make for excellent walking.

Personal retreats start Sunday night and go through Friday lunch.

Those who come are looking for a quiet time in a comfortable, natural setting. There are also Elderhostel programs dealing with Florida history, nature, and the environment. The director points out: "Camp Weed and the Cerveny Conference Center are extensions of the ministry of each congregation, a Christ-centered place set apart in natural solitude, enabling worship, renewal, education, enrichment, and education, a community for all the people of God."

Camp Weed and the
Cerveny Conference Center
11057 Camp Weed Place
Rte. 3, Box 140
Live Oak, FL 32060
(386) 364-5250
www.campweed.org

The Florida United Methodist
Life Enrichment Center
Fruitland Park, FL

On the shores of beautiful Lake Griffin, the Florida Conference of the United Methodist Church owns 87 acres and has built a most impressive adult retreat center. There is housing for 400 persons in four motel-type buildings for year-round use. Each room has two beds and private bath. There are 16 specially designed rooms for the handicapped with no steps anywhere on ground level. The cafeteria-style dining room can serve 400. Meeting rooms can handle 200, and smaller rooms as many as 90. A new $1.4 million auditorium seats 800. The buildings are spaced around the dining and conference rooms looking out to the lake.

Through the foresight and energy of former director Warren Willis, the land was purchased as parcels became available in the 1950s and 1960s. The center is envisioned as an extension of the ministry of Jesus Christ providing a setting for church-related groups to hold retreats, planning and study sessions, and other spiritual activities. The center is available for the use of all churches. Individuals can be accommodated on a space-available basis.

People come here attracted by the quiet. Life is unhurried and there is an opportunity to contemplate and reflect, a place for introspection and renewal.

We were told that occasionally there are alligators on the grounds, and that if we saw one, we should run zigzag, since they travel only in straight lines. Remarkably, for all the gators rumored to be in the lake, none showed up during our visit, but serenity, goodwill, and humor were quite evident.

The Florida United Methodist
Life Enrichment Center
4991 Picciola Road
Fruitland Park, FL 34731
Mailing: P.O. Box 490108
Leesburg, FL 34749
(866) 862-2677
www.lecretreats.org

Holy Name Monastery
St. Leo, FL

The original Holy Name convent was a three-story frame structure 140 feet long and 75 feet wide, and when the sisters acquired 40 acres next to Lake Jovita adjoining St. Leo College, they decided to have the entire building moved the half mile to the new land. A steel cable was stretched around the building and attached to a "dead-man timber" buried deep in the ground. The cable was attached to a winch and two oxen were hitched to it. The oxen walked around the winch, stepping over the cable, and as the building inched forward, a half-dozen workers pulled the rollers from the rear of the convent and set them down in front. When the convent advanced 50 feet to the winch, they unhitched the oxen, and reburied the "dead man" 50 feet farther on. It took six weeks for the convent to roll to its new location. Even more remarkable was that 13 academy students and 9 sisters lived in it all the while. "It was a long time before we had light and water," one sister wrote. This was 1911, more than 20 years after the first Benedictine sisters arrived from Allegheny, Pennsylvania, to teach in local elementary schools and start an academy for young ladies.

By 1961, the original rolling convent died of old age and was replaced by the present building, which is home to 28 sisters who teach and work at the college and go to other occupations, one by motorcycle. The three-story elevator building has guest rooms for 20 with shared baths. Excellent meals are taken with the community in the refectory. The sisters gather to pray in the chapel three times a day and guests are welcome at all services. Mass is celebrated daily.

Directed retreats can be arranged in advance and group retreats are scheduled regularly on specific topics such as Discernment, Vocation, or Monastic Experience. The sisters host Elderhostels on such topics as How Dreams Are Made, Unsung Heroes, and Myths. They teach courses in Psychology, the Testaments, Literature, and Music. One retreatant, arriving late, was concerned about whether there was room for him. "Oh, that's okay," he said, "as long as it has water and heat."

This cheerful community makes guests feel welcome and comfortable. Surrounded by orange trees near Lake Jovita and sharing the adjacent St. Leo College campus, it is a most congenial place to be.

The nearby St. Leo College is run by Benedictine monks who also have a guesthouse and retreat programs.

Holy Name Monastery
P.O. Box H
33201 State Road 52
St. Leo, FL 33574
(352) 588-8320
(352) 588-8184 (St. Leo Abbey)
www.floridabenedictines.com

Wakulla Springs Lodge and Conference Center
Wakulla Springs, FL

Only 15 miles south of Tallahassee, Wakulla Springs is like a primeval forest. It is also a haven of peace, beauty, and rest. The 4,000 acres of unspoiled wilderness is known for the spring that flows from an underground river at the rate of more than 600,000 gallons per minute into the Wakulla River, which then flows fifteen miles to the Gulf of Mexico. Mystery surrounds the spring: Where does the fresh water come from, how did the mastodon skeletons end up on its ledge, who killed "Old Joe," a 200-year-old alligator now stuffed and in a glass case in the lobby of the lodge? Visitors have plenty of time to solve these puzzles because aside from good food, comfortable beds in spacious rooms, and nature trails, the lodge has no scheduled programs. This is the ultimate natural retreat, where sightings of Florida's exotic and plentiful wildlife abound.

The property was purchased in 1933 by Ed Ball, a tycoon who managed the Dupont empire in Florida. Interested in preserving nature and serenity and being able to enjoy it conveniently and comfortably, he built the two-story Spanish-style lodge as a special retreat using marble —mostly from Tennessee—in the floors, on the steps and risers, for baseboards and bathroom walls. The ceiling beams of the lobby are southern cypress decorated with colorful Aztec and Toltec designs. Spanish tiles adorn the doorway between porch and lobby. The huge fireplace is set with gigantic logs that burn all day. The iron grillwork on the stairway features herons, ibises, and egrets. The archways and grill doors are Moorish. The gracious airy dining room is glass-enclosed, which enables diners to watch a continual flow of birds visiting the large feeders just outside. Dining is southern-style with special soups and hearty dishes, a reminder of earlier plantation days.

The property was placed under the protection of the National Audubon Society in the 1960s and the area is closed to hunting and fishing. Birds and wildlife sense the protection and many fine sights are available from the lawn, planted with magnolia and hickory trees, which goes down to the spring. Mullet jump and alligators glide by, white ibises nest across the water, and ducks of varying color and spirit poke around the bank. A pair of pileated woodpeckers work among the tall pines.

The Florida Department of Environmental Protection manages the park and Florida State University operates the lodge and conference center. Both are open to the public year-round. One regular visitor said: "It's the quiet and solitude that bring me back every year."

Wakulla Springs State Park & Lodge
550 Wakulla Park Drive
Wakulla Springs, FL 32327
(850) 926-0700
www.floridastateparks.org/wakullasprings

Abbey of Our Lady of the Holy Spirit
Conyers, GA

On the feast day of St. Benedict, March 21, 1944, a small group of Trappist monks left their monastery at Gethsemani, Kentucky, to go to the Honey Creek Plantation in rural Georgia, 30 miles east of Atlanta. This was to become the first monastery founded in the United States by another American house of the Order of Cistercians of the Strict Observance, also known as Trappists. These monks trace their lineage to an 11th-century reform movement which sought to break away from worldly entanglements and free the soul for a life of contemplation. At that time, monasticism had grown wealthy, comfortable, and worldly. Following the Benedictine Rule, the Trappists stressed the need for a life of work and prayer, penance, austerity, and expiation. More than one of the original Conyers monks had said why he chose the Trappists: "Because it was the hardest life to be found in the Church."

The first monks shared a converted barn with cows and chickens, "threatening to compete with a sharecropper's cabin as far as discomfort was concerned," wrote Thomas Merton. By December 1944, they had built a pine-board monastery. They immediately began the present monastery building and church, and in 1960 both were completed. The guesthouse was opened in 1969.

There are 2,000 acres of monastery property, undulating pastures and fields. The monks produce hay, raise cattle, bake bread, grow bonsai, and produce ornamental stained glass. The windows of the Gothic church reflect the orderliness of transcendent truth and encourage a calm atmosphere for contemplative prayer. The window patterns are geometric designs fitted together to produce nondistracting colors. Blues predominate in the nave while a golden light from white, yellow, orange, and red glass dominates the sanctuary.

There are 40 rooms for men and women who come in small groups or individually. One regular retreat offers an orientation talk and then invites retreatants to go into silence and create an atmosphere of prayer. Meals are served buffet-style and eaten in silence. The feeling here is ecumenical, it seems a place that transcends religious affiliation and provides a direct connection to the spirit.

Here are extracts from some of scores of letters received by the guest-master: "I cannot place a price on the value of my time here." "How much I feel the love of Christ here in the welcome you extend to others, especially to women and those of other faiths." "Having never been to a monastery," wrote a Protestant minister, "and not being Roman Catholic, I was apprehensive. I did not need to worry." "Both as a Protestant and a woman, I feel particularly blessed by your willingness to open this place of quiet sanctuary to me."

Abbey of Our Lady of the Holy Spirit
2625 Highway 212 SW
Conyers, GA 30094
(770) 760-0959
www.trappist.net

Convent of St. Helena
Augusta, GA

The convent complex stands on a ridge of sand hills which are part of a prehistoric beach formed eons ago. From the convent windows, you can look east to South Carolina and imagine you can still see the ocean. This 20-acre property at the end of a road is reached through quiet neighborhood streets. The Episcopal sisters who live here are of the Order of St. Helena, a religious community for women founded in 1945. The motherhouse is in Vails Gate, New York. Other convents are located in New York City and Seattle, Washington. In the order, there are four sisters who are ordained priests.

There are ten single guest rooms with shared baths. Nutritious meals are served in the refectory and daily prayers are said in the modern chapel. The community caters to small retreats, individuals, and spiritual direction. Trails lead into the woods where benches are placed for rest and reflection. This is an oasis of quiet above the bustle of Augusta. Some regular retreatants come annually to coincide with the Masters Golf Tournament at the Augusta National Golf Club not far away.

Although the convent is located in a lovely residential neighborhood, you feel as though you were in the country. And the four-sided, tentlike chapel, with its bird's-eye view of the town, beckons you to prayer.

One of the sisters here works as a hospital chaplain and sings with the Augusta Choral Society. From her mission of prayer, she's learned to "listen and try not to fix people." The simplicity of wisdom.

Convent of St. Helena
3042 Eagle Drive
P.O. Box 5645
Augusta, GA 30916
(706) 798-5201
www.osh.org
(No overnight guests now.)

Monastery of the Holy Cross
Chicago, IL

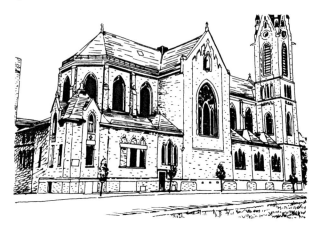

A monastery, according to Webster, is a house or place of residence occupied by a community of persons, especially monks, living in seclusion from the world under religious vows. Usually we find monasteries in rural, bucolic settings with the main buildings set on a hill looking out on a tranquil scene. So a new monastery on the south side of Chicago in the Bridgeport neighborhood causes eyebrows to raise.

This group of Catholic monks seeks to live the ancient monastic ideal of unceasing prayer in a contemporary context, not by withdrawing from the world but by bringing their prayer into the city and the city into their prayer. Part of a monastic community founded in Paris in 1975, the Monks of the Holy Cross of Jerusalem have five distinctive characteristics: They (1) are city dwellers, (2) earn wages, (3) rent their housing, (4) have no walled cloister, and (5) are part of the local church.

In the mid 1980s, three American parish priests in Minnesota heard about the French community. They first visited in 1986, spent time there, and determined to bring the concept to the United States. During that same period, churches were being closed in Chicago. When Cardinal Bernardin was contacted, he met with the priests, heard their story, and helped them lease a church from the archdiocese. The priests moved into the Gothic-style Immaculate Conception Church in July 1991 and did their own renovation. The monastery was established as a canonical entity on December 25, 1991.

The church is open for prayer morning, noon, and Eucharist in the evening to accommodate a working person's schedule. The chant is

Byzantine-style written by the contemporary French composer André Gouze. The monks have jobs as teachers, chaplains, and whatever else they are able to find. They use computers for data entry with Electronic Scriptorium, performing services for libraries.

There are 4 rooms with shared baths for retreatants in an upstairs wing of the monastery. Guests can join the community in the silent refectory where food is set out buffet-style. There is a semienclosed yard between the buildings. In good weather, grass and lawn chairs make this a most peaceful place to sit and read or ruminate, and as the sounds of city life waft over the back wall, you think, how appropriate.

Monastery of the Holy Cross
3111 S. Aberdeen Street
Chicago, IL 60608
(773) 927-7424
www.chicagomonk.org

Mary Goodwin Guest House
St. Mary-of-the-Woods, IN

On Easter Sunday 1979, the Mary Goodwin Guest House was dedicated so that visitors to the beautiful college campus would have a place to stay. Harold Goodwin, who lived in nearby Terre Haute, donated the funds in loving memory of his wife, Mary, who died in the late 1960s. The guesthouse has 19 rooms and can accommodate 38 people. Each room shares a bath with an adjoining room. The building is on two levels, and there is a kitchenette on each floor. Visitors can bring their own food or take meals cafeteria-style at nearby O'Shaughnessy dining hall, where three meals a day are catered by a professional food service.

The guesthouse is on the campus of St. Mary-of-the-Woods College, a liberal arts college founded by the Sisters of Providence. In 1840 Mother Theodore Guerin led a group of five sisters from France to southern Indiana. Living as pioneers, they answered the call to establish schools, work in hospitals and orphanages, and bring aid and spiritual comfort to European immigrants. Mother Theodore was available to every need of those around her, and in July 1992, the church decreed her "Venerable," the first step toward sainthood. There are more than 700 Providence sisters in 27 states and in Taiwan, and more than 300 live here in the motherhouse, a large brick building behind the church. The campus is as elegant as they come, with mature trees and lawns, new buildings blended with old, large with small, and a splashing fountain. The campus Church of the Immaculate Conception was built in the 1880s of Italian Renaissance design and many Providence sisters pray and worship there daily. Over the main altar, rather than a crucifixion scene, there is a smiling, fully clothed Christ, embodying the true message of Christianity: renewal and rebirth rather than death.

The sisters seem to understand the power of prayer, and this paradise of a campus reflects that. There are weekend programs that encourage people to visit the National Shrine of Our Lady of Providence and seven other shrines and groupings on the grounds. Retreats are offered regularly.

Mary Goodwin Guest House
Providence Center
St. Mary-of-the-Woods, IN 47876
(812) 535-5131 Guest House
(812) 535-2946 Hermitages

St. Meinrad Archabbey
St. Meinrad, IN

In 1854 monks from Switzerland came to southern Indiana to serve German-Catholic settlers. They named their new monastery after St. Meinrad, a ninth-century Benedictine monk known for his hospitality, who lived as a hermit deep in the forests and shared his belongings with the poor and gave spiritual counseling to those who sought him out. Following in the footsteps of their namesake, the monks have a splendid guesthouse with 25 double rooms, each with a private bath. Meals are served cafeteria-style in the lower level of the guesthouse. Weekend and midweek retreats throughout the year are an ongoing part of their ministry for those seeking renewal and growth through prayer in a conducive atmosphere.

The guesthouse is just a short walk from the abbey church, which was completed in 1907. All the stone for the romanesque church was quarried one mile northeast of here by the monks and local workers and brought to the site in mule-driven wagons. The church windows are painted glass and were executed by the Royal Bavarian Art Institute of Munich, Germany. The windows in the north and south walls depict the eight beatitudes. At the top of each window is a Benedictine saint whose life exemplified that beatitude. The southeast windows depict the martyrdom of St. Meinrad himself.

The impressive mural of Christ in the apse of the church was completed in 1943 by Dom Gregory de Wit, a Belgian monk who also painted the murals at St. Joseph Abbey in St. Benedict, Louisiana (see page 94).

The monks sing liturgy morning, noon, and evening with mass at 5:15 P.M. Monday to Friday, 8 A.M. Saturday, and 9:30 A.M. Sunday. Times for all services may vary in the summer.

More than 140 monks live here and many of them teach in the seminary. St. Meinrad's College and School of Theology prepares students for the priesthood, lay ministry, and Christian service. The monastery owns and operates Abbey Press, which manufactures and distributes religious and inspirational cards and gifts worldwide. The monks from St. Meinrad's have founded five other Benedictine monasteries in the United States located in Arkansas, Louisiana, Illinois, South Dakota, and California.

The monastery property encompasses 2,000 acres, 800 in farmland and 1,200 wooded. There are hiking and walking trails. A mile down the road is the Shrine of Our Lady of Monte Cassino, where pilgrimages are made twice a year to the century-old chapel.

St. Meinrad Archabbey Guest House
1 Hill Drive
St. Meinrad, IN 47577
(812) 357-6585
(800) 581-6905
www.saintmeinrad.edu

New Melleray Abbey
Peosta, IA

Sixteen Trappist monks left Mount Melleray Abbey in County Waterford, Ireland, in 1849 and sailed across the Atlantic to New Orleans, then up the Mississippi seeking farmland for a new foundation. They settled near Dubuque, Iowa, and theirs is probably the last Trappist monastery dependent solely on farming. Currently the monks raise 1,100 acres of corn and 700 acres of soybeans on their 1,900 acres. In the early 1990s, they set aside 250 acres from conventional farming to be certified organic. Their vision statement reads: "We commit ourselves to sustainable agriculture that will protect the ecological health of our environment and provide for the economic and social well-being of our community. We realize our land provides sustenance not only for ourselves but for the generations who will succeed us."

Visitors to the abbey are accorded the same care and concern as the land. The guesthouse wing is connected to the church and can accommodate 18 persons, all in rooms with private baths. Men and women of any race, creed, and color are welcome. The private retreats go from Monday noon to Friday morning, or any part thereof; weekends with planned conferences start Friday and go through Sunday. The weekend retreats are booked well in advance, so plan accordingly. Private retreatants can meet with a priest on request. Meals are taken cafeteria-style in the guest refectory on the lower level of the guesthouse.

The third floor of the guesthouse is set aside as a monastic center for those who would like to experience the daily life of a contemplative monk. These retreatants share fully in the life of the monastic community, which begins at 3:15 A.M. and ends after 7:30 P.M. Compline. Residence in the monastic center requires a minimum stay of four days and can last several weeks or longer.

The rectangular abbey church, with its high stone walls and beamed ceilings, seems balanced acoustically, and the voices of the monks' chanting is soothing, restful, and memorable. The community of 37 monks gathers here seven times a day for liturgy, and guests are welcome at all services. A banker who attends regularly said: "I come to hear myself think. I used to go to the health spa. Now I just sit here and listen."

New Melleray Abbey
6632 Melleray Circle
Peosta, IA 52068
(563) 588-2319
www.newmelleray.org

Our Lady of the Mississippi Abbey
Dubuque, IA

When the 13 Trappistine nuns from Wrentham, Massachusetts (see page 114), arrived in Iowa in 1964 to begin their new foundation, the Trappist monks at New Melleray held a welcoming dinner and decorated the dining room with posters that read WELCOME TO THE WILD WEST. The property just outside Dubuque had been acquired in July that same year —a 585-acre estate with dramatic views of the neighboring states of Wisconsin and Illinois and the Mississippi River. The large English-style country house was readily turned into a convent. There were 214 tillable acres and a tree farm of 85,000 Christmas trees. The main house and buildings were ideally located for privacy and quiet and the abbey was close to New Melleray, the Father Immediate—the sponsor of a new foundation—and the monks who would be chaplains to the sisters.

In 1965, the sisters went into the candy business, and over the years this has become their sustaining source of income. Their chocolate-coated caramels are irresistible. The chapel was built onto the convent and completed in 1968. During the 1970s, a new wing was added to include a library, kitchen, refectory, and dormitory with an individual cell for each nun. There are now 25 sisters living here from solemnly professed to novice. This is a young, vigorous community that has evolved in the long-standing traditions of Cistercian life to the circumstances of its contemporary setting. These developments have seen a differentiation from Wrentham, much like the relationship of a mother and daughter as it changes over time. As one writer points out: "One hopes that the principles and ideals of the mother will be followed by the daughter but their expression will differ in accordance with her developing character and personality. Thus the ideals of Wrentham have been adapted to the unique surroundings of a midwestern setting and to the particular qualities of its own members."

There are three separate houses for both men and women: In the big house there are 14 beds, a smaller house has three rooms and a kitchen, and there is a two-room hermitage for one person. All retreatants prepare their own meals from food provided. Guests are welcome to observe the liturgy in the chapel with the sisters: Vigils at 3:45 A.M., Lauds with mass at 6:45 A.M., noon prayer, Vespers at 5 P.M., and Compline at 7:15 P.M. The schedule is slightly different on Sunday and Monday. There are no formal retreats but a sister is available for discussion on request. The facilities are suited for those seeking silence, solitude, and prayer. Advance planning is required, especially during the summer and on weekends.

Our Lady of the Mississippi Abbey
8400 Abbey Hill
Dubuque, IA 52003
(563) 582-2595
www.mississippiabbey.org

Abbey of Gethsemani
Trappist, KY

There are 12 Trappist monasteries in the United States, 5 of which were founded from Gethsemani—those in Georgia, Utah, South Carolina, New York, and California. Gethsemani itself was founded in 1848 by monks from Melleray in western France. In the early 1800s, the United States was divided into four Catholic dioceses: Boston, New York, Philadelphia, and Bardstown, Kentucky. Bishop Flaget of Kentucky encouraged the 45 founding monks to purchase a farm near Bardstown and bring a monastic influence to the Midwest. Those first few years, the monks lived in log cabins, farmed the land, and began to build the abbey buildings on a knoll above a creek that wound through the property. Today the white monastery buildings are an impressive sight across the fields. The monks are perhaps best known for the outstanding cheese and fruitcake they produce and sell nationwide.

It was this monastery that Thomas Merton entered in 1941. Merton was one of the most influential spiritual writers and thinkers of the twentieth century, and his classic autobiography, *The Seven Storey Mountain*, describes in vivid detail the seekings of a young man and what led him to become a Trappist monk. That book and his other writings on social justice and spiritual formation have influenced and continue to influence countless people throughout the world.

The monastery has recently refurbished its guesthouse adjacent to the church. There are now 31 rooms available for guests, each with a private shower. Meals are taken cafeteria-style in a dining room in the guest wing. Private retreats are scheduled from Monday afternoon to Friday morning and on weekends from Friday afternoon to Sunday afternoon or Monday morning. The first and third weeks of each month are set aside for women, and the remainder of the month is for men. A monk is available for consultation and the retreat master conducts conferences on various topics. Mainly the monastery offers its hospitality for those who desire a place apart "to entertain silence in the heart and listen for the voice of God . . . to pray for your own discovery" (Thomas Merton). Retreatants are thus asked to limit talking to the times after meals and to designated areas. There are many acres of woodlands and fields for walking.

Guests are welcome to join the 75 monks who meet in the chapel seven times a day to sing the liturgical hours beginning with 3:15 A.M. Vigils and ending at 7:30 P.M. Compline. Mass is at 6:15 A.M. daily, 10:20 A.M. Sunday. The guest facilities are booked months ahead, so plan well in advance.

Abbey of Gethsemani
3642 Monks Road
Trappist, KY 40051
(502) 549-3117
www.monks.org

Center of Jesus the Lord
New Orleans, LA

On the edge of the French Quarter, high walls surround half a city block where in 1877 a group of Catholic Carmelite nuns began a cloistered existence of community prayer. For almost 100 years, the community occasionally added new members and thrived away from the world. The Rampart Street Parade passed by outside unnoticed; inside, the sisters pursued a life of prayer and meditation following a regimen of strict observance which began at 4:45 A.M. and ended at 11 P.M. In 1971, the few remaining sisters moved to smaller quarters, and the monastery stood empty.

In 1975, a center of renewal for the Catholic Church in the Archdiocese of New Orleans was established, led by Father Emile LaFranz, using the facilities and church of the former Carmelite Monastery for mass, prayer meetings, healing services, retreats, conferences, and individual counseling. Lives are being transformed daily in what is a true revival of a vital spirit exemplified by active works of charity such as feeding and clothing the poor, aiding and counseling the addicted, and developing a welcoming community. Indeed, the center is answering the daily prayers of the cloistered Carmelite sisters for intercession for the city and its people.

These contemplatives-in-action are the antithesis of cloistered contemplatives; if they can't do it themselves, they pray for someone who can, and energetic religious and laypeople are answering the call. A program at the center trains "Companions of Jesus the Lord" in practical discipleship and develops support groups for living the Christian message.

There are a number of rooms available for visitors interested in a close examination of this growing charismatic community. In nearby Ponchatoula, across Lake Pontchartrain, the Magnificat Center of the Holy Spirit (see page 270 in "Other Places") is an associated retreat setting.

Center of Jesus the Lord
1236 N. Rampart Street
New Orleans, LA 70116
(504) 529-1636
www.centerofjesusthelord.org

New Orleans Zen Temple
New Orleans, LA

In the warehouse district, a few blocks from the French Quarter, the New Orleans Zen Temple occupies the top floors of the American Zen Association Building. This is a residential Zen training center with a meditation hall on the second floor, resident quarters, offices, and work areas on the third, and kitchen and dining and more resident rooms on the fourth. Following the mandate of the late Soto Zen master Taisen Deshimaru, Zen monk Robert Livingston returned to the United States from Europe and in 1983 opened a temple to teach the practice of Zen. He came to New Orleans because he liked the place, and wanted to make it possible to practice Zen there.

After graduating from Cornell, Livingston worked as an international banker traveling around Europe. He made some money and played in the fast lane, fueled by alcohol. In 1972, he found himself depressed and in Paris and turned to AA. "You must have a spiritual way," he was advised, and he picked up a book about Zen. He discovered Deshimaru, who had a dojo in Paris, and sought him out. Livingston was drawn to the man's charisma, power, and peace. He became an aide to Deshimaru and spent ten years in Zen practice. "There were a lot of deep changes," Livingston admitted, "an interior revolution . . . changes, yes, but you're still yourself. Instead of being concentrated on oneself, you come to the point where you can forget yourself." Deshimaru had written: "Zazen is the fundamental revolution of our life. Zazen is the adult form of our life."

Livingston bought the New Orleans building in 1988; the anticipated nine months of renovation stretched into four years. But now the former studio where Fats Domino and Aaron Neville made hit records offers a soundproof room for meditation.

Daily sitting is practiced morning and evening. *Genmai* (soup) is served for breakfast after zazen every morning. One-day retreats are held every month and sesshin—a period of concentrated Zen practice and teaching—is held four times a year. There is room for 30 retreatants. Zen has come to the Big Easy.

New Orleans Zen Temple
748 Camp Street
New Orleans, LA 70130
(504) 525-3533
www.nozt.org

St. Joseph Abbey
St. Benedict, LA

A group of Benedictine monks traveled from St. Meinrad Abbey, Indiana, during 1889 and began a new foundation in St. Tammany parish. Their main purpose was to found a seminary to train American-born priests for this growing region. They came at the request of Archbishop Francis Janssens of New Orleans. In 1901 the monks acquired 1,200 acres a few miles outside Covington. Building began and school opened in 1902 with 22 students. By 1906, there were 135 students. A fire in 1907 put the monks back to square one, but when the disaster was reported in the national press, help came from everywhere. Andrew Carnegie gave a trainload of steel. The Fabacher family, owners of the Jackson Brewery, Cardinal Gibbons of Baltimore, and Governor Blanchard of Louisiana provided and facilitated financial support. The school was rebuilt, and monks and priests were educated to found and serve parishes, build churches and schools, and provide for the spiritual needs of the area.

Through the decades, buildings were added as needs arose and finances permitted. The magnificent church was completed in 1932. A new gym opened in 1952, new seminary buildings were completed in 1960. Renovations to the monastery were done in the 1970s. A separate building a short distance from the church, the Abbey Christian Life Center, was completed in 1965 so the monks could offer hospitality to retreat groups in a monastic setting. There are 40 neat and efficient rooms with baths in this self-contained building with a dining room, and retreats are held throughout the year for men, women, and couples. There are also a number of annual retreats for priests.

The gracious and welcoming monks gather for communal prayer in the church four times a day. Weekday mass is at 11:15 A.M., Sunday at 11. The interior church and the monks' dining room have magnificent murals painted by Dom Gregory de Wit between 1946 and 1955. The artist made his own paint mixtures to withstand the Louisiana humidity, and the paintings are still as sharp and bright as the day he completed them.

The monastery land is part of the Mississippi delta and the creeks on the property flow into Lake Pontchartrain. The swamps, marshes, bayous, and old-growth trees adorned with Spanish moss attract a variety of birdlife. Walker Percy, the noted writer who lived in nearby Covington, was an oblate of the abbey in his later years and is buried on the grounds.

St. Joseph Abbey
River Road
St. Benedict, LA 70457
(985) 892-1800
www.saintjosephabbey.com

St. Mary's Dominican Conference Center
New Orleans, LA

Along St. Charles Avenue, where elegant homes and mansions reflect the grandeur of this flamboyant and appealing city, there is a section where the Loyola and Tulane campuses almost adjoin. Just down Broadway, a short distance from St. Charles where streetcars run, the Dominican Center sits within the university neighborhood. Formerly Dominican College, the well-maintained and efficient building was refocused in 1985 as a retreat ministry. Directed retreats are available for individuals, as are spiritual direction, counseling, and days of renewal, a place for respite from family demands. Sabbatical housing is also available.

The center can be used for seminars, workshops, conferences, and community-building. There is one large conference room and 31 comfortable rooms for 62 persons in the elevator building. There is a patio and inner courtyard neatly planted with flowers, a quiet spot for relaxation. The recreation complex at nearby Loyola University can be visited with adequate notice. The Audubon Park and Zoo are just two blocks away. The Loyola Law School cafeteria is next door, and a few blocks down St. Charles the Camellia Grill and other New Orleans–style restaurants are plentiful.

The center offers intellectually stimulating seminar series discussing the works of T. S. Eliot, Flannery O'Connor, and Thomas Merton, and mystics such as Meister Eckhart and Teresa of Avila. Other series are thematic on Lent and Advent and there are periodic Progoff Intensive Journal retreats.

St. Mary's Dominican Conference Center
Sold to Loyola, instead try:
Rosaryville Spirit Life Center
39003 Rosaryville Road
Ponchatoula, LA 70454
(225) 294-5039
www.rosaryvillela.com

Marie Joseph Spiritual Center
Biddeford, ME

In 1948 the Sisters of the Presentation of Mary acquired the Ocean View Hotel as their provincial house. They operated a boarding school for 24 years, then ran a day-care center and held evening education classes until 1976, when they concentrated their efforts into the Spiritual Center. The center is less than 100 yards from a low, sandy shore that offers miles of beach walking.

The imposing gray building is home to 18 sisters, and has additional rooms for 70 retreatants. Guests can join the community in morning prayer at 7:30, daily mass at 8, midday prayers at 11:45, and vespers at 4:30 P.M. Inside the chapel, one feels as though one is at sea; windows on both sides look onto the ocean north and south.

The rooms are comfortable and clean, and there is an elevator to all floors. There are sitting rooms and other places for quiet reading and reflection. Meals are taken in the large dining room, where coffee, tea, and snacks are always available.

The sisters are followers of Blessed Anne Marie Rivier, whose desire to make Jesus Christ known to all inspires and sustains the endeavors of the group. The center offers programs to persons of all faiths, cultures, and lifestyles. Private and directed retreats are also available upon request.

This is a perfect place for those seeking a quiet time alone—in the chapel looking out to sea or seated at the tables above the dunes, smelling the salt air and feeling the ocean breezes.

Marie Joseph Spiritual Center
RFD 2
Biddeford, ME 04005
(207) 284-5671
www.mariejosephspiritual.org

All Saints Episcopal Convent
Catonsville, MD

This 88-acre Episcopal retreat is at the end of a neighborhood road, about 7 miles from Baltimore and 40 miles from Washington, D.C. Surrounded by Patapsco Valley State Park lands, the driveway winds gently up to the crest of a hill where the stone convent stands. The chapel was built in 1920—the first part of this impressive, rambling complex—and wings and sections were added in the 1940s and 1950s.

A community of All Saints Sisters of the Poor live here and come together in the chapel for Eucharist at 7 A.M. and Vespers at 5 P.M. Retreatants are required to attend all services and meals. The sisters are the only community in the Episcopal Church who still wear the wimple or white breast plate. Some people don't realize that there are Episcopal nuns and convents; this was illustrated at a recent Episcopal retreat in Florida, when an elderly Episcopalian woman came up to one of the sisters who was dressed in the traditional wimple, black veil, and long black habit, and said: "I'm so glad that relations between our churches have improved so we can be together like this." The sister said, "I'm an Episcopal nun." "Oh no," the woman insisted, "we don't have sisters." "But I am an Episcopal sister," the nun said again. The woman looked at her sternly and concluded: "I've been an Episcopalian for fifty years. You're mistaken."

The sisterhood was founded in 1851 in England, and in 1872 three English sisters came to Baltimore at the request of the Reverend Joseph Richey, rector of Mount Calvary Episcopal Church. The sisters founded and ran orphanages for the poor and saw the community grow as

American women entered. They came to Catonsville in 1885. Over the years, the ministry changed, and in 1972 the buildings were converted to provide retreats for adults in need of spiritual sustenance.

There are two weekend retreats per month from early September to mid July. There are three buildings on the property: the convent with rooms for 9 women guests, a small monastery building which can accommodate 3 men, and St. Gabriel's Retreat House with rooms for 24 men and women.

There are thousands of people who come here every year for spiritual renewal and the homemade breads and excellent food. Recently a phone call came from the Defense Department in nearby Washington requesting rooms for a group to consider "some exceedingly important decisions" and explaining that "they would like to make them in a place surrounded by prayer." They couldn't have made a better choice.

All Saints Episcopal Convent
1201 Hilton Avenue
P.O. Box 3127
Catonsville, MD 21228
(410) 747-4104
Monastery: (410) 747-6140
Retreat: (410) 747-6767
www.asspconvent.org

Sanctuary
Beallsville, MD

This 28 acres on a high point of Maryland countryside has been the home of religious communities since 1959. First, cloistered nuns of the Religious of the Eucharist, then for 22 years the Crozier Fathers, canons regular of the Holy Cross, lived here. From 1993 until 1997, a Carpatho-Russian Orthodox community used it as an adjunct to its Washington, D.C., monastery and then sold it to an Episcopal priest and his family, who continue to make the property available for small groups and individuals looking for a place to go.

The Civil War-era farmhouse, attached chapel, guesthouse, and cottage surrounded by neat fields are less than an hour by car from downtown Washington and make this accessible and attractive for those seeking a quiet place removed from the bustle of city life.

There are four rooms, each with two beds in the guesthouse, which has a full kitchen and dining area; the cottage also has a kitchen and a living room, with fireplace and beds for five. Small groups such as vestries, altar guilds, and parish groups who come have their own progams and agendas. There have been as many as 20 to 30 for day meetings.

The chapel has been recently redecorated: Clear windows have replaced the colored glass allowing in the light and feeling of nature. A fountain bubbles in one corner and the soft sound of the water brings the outdoors inside. The chapel space is surrounded by plants and flowers and has small, movable benches that can be arranged for a variety of uses. Native Panamanian art adorns the walls and tells the story of creation. The books of common prayer and hymnals are specifically Christian, but Sanctuary itself is nondenominational and all seekers are welcome.

Episcopal priest Guy Fouts and his wife, Barbara, a practicing psychotherapist, had both been looking for a place like this. Their professions helped them to understand that people's lives are so full that they needed and would welcome somewhere to rest and gain perspective. Though the name and those who live here have changed over four decades, the purpose remains the same.

Monastery of the Holy Cross
Beallsville, MD 20839
(Closed)

Eastern Point Retreat House
Gloucester, MA

This magnificent granite mansion was built in 1921, and looks out on Brace's Cove and the back shore of Gloucester. The Jesuit Fathers of New England acquired it in 1957 and added a wing to provide single rooms for 50 retreatants, some with a dramatic view of the sea. There is a large foyer where mass is said during retreats, and a variety of rooms are available for reading and meditation. Retreatants appreciate the many nooks and crannies inside the house and along the rocks by the shore. The dining room has bay windows looking out over the ocean. Each evening, taped classical music accompanies the buffet supper. Tea, coffee, and snacks are available all day.

There is a full schedule of guided and directed retreats throughout the year, facilitated by the staff of Jesuits and other qualified women and men directors. The length of the retreats varies from a weekend to a full month. Some weekends are reserved for AA retreats.

The aim of the programs is to help people discover where they are now and enable them to proceed to the next stage in their development, using scripture, prayer, and meditation. The 30-day retreats are conducted primarily in silence, with two "break" days. The atmosphere of silence and the closeness to the sea facilitate the process. "The longest journey," one staff member said, "is from the head to the gut."

People may come with problems or unresolved decisions, but here they have a chance to leave all this baggage at the gate and concentrate on strengthening and deepening their relationship with the Lord.

Eastern Point Retreat House
Gonzaga
37 Niles Pond Road
Gloucester, MA 10930
(978) 283-0013
www.easternpoint.org

Emery House
West Newbury, MA

In 1635, the Emery family arrived by ship from England; they acquired this property in 1680. It remained in the family until 1954, when the last Emery died and bequeathed it to the Anglican Society of St. John the Evangelist. This beautifully rustic 120 acres is at the confluence of the Merrimack and Artichoke rivers, down a quiet road on the outskirts of West Newbury. The main house dates from 1745. It has been carefully refurbished and retains its original quality and charm. A later addition is the stunning chapel with windows that look over the fields to the rivers beyond. The monks meet here to pray four times a day. After the last service, Compline, at 9 P.M., silence is observed until 9 A.M. the next day.

There are five lovely, modern hermitages nestled together some distance below the main house. Each is self-sufficient, with a kitchenette where basics are provided for a pickup breakfast, a private bath, wood-burning stove, and comfortable bed and furnishings. The hermitages are just a few minutes' walk from the main house, where meals are served; lunch is provided after Eucharist, and soup and salad after the evening prayer. The food is delicious.

The monks are a community of priests and brothers who take lifetime vows of poverty, celibacy, and obedience. The order was founded in England in 1866 by Father Richard Meux Benson, the vicar of Cowley; thus they are often referred to as the Cowley Monks, and are the oldest Anglican religious order for men. Their main monastery in the United States is St. Mary and St. John, located in Cambridge, Massachusetts.

Emery House is not only a retreat sanctuary for the Cowley Monks; it also offers regular weekend programs to laypeople and couples of any faith who seek to deepen their spiritual lives. Private retreatants are welcome. The beautifully maintained house and hermitages, the considerate and friendly staff, and the peaceful quality of the place serve its purpose well. Guests are expected to share the silence and to join the monks for the regular round of offices and celebrations of the Eucharist.

Emery House
The Society of St. John the Evangelist
Emery Lane
West Newbury, MA 01985
(978) 462-7940
www.ssje.org

Glastonbury Abbey
Hingham, MA

The Benedictine monks first came to this quiet neighborhood in 1954, when they acquired an old estate with 25 acres of woodlands bordered by stone fences. They currently own about 60 acres of very appealing landscape. The abbey buildings are dominated by a stone tower, which the original owners built for ornamental purposes and used as a giant gazebo for entertaining. All of the original buildings have been adapted for monastery use: The administration building was formerly a barn and stable; Whiting House, now one of the guesthouses, was the home of the groundskeeper; and Stonecrest, the other guesthouse, was that of a Methodist missionary.

The modern chapel, tucked away behind the monastery, is the only new building. The architect was a friend of the monks and looked on the project as a labor of love. He designed the freestanding altar, the triangular windows, the benches, and even the candlesticks. Much of the artwork is brightly colored acrylic or plaster on wood, and there are dignified, though cartoonlike, Stations of the Cross. Here the monks sing the canonical hours five times a day from 6:30 A.M. to 7:45 P.M. Mass is said at noon, except on Sunday, when it is at 9:30 A.M. About ten monks sing the liturgy in deep, rich tones, and guests are invited to join in the singing. Much of the organ music that accompanies the singing was composed by one of the resident brothers. Known as Black Benedictines because of their black, cowled habits, the monks say the office in the vernacular and devote at least three hours a day to prayer.

During the course of a week, 75 psalms will be chanted. The chapel is open from 6:30 A.M. to 9 P.M.

Private retreatants are welcome for one night, but a few days' stay is preferable. Monks are available on request for individual guidance or the Sacrament of Reconciliation. People are also encouraged to come for a weekend of spiritual restoration. These weekends begin Friday at 7 P.M. and conclude Sunday afternoon. All retreatants are requested to observe silence in the retreat houses.

Glastonbury Abbey
The Retreat House
16 Hull Street
Hingham, MA 02043
(781) 749-2155
www.glastonburyabbey.org

Insight Meditation Society
Barre, MA

In 1975 a group of Americans who had studied Vipassana (insight meditation) in Southeast Asia realized that it would be beneficial to have a center in the United States, used exclusively for Vipassana retreats. In 1976 they acquired a Georgian brick mansion built by a prominent Boston family in the early 1900s. Located on 80 acres of secluded land in central Massachusetts, near Worcester, the mansion was used as a rest home in the 1940s, and as a novitiate for Blessed Sacrament priests and brothers in the 1950s and 1960s.

The Buddha said, "We are shaped by our thoughts; we become what we think. When the mind is pure, joy follows, like a shadow that never leaves." Vipassana meditation aims to free the mind of greed, hatred, and delusion. The meditation practice at IMS is an investigation of the mind-body process through focused awareness. The student learns to observe from a place of stillness, seeing life as a constantly changing process, and seeking to accept whatever takes place with equanimity and balance.

Retreats can be as short as two days or as long as 12 weeks. Silence is observed at all times. There is a nightly discourse given by the retreat director, and individuals have an interview every other day. The single and double rooms are spartan, with foam pads for sleeping. Bring your own linens or sleeping bag. There are separate floors for men and women, with community washrooms.

A typical day on retreat begins at 5 A.M. and ends at 10 P.M. There are alternating periods of sitting (four per day) and walking meditation.

There is also a 45-minute work period devoted to tasks such as cleaning or helping with meal preparation. (All food served is vegetarian.) Students are asked to refrain from reading, writing, phone calls, and any other distractions from meditation practice.

It is an extraordinary experience to join a group of people who do not talk, listen to the radio, watch television, or escape into some other activity, but are simply content to meditate. As one retreatant expressed it, "A great feeling of bliss comes over you, and a oneness with others, a pure feeling of love." Not surprisingly, retreats at IMS are generally fully booked, so it is best to plan far ahead.

Insight Meditation Society
1230 Pleasant Street
Barre, MA 01005
(978) 355-2062
www.dharma.org

Kripalu Center for Yoga and Health
Lenox, MA

In the early 1980s the followers of Yogi Amrit Desai acquired this huge building located next to the Tanglewood Music Festival grounds. It was built in the 1950s by the Jesuits as a seminary with a capacity for 600, but very few novices materialized, and the property was left vacant for ten years until Kripalu took it over. It is so large that four acres of carpet were purchased to cover the floors. Named after Yogi Amrit Desai's teacher, Swami Kripalvananda, the center offers a wide range of programs focusing on holistic health education, yoga, and meditation. There are rest and renewal programs for those who need time to catch up with themselves, a great variety of workshops, and a three-month Spiritual Lifestyle Training Program.

There is a wide choice of accommodations from dormitory to private single or double rooms with bath. Vegetarian food is provided in the large dining hall. Meals are generally eaten in silence. There is a staff and student body of 300, and rooms for 270 guests, which are usually filled. Yet, despite the number of people coming and going, there is a lively spirit of helpfulness and consideration, and the flow of people is quiet and purposeful.

The former chapel has been turned into a large meditation hall by taking out the pews and carpeting the floor. The mosaic on the back wall of St. Ignatius Loyola, the founder of the Society of Jesus, provides an interesting backdrop to the platform in front of it.

Traditional religion has a dogma and creed suggesting that believers will be saved. In yogic practice, the spiritual and the practical go hand in hand; one lives the practice by sharing it: Show a better way; do not talk a better way. Through diet, exercise, and meditation, Kripalu attempts to quicken the spiritual energy of those who are ready. This is an invitation to discover through personal experience and experimentation what the rules of life really are. The supportive atmosphere of love and acceptance allows guests and students to observe themselves honestly, to start to cleanse their lives through attention to detail, and to handle reality in a compassionate way. The staff is available for counseling, but considerate of the need for solitude. There is also a holistic doctor and a large team of massage and other bodywork therapists; appointments with these are very popular, so bookings should be made at the time of reservation.

In 1994 Yogi Amrit Desai resigned after allegations of misconduct, and the Kripalu community is now learning to be more self-reliant and less dependent on a guru.

The center looks over a lake, a short walk downhill, which has a public beach. There are many hiking trails through the pines and the Tanglewood grounds nearby.

Kripalu Center for Yoga & Health
P.O. Box 309
Stockbridge, MA 01262
(413) 448-3152
(866) 200-5203
www.kripalu.org

Mount St. Mary's Abbey
Wrentham, MA

Forty miles west of Boston, a group of 50 Trappistine nuns live in a cloistered community, following the Rule of Saint Benedict. With traditions similar to those of Trappist monks, they devote their lives to work and prayer. The monastery dates back to the 1940s, when Cardinal Cushing wanted to have Trappistine nuns in the Boston diocese, and helped them find the property. The original 300 acres were bought from businessman John McMahon, who later canceled the mortgage and left an adjoining 300 acres and his substantial summer house to the nuns.

The front wing of the main monastery building was completed in 1949, and the community, started by 13 nuns from Ireland, has flourished and sent groups to create other foundations in the United States. Initially, the main source of income came from dairy cows, but in 1956 the nuns began to make Trappistine Quality Candy, which has proved very popular. The Butter Nut-Munch, a hard toffee hand-dipped in milk chocolate and rolled in ground nuts, is a confection inspired by heaven. The monastery no longer has dairy cows but raises and sells heifers.

About eight guests can stay on the second floor of the monastery, above the gift shop where convent-made candy, monastery-made articles, and greeting cards are always available. Fresh bread is sold twice a week, and the sweet smell of the loaves is in the air on baking days. Guest rooms are taken care of by the nuns, who have access through a maze of doors that would baffle and perplex even the most astute burglar.

The McMahon house, across the road from the monastery, has been refurbished recently, and the rooms there are clean and comfortable. Guests help themselves at mealtimes from the stocked kitchens in both guest areas.

The nuns meet to pray together eight times a day, from 3 A.M. to 7 P.M. The sound of those 50 voices raised in song is unforgettable. Guests are welcome to attend the services, but may not join in the rigorous work of the community. There is a sense of great happiness and contentment in this abbey. As one nun said, "When I entered, I thought I was giving up my liberty, but I've found more real freedom here than I have ever known."

Mount St. Mary's Abbey
300 Arnold Road
Wrentham, MA 02093
(866) 549-8929
(508) 528-1282
www.msmabbey.org

St. Joseph's Abbey
Spencer, MA

The monastic buildings of this Cistercian-Trappist abbey may have a medieval look but they date only from the early 1950s. The monks took much of the stone for the construction from the surrounding fields. The abbey is the home of more than 70 monks who sing the daily mass and divine office in the dimly lighted church to which the public is welcomed.

The property consists of 1,800 acres, 1,000 of which are wooded and the rest farmland, some of which is rented to neighboring farmers for alfalfa and field corn. The main income is derived from the famous Trappist Preserves (jams and jellies) that are made here by 15 of the monks and distributed nationwide. Another important source of income is the Holy Rood Guild, which makes liturgical vestments.

There are guest facilities for men only, in a separate wing across from the chapel. These are single rooms with private bath, furnished with bed, desk, chair, and reading lamp. Meals are taken in the guests' dining room, and coffee, tea, and snacks are available all day. Retreatants schedule their own time, are welcome at all chapel services, and may talk with the guest master each day about monastic life or for spiritual counseling.

There are two regular guest programs for men: on weekends from Friday afternoon to Sunday following lunch; and in midweek from Monday afternoon to Friday morning. Guests are not in direct contact with the monastic community, but the guest facilities and schedule follow the contemplative way of life.

This is a formal monastic community, popular with anyone seeking a close look at the Trappist lifestyle or a place of silence and prayer.

St. Joseph's Abbey
167 N. Spencer Road
Spencer, MA 01562
(508) 885-8700
www.spencerabbey.org

The Hermitage
Three Rivers, MI

Two hours from both Chicago and Detroit, this Mennonite retreat is the antithesis of city life. Set on 65 acres of gently rolling hills, just down the road from St. Gregory's Episcopal Monastery, this serene and beautiful place truly fulfills the purpose for which it was founded: uninterrupted research and thought in a setting of quiet and prayer. There are eight rooms for 12 people in a reconditioned barn with rooms on four levels with shared bathrooms. Windows in each room look out to the fields. The artful reconstruction is a credit to Mennonite craftsmanship. The attention to detail and comfort makes you feel as though you're in a well-kept home. Meals are taken family-style in the dining room. Morning and evening prayers are held in the chapel each day.

There are three hermitages well secluded by trees. Furnishings are adequate and suitable. Retreatants can either prepare their own food or go to the dining room.

Gene and Mary Herr bought the property in the mid 1980s because it was near a long-established monastery. The barn took more than four years to redo with the help of a spiritually oriented carpenter who shared the call to contemplation. The Herrs are both ordained Mennonite pastors and available for spiritual counseling. They are endorsed by the Indiana-Michigan Mennonite Conference as a sign of affirmation for their retreat work.

As you leave the property, there is a small hand-lettered sign that reads RETURN SLOWLY. After spending a day at the Hermitage, the sign inspired a pastor to write: "Return slowly. It could mean drive slowly, but I don't think so. It was a reminder that, after time spent in worship, prayer, and silence, the world was all too ready to sweep me back into the pace of doing this and going there . . . much of it needful and good. Much of it necessary. Just don't be too quick to resume it all."

The Hermitage
11321 Dutch Settlement Road
Three Rivers, MI 49093
(269) 244-8696
www.hermitagecommunity.org

St. Augustine's House
Oxford, MI

In *My Brother's Place,* a history of this Lutheran monastery, George Weckman examines whether monasticism is a legitimate lifestyle for practicing Lutherans. He compares the usefulness of a monastery to that of music or the theater. The impulse to defend monasticism comes from Martin Luther himself, who wrote that monasteries should have some measurable, practical purpose. This attitude is so deep that a Lutheran monastery is thought of as an oxymoron, a contradictory and unnecessary adjunct for a spiritual life. Yet here it is, a small but thriving community offering spiritual sustenance for those who seek it.

St. Augustine's House was founded by Father Arthur Kreinheder, an American who was ordained a Lutheran priest in Sweden in 1956, then assigned "for ecumenical work in the United States among Lutherans." Father Arthur returned to Michigan and began the monastery on property he owned in Oxford, a suburb of Detroit. After a fire destroyed the original building, a new structure was completed in 1965. The main house has five single rooms for guests, a large living/dining room with a balcony that looks across the lawn to the tops of the trees. If the feeder is empty, the local chickadees will remind you to add some food. The monastery buildings are down a tree-lined drive off a country road in a quiet and restful setting. The Quonset hut chapel, erected in 1958, has a charm enhanced by decades of prayer. Services are held there seven times daily following the liturgical office, beginning at 5:10 A.M., Eucharist at 8:30 A.M., and the last service, Compline, at 8:30 P.M. Time spent in daily prayer is about three hours with a slow, deliberate pace that helps toward reflection and meditation. Time between services is spent in reading, meditation, and work, preferably involving some physical effort or house maintenance.

Silence is the watchword here. It is observed from the end of Compline at about 9 P.M. until after Terce or the Eucharist, almost 12 hours. Another period of silence is after noon meal until None prayer. There is plenty of time for conversation at appropriate times and, as was pointed out, there is no sense in being rigid about this or any other regulation, but silence is a mechanism for turning inward and achieving the full benefits of the fundamental monastic activity of prayer.

The Fellowship of St. Augustine is a group that supports the activities of the monastery, visits when possible, retreats there regularly, and realizes how valuable a place like this can be.

St. Augustine's House
P.O. Box 125
3316 Drahner Road
Oxford, MI 48370
(248) 628-2604
(248) 628-5155 office
www.staugustineshouse.org

St. Gregory's Abbey
Three Rivers, MI

This is the oldest Episcopal Benedictine monastery in the United States. Founded by a group of American seminarians who went to study in England at Nashdom Abbey, the monks returned in the late 1930s to serve at missions in Indiana. Two of the monks were scouting southwestern Michigan for a suitable place for a monastery, became lost, and asked directions at a farmhouse. They liked what they saw and offered to buy the farm from the couple living there, but their offer was refused. The monks went back and said a novena to St. Joseph. After the novena, the farm couple accepted their offer, and the 604-acre farm was acquired in 1946. St. Gregory's became an independent abbey in 1969.

The monks emphasize being faithful to a monastic lifestyle rather than telling others how to live. St. Benedict taught the middle way: eat enough, but not too much; sleep adequately, but not too much; be involved in community life, but reserve time for solitude and prayer; and participate in the rhythm of worship, study, and prayer. The timetable of the monastery is scheduled around prayer. The monks rise at 4 A.M. for Matins and follow the canonical hours through the day to Compline at 7:45 P.M. During a normal week, the monks sing or chant all of the psalms.

There is room for 12 male retreatants in the guesthouse and 8 men and women can stay in St. Denys, a former farm building with a comfortable living/dining room and rooms on two levels with shared bathrooms. Male guests eat in the refectory in the enclosure with the monks; women prepare their food in the kitchen at St. Denys. This arrangement will change when a new building is completed and women guests will also eat with the monks.

People of all faiths are welcome. Only the desire for a deeper spirituality is necessary. Guests are required to attend daily mass and Vespers. A monk is available for discussion on request.

There is a summer vocation program from June through August when men can come for two weeks or so and follow the daily schedule of the monks' routine. Individuals attend the liturgy, work on the grounds, and perform domestic chores to maintain the monastery. The purpose is to allow individuals the chance to examine their lives in a spiritual context, to reflect on a possible religious vocation, or to see more clearly the direction of their lives.

This is a beautiful, peaceful setting with a lake and hundreds of acres for walking.

St. Gregory's Abbey
56500 Abbey Road
Three Rivers, MI 49093
(269) 244-5893
www.saintgregorysthreerivers.org

Upland Hills Ecological Awareness Center
Oxford, MI

Inspired by Buckminster Fuller's World Game Conference held in 1970, where the premise was "to make the world work for 100% of humanity without disadvantaging the natural world," Philip Moore settled in suburban Detroit and became the director of the Upland School.

In 1974, the Upland Hills Awareness Center was built on the school grounds by dedicated volunteers as a demonstration of wind and solar power. The berm-designed building has a sod roof, a heat-retaining rock wall, and south-facing windows, a good example of energy conservation, alternative technology that works in the Great Lakes bioregion.

Four times a year the center sponsors weekend retreats for people interested in developing, improving, and integrating programs that promote a responsible role toward the natural world. There have been retreats led by Matthew Fox, Elisabeth Kübler-Ross, Thomas Moore, and Wendell Berry. In 1995, Senator Thomas Hayden looked at how the old political paradigm based on vanquishing enemies is fading, as a new attitude emerges whereby one's heart turns enemies into allies and words into gifts to bring an enlivened compassion into political life. There are other programs throughout the year that celebrate the solstices and equinoxes, consecutive weekly meetings on environmental core studies, Native American influences, and a Junior World Game —an adaptation of Fuller's ideas to enable children to increase their world view.

Retreatants are housed a short distance from the center at St. Benedict Monastery, a community of Catholic Benedictine monks. The monks come together four times a day in their chapel for liturgy and daily mass. The Benedictines came to this region in 1960 and own 285 acres, a serene setting on the edge of a small lake where there is a view south to Pontiac and Detroit some 30 miles away.

Upland Hills Ecological Awareness Center
2575 Indian Lake Road
Oxford, MI 48370
(248) 693-1021
www.uheac.org

Zen Buddhist Temple
Ann Arbor, MI

Soon after Venerable Samu Sunim, a Korean-born Zen monk based in Toronto, came to Ann Arbor in the early 1980s to set up a new temple, he got a phone call from a distraught woman seeking a temporary refuge from her personal concerns. The woman spent two nights, then was able to return to her responsibilities, refreshed by her retreat. Sunim felt that being able to offer a sanctuary was one of the ways that Buddhism could reach out in the West. He believes that social responsibility must accompany expansion and recognition, and states: "Buddhism in the West will witness the transformation of monastic Buddhism into social Buddhism."

It became possible to acquire a rambling Victorian house with a large backyard surrounded by a brick wall. The house emanates a tremendous sense of peace. The resident priest, Sukha Linda Murray, ordained in 1989, has guided the development of spiritual practice here during the 1990s in a most rewarding way. A single mother with two young daughters, she balances her temple responsibilities with long days of organized activity, keeping in mind that "there is nothing to protect, no end in mind, and no desire to control things."

There are more than 100 temple members, and 60 to 70 attend services each week. Some members stay for a few weeks or months at a time, then move on.

Buddhism is immensely practical. Mental concentration developed from meditation is meant to be applied to every moment of the day, so everything becomes meditation. A local physician and longtime group member extols the benefits he's received: "A very pure, simple, and straightforward practice. If you are persistent, the results are definite and remarkable. For me, peacefulness at first, then greater understanding of myself and the beauty of each moment."

A dozen guests share rooms with communal baths. Meals are taken in the basement dining room and are usually vegetarian. There is daily meditation morning and evening. Introductory meditation courses, workshops, lecture series, and retreats are scheduled throughout the year. There is an ongoing visitors' program for those who would like to pursue a serious spiritual path.

Zen Buddhist Temple
1214 Packard Street
Ann Arbor, MI 48104
(734) 761-6520
www.zenbuddhisttemple.org

St. John's Abbey
Collegeville, MN

A few years after the Minnesota Territory opened for settlement, Benedictine monks from St. Vincent Abbey in Latrobe, Pennsylvania, took a circuitous route through St. Cloud, Minnesota, and eventually settled in an area between Lake Sagatagan and the Watab Creek. The monks set up a school for boys and young men. By 1860, in addition to the school, the monks were serving more than 50 communities in central Minnesota, reaching the scattered settlements by horseback. From this modest beginning, one of the most developed Benedictine communities has evolved. St. John's Abbey and University now occupy 2,400 acres. The monastery and campus are situated around Lake Sagatagan and Strumpf Lake, with other lakes reached by 12 miles of hiking trails winding throughout the property. More than 1,500 acres are in forest with 24 species of hardwoods. In 1894, the monks planted the first pine plantation in Minnesota. Since pine is not native to this area, any pine you see must have been planted by past or present monks or be a descendent of those trees. Observers can discover deer, foxes, squirrels, rabbits, beavers, and mink, and more than 90 species of birds have been identified. During our 1995 visit, a panther was sighted by two unimpeachable sources—a monk and a security guard.

One of the most notable features here is the abbey church. Designed by Marcel Breuer in the late 1950s and completed in 1961, this magnificent edifice stands in stark contrast to the original brick European quadrangle and the upper-Midwest "frontier gothic" of the old campus. One person used a flight analogy: "It's like having the Concorde sit next to a

DC-3." The award-winning design has attracted worldwide interest and critical comment. Opinions were and still are "as absolute and colorful as the spectrum itself." The interior was brilliantly conceived: No posts mar the view of the altar and close to 2,000 people can be seated.

The community of monks gathers in this great church four times a day to observe liturgy: 7 A.M. morning prayer, noon prayer, and mass at 5 P.M. Monday to Friday (on weekends, morning mass is said). Evening prayer is at 7 P.M. Visitors are invited to all services.

Group and private retreats are organized by the Spiritual Life Program. There is a Monastic Experience Program through which men can follow the life of a monk for extended periods to determine whether they have a vocation to this demanding life which St. Benedict described as a journey and a "labor of obedience." There is a House of Prayer on campus that schedules daily and weekend retreats on meditation themes for the curious, skeptical, and experienced. In 1994 there were programs for physicians and law-enforcement officers to help integrate their faith and spirituality with their professional responsibilities. The monastery has a dozen private rooms contiguous to the church, each with private bath. Meals are taken in the guest dining room.

St. John's Abbey
31802 County Road 159
Collegeville, MN 56321
(320) 363-2573
www.stjohnsabbey.org

Maria Fonte Solitude
High Ridge, MO

This retreat is perched on a hilltop about an hour south of St. Louis. Retreatants stay in single hermitages that cling to the sides of the hill, cozy and small and just right for one person. The only way to reach the hermitage is by holding on to ropes which are slung between the trees. Each cabin has its own special place a short distance from the next. The winter night we stayed, an ice storm swept through and we couldn't leave our cabins until late morning when ashes were scattered on the path. The ground slopes down like a barn roof and it was a sheet of ice. Jack remembers that forced incarceration wistfully, the pure solitude and quiet, the bright blue sky through the trees. Richard Lovelace's poem came to mind: "Stone walls do not a prison make, / Nor iron bars a cage; / Minds innocent and quiet take / That for an hermitage."

A community of Catholic brothers and sisters live on this ridgetop, each in his or her own hermitage in a cloistered area of the grounds. They convene in the chapel for community prayer four times a day beginning at 7:15 A.M., followed by mass at 7:30. Retreatants are welcome at all services. Meals may be collected in baskets from the dining room and taken to one's hermitage. Retreatants never mingle with the community, but a spiritual advisor is available on request. Individuals generally plan their own program of solitude and silence.

There is a library with books and tapes for use while here. There are three separate shrines to Mary on the property. Retreatants should bring sturdy walking shoes to hike the 100 acres of monastery land, seasonal clothing, alarm clock, immersion heater for hot drinks, and flashlight. Linens are provided.

As one member pointed out: "We do not look upon the hermitage as a place simply for privacy or space to breathe, but a place which exemplifies and nourishes the starkness of the desert: not its harshness, but its uncompromising refusal to provide distractions." There are no distractions here.

Maria Fonte Solitude
6150 Antire Road
High Ridge, MO 63049
(636) 677-3235
www.marythefont.org

Aryaloka
Newmarket, NH

Aryaloka is a small Buddhist retreat center tucked away in a thicket of New England bushes and trees. The main building is constructed of two connecting geodesic domes. The property was acquired in the mid-1980s from a craftsman who had built the domes for his family's personal use. The design and execution of the doors make one appreciate how elegantly wood can be worked with.

Aryaloka (which means Noble World) is run by the Friends of the Western Buddhist Order (FWBO), which is an international Buddhist movement founded by an Englishman in 1967. The founder, Sangharakshita, has developed the practice and study of Buddhism to provide for the needs of those in the West who wish to explore the traditions of, and commit themselves to, the Buddhist way of life. Meditation is the cornerstone of Buddhist practice, and Aryaloka teaches two basic techniques: Mindfulness of Breathing, which is concerned with the development of awareness and concentration; and Development of Universal Loving-Kindness, which helps to foster positive feelings of friendliness and love for all human beings.

Each member of the community must contribute in some way to the group by working in the woodshop or performing household tasks or grounds maintenance. Each person also has a financial commitment to meet, and some do outside work such as carpentry and renovations.

Aryaloka offers classes in meditation, yoga, and Buddhist studies.

Regular retreats are scheduled, as well as visitors days, which offer an opportunity to meet the people involved and just look around.

There is a beautiful meditation hall on the top floor, and various niches where one can sit quietly to read and reflect. There are footpaths cleared around the 13 acres of surrounding property, so one can enjoy the clear New Hampshire air.

Aryaloka
Friends of the Western Buddhist Order
14 Heartwood Circle
Newmarket, NH 03857
(603) 659-5456

The Common
Peterborough, NH

In 1738, ten acres of this hilltop were designated as the site of the Peterborough town center or common, but the town grew in the valley below and eventually the property became a private farm. In 1898 it was acquired by the Cheney family, who built an imposing mansion with an outdoor pool and tennis court. In the 1950s it became a girls' school, and then in 1966 it was bought by the Carmelites for use as a seminary, and converted into a retreat center in 1968.

The mansion has been lovingly restored, with beautiful guest rooms. The main floor has two chapels, conference rooms, a large dining room off the kitchen, and a study that displays historical information about the mansion and the surrounding area. Carved into the fireplace mantel in the dining room is the following message: "They eat, they drink and in common sweet—Quaff immortality and joy."

The center has splendid views to the west and southwest, looking across a valley to Mount Monadnock, which reportedly was climbed by both Thoreau and Emerson. Beyond the tennis court and pool is the cemetery that Thornton Wilder used as a setting for his play *Our Town*. The three priests and two brothers who give retreats and care for the property live in a separate monastery a short distance from the mansion.

The Common is a retreat center for people and groups of all beliefs. There are retreats scheduled regularly throughout the year, and private retreatants are welcome. The Carmelites are available for consultation. There are 173 acres of woods and meadows that make up the grounds. Two hermitages are available, set apart from the other buildings.

Traditionally, New Englanders gathered at the common to share dreams and concerns. It seems fitting that Carmelites, named for hermits who lived on Mount Carmel in Palestine, should be living on this mountain, ministering to those who are on their own spiritual journeys.

The Common
Peterborough, NH
(Closed)

St. Anselm Abbey
Manchester, NH

In 1889 the Benedictines came to New Hampshire and established a monastery and school on 300 acres of high ground overlooking the town of Manchester. The school is a liberal arts college with an enrollment now close to 2,000 students. The grounds are exceptionally well maintained, with expansive lawns leading up to the main buildings. The most prominent is the Abbey-College Church, which is connected to the monastery. The 35 to 40 monks who live here assemble daily in the splendid chapel to sing the canonical hours.

In the Benedictine tradition, the monks are self-supporting from the school and make rooms available for retreatants. Men are accommodated in the monastery, where they are expected to follow the routine of the monks; the hallways are hushed, the monks' cells comfortable but plain. There are large, arched windows surrounding a silent courtyard in which one catches an occasional glimpse of a cowled monk. At the monastery noon meal there is a *lectio* (Latin for "reading"), during which one can reflect on the words read.

The aim of the Benedictine rule is to devote every aspect of one's life to the service of God, and the atmosphere at St. Anselm is indeed one of active prayer.

St. Anselm Abbey
100 St. Anselm Drive
Manchester, NH 03102
(603) 641-7000
www.anselm.edu

Carmel Retreat
Mahwah, NJ

Nestled at the foot of the Ramapo Mountains, less than an hour from New York City, this gracious estate was built as a summer home by Clarence Chapman, a New York financier, in about 1905. A long, curving drive leads to the beautiful, newly restored mansion, which is surrounded by 35 wooded acres, abounding in native stone fences. The property, with its ponds and tall, old trees, adjoins a state park, Campgaw Reservation, so guests can glimpse the occasional wild turkey and deer while wandering the forest paths.

In 1911 the original owners added a formal garden for their daughter's wedding, and this is where the stations of the cross are located. In 1965, following Pope Paul's plea for peace at the United Nations, a rosary garden was built as a place of prayer for international peace.

The Carmelites come from a rich tradition of desert spirituality. In the late 1100s hermits from the desert came together at Mount Carmel for mutual support in following in the footsteps of Jesus. From this beginning blossomed such 16th-century mystics as St. Teresa of Avila and St. John of the Cross, and later St. Thérèse of Lisieux.

In 1954 the Carmelites bought the estate for use as a retreat center. The five Carmelites who now live here share the riches of their order's tradition, and are committed to providing an atmosphere that will nurture the reaching of God through prayer. They go out of their way to be hospitable and inclusive in welcoming both private retreatants and groups, and will organize retreats on request. Guests are invited to join them daily in the chapel for morning prayer at 8:30 A.M., Eucharist at 11:30 A.M., and evening prayer at 5 P.M.

Carmel Retreat has accommodations for up to 60 people in 29 comfortable rooms in three houses. The main house is the restored mansion, the "middle house" is a native stone carriage house with 3 bedrooms and a kitchen, available if one wants to cook, and the "lower house" has 10 bedrooms and its own kitchen. Delicious home-cooked meals are served family-style in the main house with the community, or in solitude if desired.

Maura Rossi in "A Visit to Carmel" said she comes to Carmel and wanders the property to "breathe in the beauty and peace of sky and earth . . . or to head for the serene, shadowy chapel to sit and listen for God." This is a place for people "who are looking for time and space to seek their own answers."

Carmel Retreat
1071 Ramapo Valley Road
Mahwah, NJ 07430
(201) 327-7090
www.carmelretreat.com

St. Marguerite's Retreat House
Mendham, NJ

The Episcopalian nuns of the Community of St. John Baptist came to the United States from England in 1874. Their rule is based on the Augustinian tradition of combining active work with contemplative prayer. The rambling brick building that is now St. Marguerite's Retreat House was once an orphanage that the nuns administered for almost 40 years. In 1960 the house became a retreat and conference center used mainly by Episcopalian groups, but there are also some Methodists and Lutherans who return year after year. There is a fine professional cook in charge of the kitchen—a rare treat in such surroundings. The wood paneling and the generous bedrooms and meeting rooms bespeak 19th-century charm, so one really does feel as though one has retreated from today's world.

Across the front lawn is the Convent of St. John Baptist, the home of the nine sisters who administer the retreat house. This impressive white French Gothic structure was built in 1916 and designed by a student of architect Ralph Adams Crane. The charming interior of tile floors and stucco walls with deep inset windows has a distinctly southern-European flavor. There are beautiful religious artifacts throughout. The main chapel, with its arched ceiling, contains a perfect example of an umbrella pillar. There is another, smaller chapel on the second floor, where the sisters gather daily to pray a fivefold office beginning with Lauds at 6:30 A.M. and ending with Compline at 8:30 P.M.

Ninety-three acres of woodlands surround the buildings and deepen the sense of seclusion. There is a neatly kept graveyard, reminiscent of a European churchyard, near the drive at the side of the convent.

Private retreatants are always welcome at the convent, and take their meals with the nuns. This is a small community with a deep commitment to an interior life of prayer and devotion. The nuns work to "keep a sparkle in the community," as their foundress used to say, and to share the joy of religious life.

St. Marguerite's Retreat House
Convent of St. John the Baptist
P.O. Box 240
82 West Main Street
Mendham, NJ 07945
(973) 543-4641
www.csjb.org/marg.htm

St. Mary's Abbey–Delbarton
Morristown, NJ

The former Kountze estate, Delbarton, was purchased in 1926 by Benedictine monks from Newark as a house of studies for its young monks. According to legend, another site was almost chosen, but the prior who favored Delbarton went there and planted Benedictine medals in the ground, convinced that once St. Benedict had taken root there, he would guide the choice of the community. And, indeed, the final vote was for the 400-acre Kountze property. Through the late 1920s and the 1930s, the monks farmed the land and modified the 50-room mansion for their community's needs. The armor room was transformed into the chapel (swords into plowshares) and the music studio into the refectory. In those early years, the full-scale farm helped the monks become self-sufficient.

Then the bishop, concerned with the lack of Catholic schools in the diocese, urged the Benedictines to start a boys' prep school. The first 12 students matriculated in 1939. Since that time the number of students has grown to 500, and the farmland has been turned into playing fields for soccer, lacrosse, football, and baseball. The Delbarton School has become one of the most distinguished Catholic prep schools in the United States. The school has evolved into a day school, and a former dormitory is now used as a retreat house, particularly for graduating and confirmation classes of teenagers.

The back lawn of the mansion, called Old Main, is an Italian garden with marble columns and statues; two of the latter, by Bernini, are now on loan to the Metropolitan Museum. The growth of both the school and the community necessitated the building of a new abbey. This church—which can seat 700—reflects the spirit of the Benedictines; it is entered through huge portals defining the worship area and marking the passage into the temple of God. The circular floor slopes gradually toward the center, focusing attention on the altar and encouraging participation in the liturgy. The stark simplicity of the design is complemented by the Amish-made pews. The monks meet here daily for mass and to sing the canonical hours. Retreatants and guests are welcome.

Some private retreatants are accommodated in the monastery. Meals are taken cafeteria-style with the monks, who have an excellent chef. The ordered prayer life of the community amid the spacious grounds makes this a very appealing place. On celebrating the opening of the new abbey church in 1966, one of the monks wrote, "You must in all things take your brother into account ... never come to a halt; go forward with your brothers, run toward the goal in the footprints of Christ."

St. Mary's Abbey-Delbarton
230 Mendham Road
Morristown, NJ 07960
(973) 538-3231
www.osbmonks.org

Center for Action and Contemplation
Albuquerque, NM

The Center for Action and Contemplation was founded in 1987 by a Franciscan priest, Father Richard Rohr, who saw a need for a formation center that would serve as a place of discernment and growth for peace activists and those involved in ministries of social service. There they would come, be still, and share in the center's vision, goals, and commitment to its mission: networking to promote a consistent ethic of life and the work of justice and peace; educating toward and living nonviolently, precariously, and contemplatively; actively engaging in transforming society from a faith perspective; and collaborating with other organizations endorsing a similar vision and philosophy.

Through the years, thousands of people have participated in CAC-sponsored retreats, programs, and events. They come from several countries of the world, reflect a variety of religious traditions, and represent a wide range of ages, professions, interests, and concerns. One of the most intensive of these programs is the six-week residential internship. While at the center, interns join the staff for daily prayer, participate in seminars on social activism and contemplative prayer, volunteer service at one of several social service agencies, usually visit the United States–Mexico border, spend at least three days in retreat, and are aided in reflecting on their experience through one-on-one and group interaction.

In June 1990, the center purchased the former motherhouse of the Franciscan Province of Our Lady of Guadalupe. Located in the largely Hispanic South Valley section of Albuquerque, this adobe house, called Tepeyac, is within walking distance of the CAC. A residence for a core staff group, interns, and guests, Tepeyac has a communal living and dining room and shared bedroom and bathroom space for about 20 people.

People come to Tepeyac for a variety of reasons. The Tepeyac staff attempts to create a contemplative atmosphere of quiet, safety, and support for whatever individual quests bring visitors to the center. Neither the CAC nor Tepeyac is an intentional community. However, staff members participate in and invite others to participate in the fostering of a homelike, communal environment.

Center for Action and Contemplation
P.O. Box 12464
Albuquerque, NM 87195
(505) 242-9588 info.
(505) 242-1846 reservations
www.cacradicalgrace.org

Ghost Ranch
Abiquiu, NM

Ghost Ranch, with its towering mesas, is located on 21,000 acres of magnificent high desert, 6,500 feet above sea level. Donated to the Presbyterian church by the Pack family in 1955, it operates as a spiritually oriented conference center and antidote to the dangers inherent in a technologically oriented and mechanized society. Since the early 1970s, regular seminars have been offered to all those interested in paleontology, sociology, theology, education, history, literature, music, psychology, and environmental concerns.

This area was a swamp 250 million years ago, and after important fossil remains were found, the ranch was designated a Registered Natural Landmark because "the site possesses exceptional value as an illustration of the nation's heritage and contributes to a better understanding of man's environment."

The spectacular landscape attracted the artist Georgia O'Keeffe in the 1930s. She bought land nearby in 1940 and lived here until her death in 1986 painting the cliffs and sky, bones, trees, and mountains. Her well-known masterpieces embody the grandeur, simplicity, and amazing colors of this part of the Southwest.

There is a blend of cultures in the area: the Jicarilla-Apache and Navajo in nearby pueblos, the Hispanic community, and the recently arrived Anglo-Americans. Each group lives with shared concerns for the fragile ecology.

The ranch receives an annual average of only ten inches of rain, so the land is managed with exceptional care. Neighbors can use the pasture-land to graze 400 to 600 cattle as conservation practices permit.

The guest facilities can accommodate up to 350 persons in plain but comfortable rooms with community washrooms. Meals are taken in a centrally located dining hall. During the summer season, due to the many programs offered, the rooms are often fully booked. During the rest of the year, there are conferences for smaller groups and month-long courses in photography, pottery, and the like. Private retreatants are welcomed. There is an excellent library and chapel. The real magic here is the setting for hiking and observation: seeing the early sun accentuate Chimney Rock, looking across the desert to the rock mesas outlined in the bluer-than-blue sky, and gazing at the stars in the clear New Mexican air.

Ghost Ranch
HC 77, Box 11
Abiquiu, NM 87510
(505) 685-4333
(877) 804-4678
www.ghostranch.org

Lama Foundation
San Cristobal, NM

The Lama Foundation is located 19 miles from Taos at 8,600 feet in the Sangre de Cristo Mountains. The complex of buildings sits on the side of Lama Mountain looking west across the broad expanse of the Rio Grande Gorge. In the late 1960s a group of hippie activists came here to start a community following the teachings of the Indian guru Meher Baba. They were aided and encouraged by several American teachers such as Pir Vilayat Khan, Ram Dass, and Sam Lewis, who commingled their visions to establish a place that would serve to draw all religions together to celebrate the one truth . . . many paths but one mountain.

The 100 acres of pine woods, bordering the Kit Carson National Forest, is approached along a winding dirt road that slowly works its way up the mountain. Cars are parked below the buildings and living quarters and camping areas are reached on foot. A community of about 20 hardy people live here year-round and take their meals together in the centrally positioned dining room—a rustic, charming wooden building that also serves as a meeting place. The bells on the rack outside were made from the nose cones of ballistic missiles. Just a short distance away sits the main temple or meditation hall, with its 44-foot geodesic dome, where large groups gather. There is a library in one section and a smaller cavelike meditation chamber where groups of 10 to 12 can share the synergy of their spiritual force.

There are A-frames and small domed buildings throughout the woods and an adobe structure with kitchen, dining room, prayer room, and 12 rooms for guests built around a central courtyard. Buildings are lighted by kerosene lamps and heated by wood-burning stoves, and there are outdoor privies. Community members must attend a community meditation session daily in addition to performing another practice of their own choice such as yoga or t'ai chi ch'uan. Each person has a daily work commitment such as cleaning, cooking, or wood gathering. There are cottage industries that make and sell colorful prayer flags, banners, and T-shirts, and there is also a book service. The summer season sees the community double in size to put on the summer programs, which begin about mid May and continue through September. The topics of the weekend and week-long sessions deal with spiritual development and awakening, music, ecology, and dance.

In the early 1980s, Father Thomas Keating held a retreat here with a group that evolved into the Chrysalis Movement, a network of Catholic lay communities that focus on community service, centering prayer, and contemplative living. In 1970, Ram Dass collaborated with the Lama community to produce his famous book, *Be Here Now.* Up the mountain, above the dwellings, is the final resting place of Samuel Lewis, affectionately remembered as "Sufi Sam."

The community is evolving and is a way station where pilgrims find shelter from outer-world distraction and a greenhouse where early spiritual awakening is protected and nurtured . . . it is a blending of East and West and a place of hope for peace on earth.

Lama Foundation
P.O. Box 240
San Cristobal, NM 87564
(575) 586-1269
www.lamafoundation.org

Monastery of Christ in the Desert
Abiquiu, NM

The stories of the difficulties encountered reaching this spiritual outpost are legion. Many have driven partway, become mired in the mud, and had to walk in. But once there, near the river deep in Chama Canyon, one can feel the difference in the air, "saturated in peace," as one visitor noted, "like bread soaked in wine. The obvious stillness, so striking in contrast to most other places, has a lot to do with the spectacular location . . . remote and beautiful by any standard." The monastery was founded by Father Aelred Wall, a Benedictine priest who came here with two other monks in 1964 from Mount Saviour Monastery in Pine City, NY (see page 172). George Nakashima, the famous Japanese-American woodworker, was enlisted as architect. His approach to the functional use of structure that blends with surroundings is among the highest forms of artistic achievement.

Hundreds of people come each year for a day or more, joining the 20 or so monks in the routine of their monastic life. Guests join the community for common prayer in the chapel, where the windows look out on the red cliffs of the mesa and the whole canyon appears to be a chapel.

Meals are taken with the monks in the refectory. One of the monks reads aloud at lunch and the evening meal is accompanied by taped classical music. The food is vegetarian, nourishing, and delicious.

There are no formal retreats, but guests can arrange ahead to speak with one of the monks. Those who come are encouraged to seek Christ in the desert in their own way. The monks offer hospitality and the sharing of their Benedictine way of life. The key elements are love for one another, prayer, reading, study, and manual labor. Visitors are encouraged to work at least some of the time. There are stations of the cross that zigzag up the side of one of the mesas. The 12th station, the Crucifixion, looks over the entire monastery.

An extra amount of preparation is necessary for a visit here, such as bringing proper clothing, since the snowy winters are very cold. Guest rooms are heated with woodstoves and lighted by kerosene lamps. Plans are underway to change to a solar heating system. Summer days are warm, but cool in the mornings. Shorts are not permitted in chapel, refectory, or guesthouse areas. A flashlight is useful, as are sturdy walking or hiking shoes. Musical instruments, tape and CD players, and radios should be left at home. There is no telephone—the nearest is 15 miles away at Ghost Ranch (see page 146)—but one can glory in giving up the trappings of civilization for just a little while to encounter Christ, who waits for us in the desert.

Monastery of Christ in the Desert
Att: Guestmaster
P.O. Box 270
Abiquiu, NM 87510
(801) 545-8567
cidguestmaster@christdesert.org
www.christdesert.org

Pecos Benedictine Monastery
Pecos, NM

The adobe buildings of this monastery located in the Pecos River valley blend perfectly with the surrounding Sangre de Cristo Mountains. This 900-acre property was acquired by Catholic Benedictine monks who came here in 1955 seeking a place where solitude and space were readily available. From its very beginnings, the monastery has served as a center for retreats and church renewal. The first cursillo in the United States was held here, and the community has been consistently involved with marriage encounter and family retreats.

One of the distinguishing marks of this monastery, perhaps a precursor in monastic evolution, is that in 1969 the community welcomed four monks from Benet Lake, Wisconsin, who shared a vision of establishing a Charismatic Benedictine way of life. This has become a reality here and the monastery enjoys a wide reputation for Charismatic renewal. Twice a year there are month-long training sessions called School for Charismatic Spiritual Directors, at which individuals are trained to serve their home communities. Directed and private retreats are welcome. The community gathers four times a day for prayer in the chapel, and there is daily mass. The rooms are snug and comfortable. Corridors connect the guest quarters with the dining room and the chapel. This is a bonus in the winter, when heavy snow accumulates.

Another distinguishing mark of Pecos is that monastic men and women live together following five promises: obedience, conversion of life, stability, poverty, and chastity. Men and women living together as one community has long been sanctioned by the Church. As this communal call unfolded, Pecos realized the need to join a congregation that would nurture this vision. So in 1985, after a three-year trial period, Pecos officially became part of the Olivetan Congregation of Siena, Italy. This group, founded by Blessed Father Bernard Tolamel in 1319, has from its beginning been composed of men and women.

The Pecos community believes the golden thread that holds it together is stated by St. Benedict's Rule: "Let all guests to the monastery be received as Christ Himself." The community concentrates on mystical experiences, cultivating an experiential approach rather than teaching. As one monk stated, "Religion is caught, not taught. In ten years the Catholic Church will be very different, more experiential and less based on the service station approach, more responsive and participatory. We can't afford to be myopic . . . lay ministry has to be drawn in."

Pecos Benedictine Monastery
Box 1080
143 Cowlas Highway
Pecos, NM 87552
(505) 757-6415
www.pecosmonastery.org

Abbey of the Genesee
Piffard, NY

In the early 1950s an affluent couple offered this land to the local Catholic diocese for the purpose of founding a monastery. The Cistercian order at Gethsemani, where Thomas Merton lived, sent a group of Trappist monks to Piffard to develop a monastic community. The 500 original acres were already a working farm with a main house and barns, and over the years the property has grown to approximately 2,200 acres.

The first monks modified the house to suit their communal style. They farmed the land to raise wheat, corn, and soybeans, following the Rule of St. Benedict, which demands that its followers earn their living by their own hands and make enough also to help the poor. During those early days, the cook, an ex-navy chef, made bread for the community. Visitors were so impressed with the bread's taste and quality that they wanted to take some home. So a business was started, and today the highly mechanized bakery turns out 30,000 loaves of Monk's Bread a week, on a three-day work schedule, and this is sufficient to support the community. The monks donate 1,000 loaves a week to the poor, using their own truck to deliver them to various distribution points in the Rochester area. They also make delicious fruitcakes in a variety of flavors, including an extraordinary butterscotch.

The monks lead a rigorous life that begins with prayers at 2:25 A.M. Throughout the day, they meet to sing the canonical hours and spend about three hours in community prayer and song. Visitors are welcome at these services, held in the main chapel, which was built with rocks found on the monastery land and in the Genesee River. The somber wood-and-stone interior, with its simple religious decorations and jewel-like stained-glass windows, has a natural dignity, as though a cave had been modified for worship.

There are three separate guesthouses about one-half mile from the chapel. The original monastery, called Bethlehem ("house of bread"), has single rooms, former monks' cells, each with a single bed, chair, and desk, and communal washrooms. Meals, provided by the staff, are pickup breakfasts of cereal and monk's bread, with hot water available for coffee or tea. The main meal at noon is usually a hearty stew or pasta with salads and vegetables and simple desserts. Supper is often just soup and salad, but snacks of peanut butter and jelly sandwiches, fruit, and hot drinks are always available. At the other guesthouses, Bethany and Cana, guests cook for themselves. Visitors can help with meal preparations and cleanup. Occasionally, men may work in the bakery.

This is, by reputation, one of the strictest Cistercian communities in the United States, and various monks are available for discussion and counseling. As one of the monks said, "This place allows people to look inside and examine the rhythms they are living by. Often those who come are in transition. This place allows them to step off the merry-go-round of today's fast world and take a look at their internal show."

Abbey of the Genesee
3258 River Road
Piffard, NY 14533
(585) 243-2220
www.geneseeabbey.org

Abode of the Message
New Lebanon, NY

Located on 430 acres in the Berkshire Mountains, on property bought from Shakers, the Sufi Order in the West has a thriving community of close to 100 adults and children. The Abode of the Message was founded in 1975 by Pir Vilayat Khan to provide a supportive environment for self-discovery.

The community follows the traditions of Sufism, in which life is seen as a garden where all possibilities exist for creativity and the expression of beauty. By continually developing, expanding, and refining one's ideals and overcoming self-imposed limitations, one gains a new perspective on life as one becomes aware that we are all one family, one body.

The community has restored the 18th-century Shaker buildings to serve the needs of the group. Families have apartments and meet in the main dining room for meals. The food is prepared by a rotating kitchen staff, and varies from gourmet vegetarian to cheese sandwiches. The atmosphere is cheerful and open, and visitors feel welcome and comfortable.

Meditation sessions are held every day in the meditation hall, a large, barnlike structure that can accommodate the entire community. There are regular evening sessions of special breathing techniques and exercises, conducted by the more experienced members. Services and classes are open to all, and are regularly attended by neighbors and guests.

Individuals and couples can come for visits of up to three days and live with the community. The rooms are simply but comfortably furnished. There are separate community washrooms for men and women. On the second floor of the main building is a large reading room with sofas, easy chairs, and good reading lights.

On a hill above the community buildings are hermitage retreats where individuals can spend from one to ten nights. These simple, one-room huts, each in a private natural setting, have commanding views of the valley below. Retreatants should bring sleeping bags and be prepared to use an outhouse. Food is available from the main kitchen. One spends time completely alone, except for a daily visit from the retreat master.

The community does not promote a particular creed or church, but works to unite the followers of different religions and faiths in wisdom. It believes a greater trust and confidence will be established among people in this way.

Abode of the Message
5 Adobe Road
New Lebanon, NY 12125
(518) 794-8090
www.theabode.net

Chapel House
Hamilton, NY

In the mid 1950s, an anonymous donation made it possible to build and endow Chapel House. The concept was to establish a place where anyone with initiative and interest could come to stay, have access to books of religious insight and recordings of liturgical music, be surrounded by sacred art, and have the time and space provided by a chapel for meditation and spiritual devotion.

The beautiful building is on a high point of the Colgate University grounds, away from the bustle of campus life and just across from the great lawns that used to serve as golf fairways. The chapel is simply a quiet space for prayer and contemplation. Next door is a reception room leading to the library, which holds several thousand volumes of significant books on every religion. There are comfortable reading chairs and tables for serious study. Works of art, including a Tibetan prayer mantle, grace the walls between the bookshelves, and over the stone fireplace hangs a fine sculpture of intricate brasswork depicting key themes from ancient Israel. On the other side of the reception room is a music room with a high-quality sound system and a large selection of records. The music was chosen for its religious or spiritual nature and includes works not only by Beethoven and Bach but also by those who would not generally be considered composers of sacred music. The room is decorated with Zen calligraphy, a crucifix, a superb Buddha, and many other marvelous artifacts.

Beyond the music room is the dining room, where three meals a day are served by the resident supervisor. Downstairs are seven single rooms, each with private bath, single bed, chair, desk, and more than 20 books as part of the basic furnishings. The windows look out on a quiet woodland setting.

Guests are requested to observe silence except during mealtimes. The only other requirement is that visitors use the facilities for their personal religious research and that they do not disturb the privacy of others.

The chapel has been used as a place of worship by Christians, Jews, Hindus, Buddhists, and Muslims. There is no guru or master teacher here. Visitors are expected to seek guidance in the books, music, and works of art that have been proven by time to be great teachers. The anonymous benefactor of Chapel House once said with a twinkle in her eye, "If one person a year comes and uses it for the purposes we have in mind . . . we will have a good income from our investment."

Chapel House
Colgate University
Hamilton, NY 13346
(315) 228-7675
www.departments.colgate.edu/chapelhouse

Chautauqua Institution
Chautauqua, NY

In 1874 a summer school was held on the shores of Lake Chautauqua to instruct Sunday-school teachers in organization, management, and teaching methods. From this modest beginning the programs were expanded to include political concepts, economics, literature, science, and music study. Hotels and rooming houses were built to house the ever-increasing numbers of visitors. By the early 1900s a grand hotel was built, and the summer-camp concept of a few weeks in a tent made a transition to a more genteel approach to education, which included clean sheets and an elegant dining room. Business leaders of the day, such as Henry Ford, attended, and Thomas Edison and his family came regularly.

Many religious groups either built or acquired good-sized houses and created as many rooms as possible, which they made—and still make—available for rent, with community kitchen facilities. Before the end of the 19th century, Chautauqua had become a national force as a way to reach thousands of people interested in personal growth through education. Here, in one place, grew a culture camp on the shores of a clean, clear lake where one could swim, boat, fish, and be entertained by nightly concerts and lectures from prominent speakers.

By the early 20th century, many more private homes were built on the grounds, and the 210-acre setting became a typical small town of the era. And it remains so today: an almost classic community in a sylvan setting; beautifully kept, Victorian-style houses with lush green lawns and clipped hedges, large porches with comfortable sitting arrangements, flowers growing along walkways. Many of the houses have gingerbread decorations, are painted in light pastel shades, and are in good condition and well maintained. Auto access is limited, so one can walk the streets or ride a bicycle and slow the pace of physical movement to allow the mind to rest and wonder.

The Chautauqua Program runs for nine weeks, from mid-June to the end of August. After Labor Day, things are really quiet, but there are more than 200 regular residents who stay year-round, and many of the rooming houses and some hotels are available. The fine library on Bestor Plaza remains open, as do the post office and newsstand/book-and-gift shop.

This community is a piece of Americana, an outdoor museum of late 19th- and early 20th-century life-style. One can wander for hours admiring the fine houses, look out to the lake that is never far away, sit on the well-situated benches, and be undisturbed for hours or days at a time. A perfect place to read, relax, ruminate, and get one's internal wheels balanced.

Chautauqua Institution
P.O. Box 28
Chautauqua, NY 14722
(716) 357-6200
www.ciweb.org

Cormaria Center
Sag Harbor, NY

Set on 17 acres fronting Northwest Bay is the Catholic retreat house called Cormaria. The main section was built in the early 1900s by a sea captain for his private residence. The story goes that the captain got his ship's carpenter to do the fine interior woodwork, and it is splendid. There is elegant Tiffany glass around the dining room ceiling and windows, which command a spectacular uninterrupted view of the bay.

Off the main entrance is the chapel, decorated in a nautical motif. A back corner is hung with fishing nets and shells placed on the wall; boat oars separate the altar from the pews. The windows offer a glimpse of the sea. To the other side of the entrance foyer is the large dining room, a section added to the original house, where home-cooked meals are served cafeteria-style. There is a residence wing for up to 75 persons in clean, comfortable single rooms with community washrooms. Meeting and crafts rooms are on the lower level.

The nuns of the Religious of the Sacred Heart of Mary see hospitality to a large variety of guests as a natural part of their mission. Their regular retreat programs cover every need, including continuous spiritual direction.

At the edge of the property is a small building that has two separate hermitages for those who prefer to spend their time alone.

Cormaria, in its tranquil setting, offers a variety of opportunities for spiritual sustenance and rebirth. One retreatant, a Brahmin, wrote a thank you note to the director in which he said, "The peace that I found hasn't left me."

Cormaria Retreat House
Bay Street
P.O. Box 1993
Sag Harbor, NY 11963
(631) 725-4206
www.cormaria.org

Dai Bosatsu Zendo
Livingston Manor, NY

The approach to the zendo winds along a narrow road for 20 miles, and by the time you reach it, it is as though you have passed through a time warp and come upon a place deep in the mountains of Japan; only there, it seems, could one find such a magnificent temple. The monastery is at the edge of Beecher Lake, the highest lake in the Catskill Mountains, which the naturalist John Burroughs described in 1868: "As beautiful as a dream . . . the mind is delighted as an escaped bird, and darts gleefully from point to point." The 30-acre lake has changed little since then, or even since the time it was revered by the Leni-Lenape Indians, who believed that the mountain waters restored vitality to both mind and body. The monastery was completed in 1976, and since then has offered students the opportunity for intensive training in a traditional Zen monastery environment. As authentic inside as out, the quality of its construction is evident from the gleaming oak floors to the windows that act as picture frames for the forest, the lake, and the abundant wildlife.

As part of the Zen Studies Society established to aid D. T. Suzuki in his efforts to introduce Zen Buddhism to the West, this zendo, only three hours from New York City, has a full schedule of retreats ranging from weekends to full weeks. Anyone is welcome to visit the monastery or guesthouses and to join in the daily sitting sessions in the meditation room. In twice-weekly classes, the 17 monks and students in residence ponder how to become a stronger and more compassionate Buddhist community. One way has been to invite outside groups, such as AA, to come to meetings. The program that began in 1988 was so successful it has more than doubled in size. Participants who came with no knowledge or experience of Zen training have returned again and again, and many now sit regularly.

As a result of reaching out to this and other groups, the monks have become less isolated, and the awareness of Zen practice is growing in the world. As one monk wrote, "Real Zen practice opens out. It is wisdom and compassion in action. . . . If compassion in action is present in society, it will become clearly evident in the actions of that society."

In addition to the monastery and the 14-room lakeside guesthouse, there is also a lovely cottage for one or two in the woods.

Dai Bosatsu Zendo
223 Beecher Lake Road
HCR 1, Box 171
Livingston Manor, NY 12758
www.daibosatsu.org

Elat Chayyim
Accord, NY

Nestled in the foothills of the Catskill Mountains, Elat Chayyim, "tree of life" in Hebrew, is located on 35 acres along a quiet country lane lined with sheltering trees. Founded in 1992 by two Reconstructionist rabbis, this center, once a Jewish bungalow colony called Chait's Hotel, celebrates Jewish renewal and welcomes people from all branches of Judaism—Reform, Conservative, Reconstructionist, Orthodox, Post-Modern, and secular.

Rabbi Joanna Katz and Rabbi Jeff Roth have created the first real Jewish retreat as a sanctuary to promote what they feel is a much needed transformation in Jewish practice and spirituality. They, along with others in this movement for Jewish renewal, bring the teachings of Jewish mysticism to the center, rather than leaving them on the periphery. They are building on contemporary spiritual sensibilities including the experiences of women, and their programs reflect humanism, transpersonal psychology, and an openness to other spiritual traditions. They aim to develop an authentic Jewish practice for our time and for those who feel alienated from their Jewish roots. This will, they hope, have a healing effect on the individual, the family, the community, and the planet.

The centerpiece of the main lodge is a ceiling-high stone fireplace surrounded by picture windows that look out over the flower and vegetable gardens to the Catskills beyond. The spirit here is warm and welcoming, and guests gather in front of the fireplace after dinner to share stories, songs, poems, and dancing. Those who prefer quiet may wear a special button to indicate that they are observing silence, and may dine in a separate room. No matter which dining room guests choose, they will savor the gourmet vegetarian meals made with home-grown produce of which the center is justly proud.

Friday night and Saturday Shabbat services are held with much joyful singing and prayer, using a new Or Chadash, a prayer book with completely revised Psalms and prayers. Lovely walks are available along country roads and through surrounding fields, and quiet places inside and out abound for reflection and contemplation.

A variety of retreats are held here throughout the year, in addition to those for the Jewish holidays, including unique meditation retreats with visiting Buddhist teachers, a men's retreat, a retreat for singles, and a training for spiritual facilitators. Separate children's programs are provided as part of the weekend Shabbaton.

Elat Chayyim
Isabella Freedman Jewish Retreat Center
116 Johnson Road
Falls Village, CT 06031
(800) 398-2630
www.isabellafreedman.org
(New location & affiliation)

Holy Cross Monastery
West Park, NY

From the entrance plaque, which reads *Crux est mundi medicina* ("The Cross is the healing of the world"), to the request that guests offer a prayer for the person who will next occupy their room, this monastery reaches out to offer solace and comfort to all who come here.

Holy Cross Monastery is an Episcopalian community of monks who follow the Benedictine traditions of monasticism. The monastery is perched on 26 acres bordering the Hudson River. The original building, a large, rambling brick mansion, was completed in 1904, and there have been additions and modifications over the years. The refectory is of superb design, with seven large arched windows looking out to meadows and woods with the river beyond, an ever-changing art gallery of the Hudson River School, painted daily by nature.

The guest rooms are generous by monastic standards, and can be reached by elevator. They are clean, neat, and comfortable, many with a river view. The monks observe a daily schedule of community prayer in the chapel beginning at 6 A.M., with the last prayer service at 7:30 P.M. The Great Silence begins at 9 P.M. and is observed until 8:15 the next morning.

There is a regular series of retreats that explore subjects such as the spiritual dimensions of writing and art, and examine the Benedictine monastic experience, which emphasizes a balanced life of work, prayer, and relaxation. Another program focuses on healing and reaching out to those in recovery.

There is an ongoing artist-in-residence program in which serious, accomplished artists are given room and board and a place to work, based on their talent and need.

Below the chapel is the crypt where the founder of the community is interred. There is a magnificent folk-art icon donated by two artists, free spirits who had borrowed the car of an Episcopal priest in Michigan, and were grounded nearby. Rather than returning to the Midwest to explain their lengthy absence and the condition of the vehicle, which they had crashed into a tree, the artists agreed to take refuge at Holy Cross and donate their artistic talents, which were considerable, to making icons for all of the monasteries in the order. This one depicts Father James Huntington, the founder of the Order of the Holy Cross, with scenes of New York City, where the order began.

In any season, this is a lovely place to be. From the solitary walks along the river to the many quiet nooks inside, where one can read quietly, the monks maintain a warm and inviting hospitality.

Holy Cross Monastery
Box 99, Rte. 9W
West Park, NY 12493
(845) 384-6660
www.holycrossmonastery.com

Mount Irenaeus
Franciscan Mountain Retreat
West Clarksville, NY

This mountain retreat, named after a revered Franciscan friar, is a 228-acre farm high in the Allegheny Mountains, with views to the south and east over the magnificently wooded western edges of the Appalachian Range. The main house, which has a large living room with fireplace and adjoining dining room and sun porch, is a gathering space for meals. Cabins, off in the woods a respectable distance from the main house and from each other, have kitchens where visitors can cook and fend for themselves. Self-sufficiency in the context of community is encouraged at Mount Irenaeus, and pitching a tent is also possible if visitors are so inclined.

The chapel was framed in one weekend by a loyal group of people who wanted to contribute their energy by helping to build a communal house of worship. The lovely structure was raised in a nondenominational spirit for the enjoyment of people of all religious persuasions. Set apart from the main house and cabins, on one of the highest spots on the farm, it looks down over the hills and valley.

The altar is in the center of the chapel; low steps lead down to it. Window seats are built beneath the large, clear windows which frame the vistas beyond. Pillows are scattered about, as though someone's comfortable home were temporarily being used as a place of worship. The lower level of the chapel is a library where one may choose a book to read.

Many of the programs are inspired by the thoughts and actions of St. Francis of Assisi, who, with his early followers, went to the woods and mountains to seek a clearer vision of life. There are also evenings of prayer and reflection from the writings of Thomas Merton, who taught at St. Bonaventure University before becoming a Trappist.

There is much to be done at this young retreat haven, and help is always appreciated, whether it is weeding the garden, clearing brush, helping to cook or clean, chopping wood, or maintaining the hiking trails. Yet none of this is required. The earnest hope of Mount Irenaeus is that people will come to enjoy the serenity and peace that is there, and thus find it within themselves. This is a contemplative community that invites people to share its life and prayer.

Mt. Irenaeus
Franciscan Mountain Retreat
Box 100
West Clarksville, NY 14786
(585) 973-2470
www.mounti.com

Mount Saviour Monastery
Pine City, NY

The tree-lined road to Mount Saviour winds through long, rolling green fields, dotted with grazing sheep, almost as if an artist had painted them there to add color and poignancy. The Catholic Benedictine monks first came to the top of this mountain, near Elmira, in 1951. They acquired a farm, and now hold close to 1,000 acres, about 250 of which are cleared and fenced to maintain 600 sheep. To keep the monastery self-sufficient, the wool is sold as yarn, rugs, and sleeping pads. The spring shearing is an exciting time, when the monks round up the balky flock to relieve them of their winter coats.

The monastery complex is built around an octagonal chapel whose tall spire rises above the central altar. The monks sing the canonical hours here, and guests are welcome at all services. A bell is rung to call all to worship, and the monks file in, wearing gray cowled habits. The liturgy sung by these devout men is a moving and holy experience. At the conclusion of Compline, the last service of the day, the monks descend to the crypt, guests following, to sing the final prayer around the candlelit 14th-century statue of Our Lady, Queen of Peace.

Single men stay in St. Joseph's, which was the first monastery building. Each room has a cot, a desk, a chair, and a small closet. The common washroom is at the end of the corridor. On the lower level is a library and a large living room with chairs grouped or set singly by windows that look onto the lawns and pastures. Coffee and tea can be made in the kitchen, and meals are taken with the monks in the new monastery nearby.

Women and couples stay at St. Gertrude's, a refurbished farmhouse 15 minutes' walk up the road from the chapel. This charming house has clean, fresh rooms, watercolors of monastery scenes hung on the walls, and homelike furnishings. Meals are served family-style in a glass-enclosed porch.

Guests are expected to structure their own time in a way that suits their need for quiet and reflection. There are many places on the property, indoors and out, to find solitude. One can wander into the fields and in the evening look down to the Elmira Airport and watch the lights of the far-off planes, or sit on lawn chairs, looking to the south, and see the glow from the villages in the valley below. The chapel is open all day, and in the crypt there are several altars, with one section set apart for the Blessed Sacrament.

Mount Saviour Monastery
231 Monastery Road
Pine City, NY 14871
(607) 734-1688
www.msaviour.org

New Skete Communities
Cambridge, NY

The term *skete,* originally the name of a remote settlement in the Egyptian desert, has come to mean a small, family-style monastic community with one spiritual father. New Skete belongs to the Orthodox Church in America led by His Beatitude, Theodosius, Archbishop of Washington and Metropolitan of All America and Canada.

In 1967, New Skete moved to 500 remote acres of steep, rocky land in northern New York State. The monks have built two beautifully crafted temples, both of unfinished wood. The first, erected in 1970, is topped by gold cupolas or "onion" domes, giving the feeling of eastern Europe. The interior is adorned with Byzantine icons, many painted by the monks. This temple is always open to visitors. A few steps away is the second temple, dedicated in 1983 to Christ, the Wisdom of God. The floors are of Italian marble, and the furniture and altar screen are carved from ash, zebrawood, basswood, white oak, English brown oak—each piece a work of art. In the center of the altar stands the holy table of red oak, in which relics of martyrs are sealed as a reminder of the Church's baptism in blood. The high white walls give a sense of light-filled openness, and the acoustics are perfect. Given the rusticity of the outer structure and the remoteness of the location, this temple is like a jewel on a mountaintop.

New Skete is three separate communities governed by one spiritual leader. Each community has separate quarters and works to contribute its skills for the good of the whole. The monks have their living quarters next to the main temple. Nearby is a separate guesthouse with room for six. Visitors are expected to join the community for prayer and meals. They can help with grounds maintenance, office, and kennel work (see below), but this is not required. The nuns of New Skete have their own convent a few miles away, where they bake world-class cheesecake that is sold in their shop or by mail order. The Companions of New Skete, the third group, are married couples who live in Emmaus House, a separate residence on the property. They follow a religious rule, living and working in community, worshiping daily with the monks and nuns, and support themselves by sewing, weaving, and some outside jobs.

For years New Skete monks have bred, raised, and trained German shepherd dogs, for which they are known worldwide. Their definitive book, *How to Be Your Dog's Best Friend,* has sold thousands of copies. The monks also run a thriving mail-order business selling cured meats like ham, bacon, and sausage, plus cheeses and condiments.

The quality of their food products is reflected in their meals. Eating properly is as important at New Skete as praying and working well. The communities believe and practice that spirituality is a lived experience rather than a perceived one. As one monk said, "Having to care for other human beings roots you in spirituality."

New Skete Communities
P.O. Box 128
Cambridge, NY 12816
(518) 677-3928
www.newskete.com

Our Lady of the Resurrection Monastery
La Grangeville, NY

In a secluded area of Dutchess County, 22 acres of hilltop land are the site of a rambling wooden Benedictine monastery. It was founded by Brother Victor-Antoine d'Avila-Latourette, who had a vision of how a monk should live. The result is a beautiful and simple place that continually reminds one of man's connection to prayer, nature, art, and spirituality. A small flock of sheep keep the grass under control around the monastery and guesthouse; an herb and flower garden provides joy to the eye and zest to the cooking; the bedrooms are decorated with warm colors, and the living and dining rooms resemble a French country farmhouse. The chapel was constructed from stones found in the fields.

Brother Victor, who holds degrees in music, psychology, and education, was inspired by Father Peter Minard, a hermit and ascetic who seemed to him a living icon. Victor felt called to this simple way of life, following the duties and obligations of the Benedictine rules of hospitality, counsel, compassion, and concern for the environment.

The chapel has a European flavor, and the design and decorative touches are those of a master. Daily prayer services are held here, morning, noon, and evening. Both Gregorian chant and High Church Slavonic are used in the services. Meals are taken in the refectory, whose windows and skylight look out to the trees and grounds. The food is delicious, and many of the recipes can be found in Brother Victor's popular cookbook, *From a Monastery Kitchen*. Guests can stay either in the monastery, where there are six single rooms, or in the plain St. Scholastica Guest House, which has a separate kitchen for pickup breakfast and snacks. Guesthouse visitors come to the monastery for lunch and supper. An excellent library is available. There is one hermitage set off in the woods for anyone wanting to be completely alone.

The monastery is devoted to contemplation and simplicity. Each person will approach this in a different way, but the monastery provides an opportunity for all to rest and withdraw for a while, to escape the noise and busy-ness of their lives.

Our Lady of the Resurrection Monastery
Barmore Road
La Grangeville, NY 12540
(Write & include s.a.s.e.)

St. Cuthbert's Retreat House
Brewster, NY

In 1959 a group of Episcopalian nuns of the Community of the Holy Spirit discovered this property on a quiet country road with drystone walls. The nuns had been seaching for a country retreat house where they could find some respite from the strenuous life of teaching and administering their New York City school. The neighbors soon became used to seeing the nuns go back and forth in Beulah, their old Buick convertible with the gleaming chrome teeth. The car had a leaky top, so when it rained the nuns would open up their umbrellas inside the car to keep their habits dry.

On this 127 acres of woods and fields is the original farm—now called St. Cuthbert's—owned by the Sears family from 1810 to 1940. In the mid-1800s, after a trip to the West Indies, the senior Sears decided to build a veranda and a mansard roof, which meant adding a third story. The spacious and well-made house was ideal for the nuns, and it has been beautifully restored. The rooms still have 19th-century furnishings, and there are rumors of a friendly ghost who can be heard occasionally walking up the stairs during the day.

It seemed a natural step to open a day school here, as a means of supporting the country place, and to carry out the order's mission to educate. In the early 1960s the nuns founded Melrose, with a few grades of elementary school, and by 1970 they had to construct an entire building to accommodate more than 100 students, from kindergarten to eighth grade. A convent wing was added to the new school building, and the nuns now live there.

Just across the road is the more modern St. Aidan's, which is used for smaller groups and private retreatants who want a few days in a beautiful country setting.

Morning and evening prayers are offered by the community in two chapels: one, used year-round, is in the school; the other, just behind St. Cuthbert's and used mainly in mild weather, is a charming wooden prayer house, built like a giant gazebo.

The nuns who live and work here have managed to establish a successful educational program for the young while fulfilling their desire for a spiritual life. It is this place and time for meditation and prayer that they share with retreatants.

They also have a retreat house in New York City that welcomes those who seek quiet.

St. Cuthbert's Retreat House
Federal Hill Road
Brewster, NY 10509
(845) 278-9777
www.chsisters.org
St. Hilda's House, NYC
(212) 666-8249

Springwater Center
Springwater, NY

The Springwater Center began in 1982, when Toni Packer, then a teacher at the Rochester Zen Center, left with a group of students to form the Genesee Valley Zen Center. Subsequently, the name was changed to Springwater Center for Meditative Inquiry and Retreats. The new center, as Toni Packer explains, was born out of the need to question the forms of inherited Zen practice and the authority vested in religious teachers and traditions. This process of inquiry has continued to shape the activity of the center, responding to the needs of people working together, both in and out of retreats. The traditional Zen forms have been dropped. Toni is available to meet with people, both individually and in groups, during seven-day retreats and when she is in residence.

There is a spacious meditation room with tall windows that bathe the wood floors and walls in generous light. There is a solarium and a large kitchen as well as a room set aside for exercise, listening to taped talks, and reading. There are sleeping quarters for up to 40 people, many in dormitory style, and guests bring their own linens or a sleeping bag.

Retreats lasting from four to ten days are scheduled regularly. Silence is observed throughout to provide the opportunity for introspection that is so difficult in an active, busy life. There are sitting periods, a daily talk, and individual and group meetings with Toni Packer, as well as communal work (meal preparation, housecleaning, and grounds maintenance). Except for the work periods, all activities are optional. Time is set aside for exercise and rest. It is also possible to visit as a guest outside of retreat times.

The property has ample space for walking, hiking, or cross-country skiing. One can explore the old farm ponds or just find a quiet place beneath a tree. The center is on 200 acres in a beautifully remote section of western New York, yet within an hour's drive of Rochester. It has superb views of the surrounding hills and valley.

Springwater Center
7179 Mill Street
Springwater, NY 14560
(585) 669-2141
www.springwatercenter.org

Still Point House of Prayer
Stillwater, NY

Taking the name "Still Point" from T. S. Eliot's *Four Quartets*, in 1972 Dominican sister Sylvia Rosell wrote a proposal to her order for a house of prayer, seeking support for one year. After only six months, the venture became self-sufficient, and her ministry of bringing life and prayer closer together continues to grow. Her directed and guided retreats are combined with holistic health programs, yoga, meditation (the Jesus prayer), and zazen, with some time for winter and summer sports.

Still Point is one of the quietest places imaginable. The 30-acre property appears neighborless, a spot completely overlooked by the rest of the world. The main building, Hospitality House—a reconditioned farmhouse—has space for seven to sleep in small, comfortable rooms. There is a chapel with a circular window behind the altar that looks out on the woods. Morning and evening prayer sessions include Matins at 7:30 A.M. and Vespers and meditation in the late afternoon, just before supper. A priest comes to say mass three times a week. Down the hall from the chapel is the dining/living room where guests meet to share an evening vegetarian meal. Breakfast and lunch are pickup style in the kitchen.

There are five small hermitages off in the woods, a short walk from the main house. Those on hermitage retreat can take food back or join the other guests at the evening meal. Just below the main house is a tranquil pond next to Meditation Park, a landscaped area with benches for quiet contemplation. Beyond the park, on a little hill, are outdoor stations of the cross and a Native American medicine wheel.

Still Point's focus is spiritual growth through the healing process of meditation, prayer, solitude, and quiet. The name of the community truly reflects its purpose. As Sister Sylvia says, "As soon as you stop the train, you can see what cargo you're carrying."

Still Point House of Prayer
Interfaith Retreat Center
20 Still Point Road
Mechanicville, NY 12118
(518) 587-4967
Stillpointretreatcenter.com
(New location)

Transfiguration Monastery
Windsor, NY

In 1979 three Benedictine nuns joined together to live a simple monastic life on 100 acres of fields and woodland in the Susquehanna Valley, near Binghamton. One of these three, Sister Mary Placid, remembers back in 1930 meeting two young American boys who were taking apples from her backyard in her native France. The boys subsequently became her friends, and after she entered the convent she continued to pray for them. Years later, when she read *The Seven Storey Mountain*, she discovered that her childhood friends were Thomas Merton and his brother John Paul.

Both the monastery and the cozy guesthouse are built of logs and heated by woodstoves. The guesthouse has a kitchen where visitors may prepare their own breakfast with the basics provided. Prepared food is brought to the guesthouse kitchen in a picnic basket for lunch and supper. Sometimes, on Sundays and other special occasions, guests eat with the community in the monastery refectory.

The community meets four times a day to sing the liturgy in the chapel, which is decorated with extraordinary icons. Guests are welcome at all services.

There is a golf course adjacent to the property, where one of the nuns regularly strolls the border, a good place to pray. If she finds a golf ball, she brings it back and adds it to the monastery's collection. These balls are cleaned, put into egg cartons, and sold back to the world, labeled "Holy in One." The sisters have a winery with wine bottled under the St. Benedict Winery label. One sister does superb icon painting, and periodically the monastery sponsors retreats and conferences. For a while the nuns operated a catering business, but this took them away from home too much. However, they still provide delicious food and it's worth a visit just for that. But there's more here. As one nun said, "A monastery is a sacred space for sacred time. People are attracted for that reason."

Transfiguration Monastery
701 N.Y. Route 79
Windsor, NY 13865
(607) 655-2366
www.transfigurationmonastery.org

Zen Mountain Monastery
Mount Tremper, NY

Located deep in the Catskill Mountains, the 200 acres of nature sanctuary that make up the monastery grounds are bordered by the Beaverkill and Esopus rivers. The property is surrounded by thousands of acres of New York State Forest preserve and has miles of hiking trails. The main building, a well-crafted four-story stone structure built in the early 20th century, contains a large meditation hall, classrooms, a dining room, and a library. Here too are the sleeping quarters for guests and retreatants, in dormitories with communal bathrooms. Visitors should bring a sleeping bag or blanket, a towel, and loose, comfortable clothing for sitting and outside work.

Since the monastery opened ten years ago, it has become known for one of the most rigorous and authentic Zen training programs in the United States. Retreatants for weekend or week-long programs enter the routine of the monastery itself. The emphasis here is on practice rather than on formal teaching. Each activity provides a mirror to study the self, from the moment the wake-up bell sounds for early-morning zazen, followed by chanting and a ceremonial breakfast that provides an opportunity to observe the effect of the foods on the body, and so on throughout the day. Staff and guests work silently together doing care-taking, a practice of giving back to the buildings and grounds some of the benefits received from them.

All meals are taken buffet-style in the dining hall, and each person helps to clean up afterward. The afternoons are spent according to the retreat schedule, either with continuing work practice, classical Zen art and contemporary art, martial arts, or reading. The focus of each and every moment is the "still point" of Zen; the ultimate aim, to make of one's life an expression of one's practice.

The concentrated simplicity of Zen is more than a philosophy; it is a way of life tracing back to the Buddha himself. The path of concentration development, through sitting zazen, helps bring body, breathing, and mind into harmony so that we may realize that we are not separate from other people. Neither are we limited to any one religion or cultural tradition. From this understanding, compassion and empathy for all human beings arises naturally.

Zen Mountain Monastery
Box 197, South Plank Road
Mount Tremper, NY 12457
(845) 688-2228
www.mro.org

Avila Retreat Center
Durham, NC

Originally founded in 1958 as a Carmelite monastery for cloistered nuns, Avila is now owned and operated by the Catholic Diocese of Raleigh as an ecumenical retreat center. A one-mile meditation trail winds through the gently sloping 51 acres of woods and meadows. Named after St. Teresa of Avila, who lived in Spain during the 16th century, the original building was designed like a European monastery. The main building acts as a buffer from the outside world, protecting the peaceful inner courtyard of landscaped lawns, bushes, and flowers. Walkways lead back to comfortable cottages built a short distance from the main building, which has a dining room (the food is excellent), meeting rooms (with cushioned rocking chairs), and a chapel. A small community of sisters lives here and, with the help of many local volunteers, offers groups and individuals a place of hospitality, healing, and unity. "There is a healing process here, a spiritual energy noticed by many," said the director, Sister Damian Jackson.

The center was the first in the diocese to offer retreats for separated, divorced, and widowed persons, charismatic retreats, and one called "The Joyful Christ" which focuses on humor in religion. There are a variety of programs for people of all denominations including special programs for abused women and adult children of alcoholics, refresher days for young mothers, and retreats for teenagers, disabled people, teachers, families, and senior adults. They have "programs that touch every human need." Directed and private retreats are available on request. Since 1983, more than 20,000 people have spent time here.

Many put away their watches and follow the rhythm of the bells that call to meals, meetings, and prayer.

Avila's ecumenism may have peaked recently when the sisters were invited to be spiritual leaders at another retreat center. One described it: "So here were Catholic nuns giving a retreat to Methodists at a Baptist retreat center!"

Sister Damian has won wide recognition for her efforts here. She has been nominated two consecutive years for Durham's Woman of Achievement Silver Medallion Award and honored as "a role model and inspiration to the women of Durham community, demonstrating unusual and extraordinary accomplishments in her chosen field." Avila reflects that.

Avila Retreat Center
711 Mason Road
Durham, NC 27712
(919) 477-1285
www.avila-retreat-center.com

Southern Dharma Retreat Center
Hot Springs, NC

About one and a half hours north of Asheville, in the rugged and remote mountains of western North Carolina, at the end of a long, winding dirt drive, is an upper valley of Hap Mountain. The center is located in a place far removed from the distractions of everyday life. Here individuals can come to nurture a sense of peace and uncover the truth within the heart, to study and practice the dharma and do the inner work we are all sooner or later called to do.

In the late 1970s, after some time studying in California, Elizabeth Kent and Melinda Guyol shared the idea of starting a retreat center somewhere in the mountains. They both wanted to work at something they believed in and felt was worthwhile. The land was acquired in 1978 and five years were spent clearing, building, remodeling, and improving roads. During this phase, a few programs were sponsored, and gradually the new retreat center became known. More and more people visited, offering help, caring about the place, and in 1995 there were 22 retreats scheduled.

A small community lives here, maintains the buildings, and prepares for retreatants. Individuals can come for their own spiritual purposes in between scheduled groups. There are a few private rooms with shared baths and a dormitory in a finely constructed main house. The kitchen is off the dining room where a potbelly stove warms the body and the heart. The meditation hall with polished wood floors is a short distance from the main house and was being modified in 1995 to be accessible to the handicapped.

This is not a facility that follows one tradition or follows a single spiritual leader. Teachers from a variety of traditions are invited to give meditation retreats. The facility is maintained as a supportive environment where truth is expressed in many forms, acknowledging that spiritual growth is individual, each person's response is unique, and different spiritual paths answer different needs. The unifying theme here is an emphasis on meditation, contemplation, and silence.

Southern Dharma Retreat Center
1661 West Road
Rte. 1, Box 34H
Hot Springs, NC 28743
(828) 622-7112
www.southerndharma.org

Annunciation Priory
Bismarck, ND

In June 1944, sisters from St. Benedict's Convent in St. Joseph, Minnesota (see page 277), gathered in the Bismarck, North Dakota, diocese to start an independent foundation. They committed themselves to serve the people of the region. As Kathleen Norris wrote in *Dakota*, "The High Plains, the beginning of the desert west, often act as a crucible for those who inhabit them. Like Jacob's angel, the region requires that you wrestle with it before it bestows a blessing." Fifty years later, the blessings are evident: a hospital, a medical center, and the University of Mary.

In the 1950s, the sisters acquired land a few miles south of Bismarck, on a bluff looking over the Missouri River and the plains beyond. They were able to persuade Marcel Breuer, who was working on the design for St. John's Abbey church (see page 128) in Collegeville, Minnesota, to be the architect. Internationally known, Breuer designed the UNESCO building in Paris and the Whitney Museum in New York. One sister remembers him sitting alone for hours on the spot where the priory now stands, allowing his imagination to express "in static materials— stone, concrete, glass—the drive toward the spiritual." He mused: "The inanimate structure should reflect vibration of thought, emotion, and belief." The design also reflects Benedictine values of permanence, stability, and simplicity. Breuer used sun and shadow as metaphors to blend oppositions without diminishing either. He worked fieldstone and flagstone, reinforced concrete, and cantilevered stairways into a unified whole. The 100-foot-high bell banner makes a distinctive silhouette on the landscape and marks the approach to the chapel. The V-shaped concrete supports for the cloister walkway rest on native flagstone, and the flue tiles across the building front give a sense of enclosure. Breuer suggested that no trees or bushes be allowed to interfere with the lines of the structure. Carpets of grass are carefully tended. The hand of a master designer is evident everywhere outside and in. The main chapel has a west window predominantly amber and violet (setting of the sun), and the east window is rose with blue (rising sun).

The sisters have a few rooms for guests who share cafeteria-style meals with the community. There is morning, noon, and evening prayer and daily mass with times varying according to the season. Private and directed retreats can be arranged for both men and women. The 90-acre property, which includes the University of Mary campus, offers many pleasant walks with serene views from the bluff down and across the wide Missouri.

Annunciation Monastery
7250 University Drive
Bismarck, ND 58504
(701) 255-1520
www.annunciationmonastery.org

Assumption Abbey
Richardton, ND

In 1993, Assumption Abbey celebrated its 100th anniversary as a monastic community. Back in 1899, Benedictine monks from Devil's Lake, North Dakota, moved here and became an integral part of the settling of the Dakota Territory. The pioneer spirit and zeal of the missionary monks, soon joined by Native Americans, developed a strength and character still exemplified by their work. The monks purchased land on the edge of the village, served as missionary priests to the German-Russian and German-Hungarian settlers, founded schools that became a college and seminary, suffered through financial difficulties in the 1920s brought on by overexpansion, then stuck it out with resourcefulness. Today the school has closed, and the monks work as farmers and printers, as pastors to local churches, and as teachers at midwestern colleges.

The abbey has 2,000 acres on which the monks raise cattle for market and ducks and geese for their own table. They sell wine under their own label, produce their own honey, grow their own vegetables, and bake their own bread. Visitors take meals cafeteria-style with the monks in the dining room, where a wall of windows looks north across the prairie 40 miles to the Killdeer Mountains. The monastery sits on a bluff at the edge of the prairie sea. At night, the lights of an occasional car along a road a few miles west look like a small boat crossing.

The community and guests pray together in the church morning, noon, and evening and mass is at 5 P.M. Monastery guests can join the monks in the choir stalls.

There are seven guest rooms in the monastery with private baths. A guesthouse has room for another 20 with shared bathrooms, and from June through October there is a dormitory that can accommodate a large group. There are no organized retreats, so individuals should be prepared to plan their own time. A monk is available for discussion if requested. There is a program for single men who would like to experience the Benedictine way of life.

There are many advantages to living on the northern Great Plains, one monk explained: "We have four distinct seasons here, and we get each one several times a year." No matter what the weather, it's a fine place to visit. In between sleep, prayer, and meals, there are acres of prairie to explore. Author Kathleen Norris, who wrote much of *Dakota* here, advises: "Check where the bulls are before hiking the pastures!"

Assumption Abbey
418 Third Avenue
Richardton, ND 58652
(701) 974-3315
assumptionabbey.com

Jesuit Retreat House
Cleveland, OH

In the Cleveland suburb of Parma, there are 50 acres of forest, much of it native hardwoods, a substantial part in old-growth oak trees, surrounded by fences that mark this 100-year-old retreat. The property was acquired in 1893 to be used for Jesuit scholars. In 1898, three laymen came seeking spiritual direction in the Exercises of St. Ignatius. This was the first lay retreat given here and probably one of the first in the Midwest. Since then, the retreat programs have grown and evolved following the Jesuit philosophy of "finding God in all things."

Until 1967, the facilities had a dual function as a seminary and retreat house. In that year, the seminary program was moved to Colombiere, Michigan, and the mission of the retreat house evolved more fully. Maintaining the ministry of St. Ignatius's Spiritual Exercises, the programs foster spiritual and personal growth in men, women, and children, religious and clergy. The first women's retreat was held in 1968, and in the following year, 1,500 high school students attended. In addition, there are individually directed weekend retreats, 6-, 8-, and 30-day retreats, and weekly meetings over an eight-month period that offer the 19th Annotation form of the Spiritual Exercises.

There are days of recollection for senior citizens, priests, and teachers; many programs that encourage spiritual self-expression through poetry, journaling, and autobiography. There are family-oriented weekends such as Engaged Encounter, Mother-Daughter Retreats, and Couples Night Out. There are programs specifically for women, and others such as Strategy: Planning from a Business Perspective with God's Approval.

Here you feel as though you've entered an oasis, buffered from the outside world by the trees; the beauty of the well-tended landscape, the paths through the woods, the comfortable rooms and generous food, all combine for an opportunity for spiritual sustenance.

Jesuit Retreat House
Cleveland, OH
www.jrh-cleveland.org
(Don't want travelers)

Osage+Monastery Forest of Peace
Sand Springs, OK

This is a community founded with the specific purpose of uniting the spiritual traditions of East and West. The concept took visible shape in 1975 when Sister Pascaline Coff, a former prioress general of the Benedictine Congregation, along with other sisters, acquired 40 acres of secluded, wooded property 25 miles west of Tulsa, Oklahoma. Named Osage Monastery, after the American Indian territory it is in, its initials, OM, form the sacred Eastern word for the Divine.

This American Christian ashram has drawn a composite from many spiritual paths. The chapel has icons and symbols from Native American, Hindu, Jewish, and Buddhist traditions. A transparent tabernacle is in the front corner of the room with a lighted candle marking the resting place for the Eucharist. The large windows look out to the forest, and there are warm wooden floors and a sunken circle which holds the polished wood-slab altar. One can sit on the circle's edge or use meditation *zafus* or mats. The community meets here for meditation, prayer services, *satsang,* and daily Eucharist. Visitors and guests are welcome at all services.

Retreatants stay in individual cabins with showers and toilets. Meals are self-serve breakfast with dinner and supper taken with the community in the Long House. Food can be arranged for those who wish for complete solitude. There are no formal retreats, but spiritual direction is available if requested.

The pattern of each day follows the goals of the founding members. First is to give priority to contemplative prayer for the community and those who come to pray; second, a process that is ongoing to create a monastic ashram community, which is a place of simple lifestyle and intense spiritual exercises, open to all religions; third, to adore as a way of life, not just a period of time but the whole of life; and fourth, "to seek after peace and pursue it," to realistically pursue peace and justice, and what's fitting for this particular lifestyle.

The noted writer Father Bede Griffiths spent a month here in 1992, and he called it the most peaceful place he'd ever been. This astonished the community since they felt he had been a gift and joy for them. One sister was asked, "What are your dreams for the future?" She laughed and replied: "This is it. We're not dreaming. We're living." Here the future is now, and what a beautiful future it is.

Osage+Forest of Peace
141 Monastery Road
Sand Springs, OK 74063
(918) 245-2734
osageforest@gmail.com

Breitenbush Hot Springs
Detroit, OR

Named after Peter Breitenbush, who explored the Willamette Valley in the 1840s, these hot springs were used by Native Americans for centuries. The different tribes set aside their rivalries and feuds during their time here, recognizing this to be a sacred place for healing. Located in the Cascade Mountains, the springs are surrounded by the Willamette National Forest with its mountains, canyons, cascading streams, and rivers. The Breitenbush River flows through the 86 acres of the retreat, and these rushing waters, through the use of an ingenious hydroelectric plant, provide the electricity for the center; geothermal heat is taken from the same source that provides the artesian-flow hot springs.

A group of 45 people lives on the grounds, maintains the more than 40 rustic cabins, provides three well-prepared vegetarian meals a day, and organizes an array of programs and services that satisfy the most eclectic tastes. The community is committed to sharing its spiritual practice with all guests. There is daily morning meditation, a yoga session, and a spiritual spinal-maintenance program called EDGU—a series of upper-body movements that is excellent for rehabilitating the back.

The scheduled events, usually around weekends, offer courses in relationships, including men's and women's issues, healing arts, massage and bodywork, the environment, and self-transformation such as holotropic breathwork. Evening activities include concerts, storytelling, drumming circles, sing-alongs, and dancing. There is a monthly sweat lodge ceremony. Elderhostel courses are also offered through Western Oregon State College.

There is a parking area at the edge of the property where you transfer bags into a cart in order to reach the snug wooden cabins, all of which have heat and electricity and basic furnishings but only about half of which have plumbing. There are community bathhouses nearby. Bedding can be rented or you can bring your own sleeping bag.

The staff offers full-body or focused-area massage, as well as hydrotherapy and herbal wrap. The several hot springs are a delight to slip into on a cold night, with only the sounds of the river flowing nearby, the outline of the mountains delineated against the clear, star-marked sky.

"Breitenbush," as founder Alex Beamer wrote, "is a grand experiment to find better ways for people to live, work, and play together. We explore and practice helping others evolve to their highest potential, through psychological processing, spiritual practice, having fun, serving others, and taking good care of the body. We honor all paths respectful of people and the earth."

Breitenbush Hot Springs
P.O. Box 578
Detroit, OR 97342
(503) 854-3314
www.breitenbush.com

Menucha Retreat and Conference Center
Corbett, OR

One of the approaches to Menucha from Portland, only 22 miles to the west, is along the old scenic highway that follows the contour of the Columbia River past waterfalls that tumble from heights of more than 100 feet. This 99-acre retreat is on a bluff 800 feet above the river where the views east and west of the great gorge are awesome. The site was purchased in 1950 by Portland's First Presbyterian Church as a place where individuals and groups could get away for a while to study, reflect, and renew. The Hebrew word *menucha* means rest, peace, or repose—an apt description for this inspirational location. One can't help but be calmed and quieted by the vast panoramas.

This was once the private home of Julius L. Meier, governor of Oregon from 1930 to 1934, and presidents Herbert Hoover and Franklin Delano Roosevelt were guests here. The building, now called Wright Hall, was completed in 1927 and contains the central dining room as well as a meeting area. The great hall, with its huge stone fireplace, is large enough to hold 100 people. There are also eight dormitory rooms with adjoining bathrooms for up to 48 persons in this pleasant building. Other facilities on the property offer homelike accommodations from an apartment for individuals or families to dormitory sleeping arrangements. There is an array of group meeting spaces for 10 to 50 in eight different buildings.

The professional staff that manages the facility seems unflappable while maintaining a country home atmosphere and making it possible for many to come and share the place. The spirituality of the setting seems to touch all who visit. As one guest noted, "This is the most nurturing center I've ever been in, and I've been in a bunch of 'em!"

There are trails through the woods and different viewpoints for looking across the gorge to the far mountains. Here tensions decrease and the mind becomes still. On the wall of the manager's office hangs a reminder: "What I do today is very important, because I am exchanging a day of my life for it."

Menucha Retreat and
Conference Center
38711 Historic Columbia
River Highway
Corbett, OR 97019
(503) 695-2243
www.menucha.org

Mount Angel Abbey Retreat House
St. Benedict, OR

In the lush Willamette Valley, between the Cascades and the Coast Range, there has been a community of Benedictine monks for more than 100 years. In 1882, a contingent from Engelberg, Switzerland, came to the little town of Fillmore—the name was later changed to Mount Angel—and acquired more than 1,000 acres of land. The buildings of the abbey were eventually constructed on a butte overlooking the valley to meet the needs of the growing community, whose history as a place of education is an integral part of the Northwest. Twice major fires destroyed part of the complex, but now the hilltop resembles a college campus where the main church is the focal point. Here the 55 monks sing the canonical hours. The church has a high vaulted roof over the altar and a choir section where the monks' double-row pews face each other, one side responding to the other during the sung liturgy. There is seating for hundreds in the main section, and Sunday services are very popular.

In 1970, the library building was completed. This 44,000-square-foot three-story structure was designed by the Finnish architect Alvar Aalto. Made possible by a donation from the Vollum family, which founded Tektronix, the library houses more than 250,000 volumes in theology, language, philosophy, the arts, social sciences, and natural history. Designed to be user-friendly, the collection is on a state-of-the-art computer system and there are 70 nooks for individual study. There is a comfortable reading room with 600 current periodicals, a music listening room, and an auditorium that is an acoustically perfect space. There are more than 100 seminary students who live at the abbey and are engaged in undergraduate and graduate studies.

A few steps from the church is a retreat and guesthouse with 30 rooms, each with private bath. The rooms are nicely furnished and well maintained. A lower lounge has a snack area where hot drinks are always available. Meals are provided here or in the seminary dining room across the lawn. There is a chapel for quiet meditation and prayer.

The retreat programs are designed for contemporary spiritual needs, and reach out to mothers and daughters, fathers and sons, married couples, professional groups, and groups from other religious denominations. Private retreatants are accommodated.

Years ago, stone seats were found on top of the hill where the buildings now stand. Local Indians revealed that their ancestors had used these stones when they wanted to speak with the Great Spirit. In those days the butte was called Tap-a-Lam-a-Ho, the Mount of Communion. "You call it Mount Angel," one Indian said, "and you built a more elaborate structure than the stone seats of the natives, but its purpose will forever be the same —a mount of communion and prayer for unknown ages."

Down the road is the Shalom Prayer Center at Queen of Angels Monastery, a smaller center run by Benedictine nuns. See page 289 in "Other Places" for details.

Mount Angel Abbey
Retreat House
1 Abbey Drive
St. Benedict, OR 97373
(503) 845-3025/3030
www.mountangelabbey.org

Our Lady of Guadalupe Trappist Abbey
Lafayette, OR

In 1955, after seven years in New Mexico, this community moved to Oregon seeking greater seclusion. Their property is 900 acres of woods and 400 acres of farmland. The long driveway winds through the fields to the monastery complex, which sits alone on the hilltop. The church over-looks a large courtyard, the guest refectory, and the bookstore. A passageway from the refectory leads to the four duplex guest cottages, which share a bath at midlevel. They are beautifully designed and connected by wooden decks, and look out over ponds and woods. The rooms are very comfortable with single bed, desk, reading lamp, and rocking chair. Meals are served in the refectory, where the monks set the tables and clear away afterward, kindly discouraging would-be helpers. The food is hearty, vegetarian, and delicious (especially the home-baked bread). Dinner, when we visited, was cooked by a doctor on their sabbatical residency program. Coffee and tea are always available in the dining area.

The 37 monks in the community—17 priests and 20 brothers—meet in the chapel to sing the canonical hours five times a day, with mass following 6:30 A.M. Lauds. On Sunday, mass is at 9:15 A.M. The excellent acoustics of the wooden interior of the church accentuate the organ or guitar accompaniment; two monks can play the organ, two others are guitarists. The liturgy is beautifully arranged and sung.

Visitors are expected to structure their own time, but monks are available for discussion by appointment. There is a small library and tape selection in a pleasant reading room. Thomas Merton once wrote: "There is an advantage to the monastery by inviting people in and being in touch." The guestmaster paraphrased that statement by saying, "Guests have been an enrichment to us."

Retreatants can come for one to seven days. "It really takes two days to wind down," one monk noted, "stress being one of the main addictions of our society. Visitors should leave their books at home; whatever they need for security, leave it behind. Try to let it go and accept that it's okay without anything to do. Don't just do something, stand there! Many who come have reached a point in life where they have to change. Once they admit that, they'll be able to accept the process, let the transformation happen. As people work prayer into their schedule, then everything is prayer, all the time."

The main business of the monastery is bookbinding. About 20 of the monks produce as many as 1,000 volumes a week. More than 1,000 Douglas fir trees are planted on the property every year to replace the aging trees, and the community tends an extensive vegetable garden. There is also a mail-order fruitcake business and a wine warehouse.

The grounds are exceptionally peaceful to wander through. Trails lead past a large cottonwood tree and to ponds, and from the top of one of the hills the frosty peak of Mount Hood is visible. At night, frogs, coyotes, and hoot owls can be heard chanting their own litany.

Our Lady of Guadalupe
Trappist Abbey
P.O. Box 97
Lafayette, OR 97127
www.trappistabbey.org

Daylesford Abbey
Paoli, PA

At the center of 120 acres of beautiful lawns and fields is a large, modern abbey church where well-attended Sunday services are held. There is a small chapel beside the main church where the Norbertine monks pray morning and evening and guests are welcome. Behind the church and connected to it is a three-story building that has several large meeting rooms on the first floor, and 57 rooms for guests on the second and third floors.

There is a small house called Emmaus for private retreats or small groups, set away from the main complex. It has a small chapel, a kitchen-dining area stocked with basics, five bedrooms with three baths and two parlors. Nearby, through the trees and across a meadow, is a lovely hermitage, and behind that a pond with an exquisite stone chapel for prayer and meditation.

The abbey serves the community by administering and teaching in local schools, providing parish priests, and supporting facilities in Philadelphia for homeless men and women. It also sends chaplains to local hospitals and conducts retreats and programs dedicated to religious and cultural renewal.

While making their facilities available for private retreats and outside groups, the Norbertines themselves offer a series of retreat evenings and weekends ranging from programs of investigative reading on works of Christian mystics to workshops on the Enneagram, exploring the motivation of thought and action.

The Order of Premontre, founded by St. Norbert in 12th-century

France, established its first successful American community in Wisconsin, working with immigrants from Holland, Belgium, and France. The Norbertines founded parishes and schools and soon attracted young Americans into their communities. From these new monks a group moved to Delaware in 1932, and two years later, at the request of the diocese, the Norbertines came to Philadelphia as teachers. In 1954 a group came to Paoli and founded Daylesford Abbey. These Catholic priests and brothers are sworn to seek Christ through community living, poverty, obedience, celibacy, and a dedication to the ministry. The underlying belief is that an active religious life needs an ascetic and contemplative haven, and this is what the abbey offers, not only to its residents but to visitors as well.

Daylesford Abbey
220 S. Valley Road
Paoli, PA 19301
(610) 647-2530
www.daylesford.org

Pendle Hill
Wallingford, PA

A Quaker center for study and contemplation, Pendle Hill offers an opportunity to live in an educational community, attend classes, worship daily, and do cooperative work. It was founded in 1930 by members of the Religious Society of Friends, and its philosophy comes from the four basic social testimonies of the Friends: equality of opportunity, simplicity of environment, harmony of inward and outward action, and community of daily interdependence of individuals and the spirit.

Pendle Hill is made up of 16 buildings on 23 acres in a suburban neighborhood outside Philadelphia. The quiet campus is planted with more than 140 different kinds of trees and shrubs that make it seem like a family compound. The community gathers in the dining room for three meals a day, sitting together at long tables. The food is served buffet-style and is delicious; there is often freshly baked bread and always attention to a balanced diet. The staff of 30 come from different professional backgrounds, and are highly qualified to present diverse courses in Quaker faith and practice, Bible studies, pottery, poetry, and weaving, as well as exploring one's vocation, looking to answer questions like What am I called to do now? How can I find the place to do it? and Who am I becoming?

There are rooms for 30 to 35 students who range in age from teenagers to youngsters of 75. The serious, committed students and staff demonstrate a spirit of fellowship in everything from their interplay at mealtime to their singing together as they clean up the kitchen.

Each morning there is a meeting for worship in silence, which may be broken by spoken ministry as the spirit moves those gathered together. The tradition is that ritual of service and place is unnecessary; one should live fully in the present, with truth and love.

One visitor observed that the spiritual should draw one into the world and be combined with regular life; people come here to develop spiritually and intellectually and take that to the home, office, and community. Even though "we often walk the lonesome valley by ourselves, we can learn to walk cheerfully over the earth, responding to the God in everyone. . . . Religion is not only a beatific vision, it is getting on with it."

Pendle Hill
338 Plush Mill Road
Wallingford, PA 19086
(610) 566-4507
(800) 742-3150
www.pendlehill.org

St. Raphaela Mary Retreat House
Haverford, PA

This three-story stone mansion was built in a quiet suburban neighborhood of Philadelphia's Main Line in the early 20th century. Catholic nuns acquired it in 1957 and immediately started a retreat center that, in its first year, had 360 retreatants. The center now receives 3,600 annually and is self-supporting. The nuns make their facilities available to any denomination or group seeking a quiet, restful place to concentrate in relaxed surroundings. Their service is hospitality, and they celebrate people's desire to be renewed and refreshed.

Major renovations were completed in 1989. The stunningly beautiful main rooms have a soothing and harmonious blend of colors and textures that invite tranquillity and reflect the vision of the community and architect Agnes Kan. Up to 70 persons can be accommodated in comfortable single and double rooms. New washrooms were added, as well as sinks in each room, new plumbing and electricity, and air-conditioning.

The sisters are called Handmaids of the Sacred Heart of Jesus. Their order was founded in 1877 in Spain by St. Raphaela Mary. Following the rule of St. Ignatius Loyola, their main mission is to educate. Their schools for wealthy children support those for the poor. They were attracted to this property because of the nearby Catholic colleges, Rosemont and Villanova, which make it easier for community members to continue their education.

The grounds behind the house are spacious and well kept. Some 70 yards back is a grotto, a statue of Blessed Mary with a covering built by a group of young men who came for a retreat and donated their time and skill.

The resident community has morning and evening prayer sessions that retreatants are welcome to attend. The nuns have an obligation to sit before the Blessed Sacrament an hour a day, and this they perform according to their individual schedules. When asked if there were special prayers to say at this time, one nun replied: "Oh, no . . . I just look at Him and He looks at me."

St. Raphaela Mary Retreat House
616 Coopertown Road
Haverford, PA 19041
(610) 642-5715
www.straphaelacenter.org

Mount St. Joseph Spiritual Life Center
Bristol, RI

Situated on 25 acres of woods and well-tended lawns, this retreat House overlooks Mount Hope Bay and the Mount Hope Bridge. Acquired in 1967 by the Sisters of St. Dorothy, a congregation of Roman Catholic sisters, the house was initially used as a house of religious formation and then evolved into a home for the community. In 1986, the sisters began to share their peaceful and beautiful environment with individuals and groups seeking a place of tranquility in which to relax, reflect, and pray.

Today the sisters host days of reflection, prayer, and renewal. Groups and individuals may schedule days and weekends of retreat, staff meetings, or just plain "getaways" throughout the year.

The sisters have a strong commitment to hospitality and a welcoming spirit inherited from their founder, St. Paula Frassinetti. They provide an atmosphere in which one can commune peacefully with God, nature, and other people. The sisters also work in Massachusetts, New York, New Jersey, Ohio, and Texas, and in fourteen other countries throughout the world. Their charism is evangelization through education in all its forms and they share this gift with the larger community through Catholic schools, religious education programs, parish ministry, retreat work, and hospital chaplaincy.

Mt. St. Joseph Spiritual Life Center
13 Monkey Wrench Lane
Bristol, RI 02809
(401) 253-5434

Portsmouth Abbey
Portsmouth, RI

Portsmouth Abbey is a community of Benedictine monks located on 500 acres of shorefront on Narragansett Bay. The monastery, just seven miles north of Newport, was founded in 1918. Following the English Benedictine tradition, in 1926 the monks opened a college prep school for boys modeled on the British boarding-school system. The school has now become coeducational and aims to develop informed and open-minded leaders educated in the Christian tradition and prepared to meet the challenges and responsibilities of life. The school has grown from a student body of 20 to its current number of more than 300 students, 80 percent of whom are Catholic. All students go on to college.

There are several rooms available for male guests. Meals are taken with the monks. During the summer, group retreats are held for up to 80 people, using the boys' dormitory and cafeteria. This is one of the most traditional of the Benedictine communities in the United States. The monks still observe the rule of requesting permission from the abbot before they leave the property; they also observe the Chapter of Faults, every Wednesday evening, when monks acknowledge before the community any transgression of monastery rules.

The monks sing the canonical hours beginning at 5:45 A.M., and assemble six times a day in the magnificent stone and wood chapel. The church is octagonal, with a tall spire. Inside there is seating for several hundred arranged in tiers facing the central altar, above which a gold crucifix, designed by sculptor Richard Lippold, is suspended from a multitude of fine wires radiating out like beams of light. The solemnity and power of the liturgy seem to take on a new dimension in such a dramatic setting.

Even when school is in session, this is a good place for reflective time: the lovely chapel, the example of the monks' prayerful life, and the spacious grounds to wander in.

To celebrate the graduation of his son, American artist Harry Jackson donated a sculpture that is in the main lobby. The bronze statue, a cowboy on horseback swinging a lariat, is inscribed "When you rope a dream, tie hard 'n fast 'n never turn it loose."

Portsmouth Abbey
285 Cory's Lane
Portsmouth, RI 02871
(401) 683-2000
www.portsmouthabbey.org

Mepkin Abbey
Moncks Corner, SC

In 1949 Trappist monks came from Gethsemani, Kentucky, to the low country of South Carolina, along the banks of the Cooper River. The Catholic Diocese of Charleston had been given 3,000 acres of land by the Henry Luce family, and Bishop Walsh, seeking a contemplative presence in the region, invited the Trappists. This land was originally a rice plantation, and now there are 1,400 acres in forest, 1,000 acres clear, and 600 acres under water (the former rice fields). The Mepkin method of flooding the fields along a tidal river was once the model of rice cultivation. The technique was copied by other plantations, but now that growing rice as a commercial crop is no longer viable for them, the monks raise chickens whose eggs they sell as their main source of income.

A long avenue of Spanish moss–clad oaks border the drive into the monastery grounds. The road winds around to the refectory next to the church and bell tower. Recently remodeled after severe damage from Hurricane Hugo, the church is the essence of understatement and practicality, a most appealing sanctum where the monks gather six times a day to sing the canonical hours. Retreatants are invited to join the monks in the prayer stalls and sing the liturgy. A guitar carries the melody for most services and sometimes the abbot, a graduate of the Juilliard School of Music, plays the organ.

Meals are taken in an alcove off the monks' dining room, so participation in monastic life is very real. Home-produced eggs are served every day for breakfast and the noon main meal is shared with the monks; guests follow them in line for the buffet and eat in silence while a monk reads from a spiritual book (during our visit it was *Dakota* by Kathleen Norris).

There are 12 guest rooms for men and women in two different houses, a short walk from the refectory and church. You design your own program within the monastery routine. Spiritual counseling is available on request. There is a 30-day monastic guest program for men only, during which participants follow the schedule of the monastery, working four hours a day, attending services, and observing places and times of monastic silence. TV, radio, alcohol, and tobacco are not allowed.

"These are the places that keep the whole world together," one guest observed. And a monk explained his feelings this way: "All creation is praising God, but you couldn't pay me to do this."

In the serene terraced gardens near the river—remnants of past splendor—Henry and Clare Boothe Luce are laid to rest with other family members. Their marble headstone has a live-oak carving.

Mepkin Abbey
1098 Mepkin Abbey Road
Monck's Corner, SC 29461
(843) 761-8509
www.mepkinabbey.org

St. Christopher Camp and Conference Center
Seabrook Island, SC

On the beautiful barrier island of Seabrook, just 25 miles from Charleston, the St. Christopher Center has 308 acres of oceanfront, marsh, and river dotted with century-old oaks and stately palmettos. In 1684, the Stono Indians traded the island for beads, trinkets, and cloth to the government of South Carolina, which distributed the land to settlers. British soldiers landed here during the Revolutionary War. In 1951, the widow of Victor Morawetz gave 1,408 acres to the Episcopal Church, and in 1970 the Church sold 1,100 acres to finance the present center on the remaining acreage.

The weathered wood buildings can house 60 and are designed to blend with the island setting. The conference accommodations are first-rate and the 60 rooms all have private bath and are well furnished. The rustic cabins for the young are functional and snug. Bring sleeping gear for the cabins. Food is prepared by chef Stephen Boyle, recipient of Charleston's 1989 Chef-of-the-Year Award. There are annual retreats for families and individuals at Thanksgiving, Lent, and Advent. Some families have been coming for years. Private retreatants should plan their own programs.

The director and staff of six give Elderhostel programs on the environment and the Civil War. September through May, there are educational programs for school groups, and June through August summer camp programs encourage the young to learn respect for all life and to commune with nature. The pristine mile-long beach where bottlenose dolphins come within 20 feet of the shore adds to the pleasure of being here.

St. Christopher Camp &
Conference Center
2810 Seabrook Island Road
Johns Island, SC 29455
(843) 768-0429
www.stchristopher.org

Springbank Retreat Center
Kingstree, SC

This 65-acre retreat is part of a southern plantation of thousands of acres which were given to John Burgess by the king of England in 1773 and remained in the Burgess family for five generations. In 1931 it was bought by Edward Hadden, the co-founder of Time, Inc., as a wedding gift for his wife, Agnes. The grounds were planted as gardens. All were welcome, rich and poor, black and white. At Christmastime, the driveway was filled with people who came to receive Mrs. Hadden's food baskets. In 1955 after her husband died, Mrs. Hadden donated the property to the Dominican order. She lived here till she died and is buried next to her husband on the grounds under a favorite live oak tree.

In the early 1980s, a committed group of Catholic sisters from various orders began the process of developing a retreat center, using the grand mansion where the chapel is as the focal point. Behind the mansion, there is a separate building with large windows looking out onto an open field with old-growth trees, draped with Spanish moss. Other buildings are used as studios for painting, pottery, and weaving. The philosophy here centers on the power of creative energy and the importance of spiritual, mental, and physical health.

The retreats range from weekend specialty topics to 60-day sabbatical programs open to anyone seeking renewal and revitalization. Topics include journal writing, Native American spirituality, poetry, men-only inner journey, and a women's weekend that focuses on the creative arts as meditation. A sweat lodge ceremony is held ten times a year.

There are walking trails through the grounds where live oaks, camelias, and azaleas abound. As one sister pointed out: "In the past, people didn't want to waste their vacation going on retreat. Now people don't want to waste their vacation getting worn out. They appreciate the time for rest and solitude." And that's reflected in the growth here. The mailing list has swelled from 700 to 5,000.

The center is owned and run by an ecumenical board of clergy and laypeople including Methodist and Baptist ministers, a bank officer, and a lawyer, each of whom has a strong commitment to Springbank's future.

Springbank Retreat Center
1345 Springbank Road
Kingstree, SC 29556
(800) 671-0361
www.springbankretreat.org

St. Mary's Episcopal Retreat and Conference Center
Sewanee, TN

In 1888, the Episcopal Sisters of St. Mary opened a girls' school on this secluded 200 acres on a ridgetop in the Cumberland Plateau. The school closed in 1968 and the sisters directed their mission to retreat and conference work using the school buildings. In 1985, they arranged the sale of the property to the Episcopal Diocese of Tennessee and the nearby University of the South, which jointly manage and operate the center. The laypeople who work here feel it's a sacred mountain. As they drive out the gate, they touch the car roof to take an angel with them. When they come back, they return the angel because, they explain, you don't need it when you're on the grounds.

From the lawn, the view over the peaceful, rolling Tennessee hills and wide valley below is magnificent. There are nature trails winding through the woods down to the valley.

Groups of varying sizes up to 100 can stay in the efficient and comfortable rooms. Meals are provided for groups but individuals need to bring their own food or drive to the restaurants in Sewanee only 2½ miles down the hill. There is a separate building for use as a hermitage.

The sisters live in a convent at the end of the road. They come together for morning and evening prayer in a stunning chapel, and visitors are welcome.

St. Mary's Episcopal Retreat &
Conference Center
770 St. Mary's Lane
Sewanee, TN 37375
(800) 728-1659
(931) 598-5342
www.stmaryssewanee.org

Corpus Christi Abbey
Sandia, TX

Benedictine monks from Arkansas came to Corpus Christi diocese in the 1920s at the request of the local bishop to establish a school, which they ran until 1972. The community relocated in 1974 to their present location on the shores of Lake Corpus Christi with a new mission. The abbot outlined the hopes of the relocating community: "This monastery is to be a house of prayer, a liturgical center, a house of personal, spiritual renewal." The outreach started at the previous monastery—the first to introduce retreats to laypeople in southern Texas—has expanded in many directions. The monks welcome anyone regardless of race, creed, or national origin. They have seen the charismatic group that started here in 1985 with a handful of people grow to hundreds which meet regularly. They offer a variety of retreats in English and Spanish to accommodate the large Hispanic population, and use earthy analogies to put spiritual life into an easily understood perspective. Their early retreat literature used the analogy of a football game: "In the game of life, a retreat is a timeout period away from the hurly-burly of the game. More importantly, it is a huddle with Jesus Christ, the greatest coach ever . . . many games are won not on the field but in the huddle of the timeout period."

Located 50 miles northwest of Corpus Christi, the abbey grounds have 110 lakeside acres with a pier and observation deck. Lake Corpus Christi is noted for catfish, bass, gaspergon, and perch. This region of Texas has a moderate climate, with temperatures in the mid 80s most of the year and in the mid 50s during winter. The area is primarily used for growing corn, milo, and cotton, and for grazing cattle.

The abbey buildings are Quonset-style, a practical adaptation for a growing community. There is the abbey church, an extensive library, a newly renovated dining room, conference rooms, and space for 50 retreatants in double rooms, most with private baths. All are air-conditioned.

The monks have a daily prayer schedule starting with 6:20 morning prayer and mass, midday prayer just before lunch, Vespers at 5:20 P.M., and Compline at 7:20 P.M., followed by the Great Silence. Retreatants are welcome at all services. Programs include weekend retreats, days of reflection, prayer groups, and private and directed retreats. One weekend in October there is the annual "medieval" Abbeyfest with local food and entertainment put on by the Society for Creative Anachronism.

Corpus Christi Abbey
101 S. Vista Drive
Sandia, TX 78383
(361) 547-3257

Abbey of Our Lady of the Holy Trinity
Huntsville, UT

In *The Waters of Siloe*, Thomas Merton described how the Trappist scout Dom Frederic discovered the place for a new foundation in Utah: "Finally he came upon a ranch which seemed to have been created for contemplative monks. Eighteen miles east of Ogden, after a long climb through Ogden Canyon, the valley opened out into a mile-wide bowl between mountains. The clean air of high altitudes breathed silently over these fields. Not a home was in sight. The snowy ridge of Mount Ogden stood up stark against the sky, as if it were the sentinel of this wilderness. Eastward was a no-man's land of snow and sagebrush, and there were deer tracks in the snow. There were 1,600 acres of land with good springs . . . the very silence of the place cried out for Trappists."

The ranch was purchased in March 1947 and a group of monks from Gethsemani, Kentucky, arrived in July that same year. Almost immediately they began to assemble their Quonset monastery. The quadrangle of Quonset buildings is functional and unique to monastic architecture. The exterior surfaces have been sprayed with urethane foam insulation and painted off-white with brown trim. Today the 22 monks sell liquid and creamed honey by mail and in their gift shop, and raise chickens and beef commercially. They farm 750 acres of irrigated fields raising alfalfa, barley, and wheat, and make whole-wheat and raisin bread in their bakery from their own wheat. The remaining acreage is pasture. Guests find hiking at 6,000 feet above sea level invigorating and the views rewarding.

There are 12 rooms for men only, all of which have private baths.

Meals are provided in the guest dining room. The guest wing also has a lounge and library. The monks celebrate the liturgy of the hours daily in the chapel, starting with Lauds at 6 A.M., followed by mass; Compline at 7:30 P.M. is the last service of the day. Guests and visitors are welcome at all services.

The description of a monk's life, written by the 12th-century Cistercian St. Aelred, still seems apt today: "You have chosen solitude and silence, a life of fraternal love and voluntary poverty; you have escaped, in fact, the tumult of the world." For men interested in listening to the silence of the mountains, this is a place well suited for seclusion, giving one a chance to sort things out, or just come away and rest a while.

Abbey of Our Lady of
the Holy Trinity
1250 S. 9500 E.
Huntsville, UT 84317
(801) 745-3784
www.holytrinityabbey.org

Karmê-Chöling
Barnet, VT

About one hour north of White River Junction in northern Vermont, just outside the town of Barnet, is Karmê-Chöling (Tail of the Tiger), a Tibetan Buddhist meditation and retreat center. Founded in the early 1970s by the late Chögyam Trungpa, Rinpoche, this was one of the first Vajrayana centers outside of India. Guidance is offered in meditation practice, the study of Buddhist philosophy and psychology, and the application of those teachings in daily life.

The center is on 540 acres of wooded country. As you approach, you look across a pond to buildings with an unmistakable Tibetan design—one of which is emblazoned with a large red and gold circle. The main buildings house the staff, a large dining room where meals are taken cafeteria-style, plus the sitting hall, conference rooms, guest rooms, and private meditation rooms.

There are many levels of meditation practice available: introductory weekends for those with little or no experience; the *dathün* or one-month group meditation retreat; Shambhala training; and in-house or residence retreats where visitors may come for any length of time and follow the daily schedule of five hours of meditation and three and a half hours of work, plus evening classes. This has the benefit of group support and close contact with a meditation instructor. The center also owns a charming hotel in the town of Barnet, usually used for groups.

This is a bustling, well-organized and well-managed school that can deal with large numbers of students and practitioners. Child care is available at a moderate charge for children two years and older. There is plenty of space to wander on the property, especially for the conditioned hiker. From the main buildings a dirt road winds up the hill with small shrines along the way, past the concealed hermitages to an open field where there is a large outdoor shrine. Convocations are held here in the summer, and hundreds gather for special events.

Karme-Choling
369 Patneaude Lane
Barnet, VT 05821
(802) 633-2384
www.karmacholing.org

Weston Priory
Weston, VT

Weston Priory, a community of Benedictine monks, is located at the edge of the Green Mountain National Forest, four miles north of Weston. It was founded in 1953 by a brother from Dormition Abbey in Jerusalem, and other brothers have come from all parts of the United States, Canada, and Latin America. The many recordings of the monastery's extraordinary choir are sold as a means of financial support and a way to share the joy of community spirit. The monks also create woodcrafts and greeting cards and have a gallery of high-quality thematic pieces that demonstrate their social conscience. In 1984 the monastery was declared a public sanctuary for Central American refugees. The monks have given sanctuary to one Guatemalan family for over eleven years.

Down a quiet, tree-lined road are three guesthouses, each accommodating from three to six adults. These beautifully furnished houses are set off from one another only a few minutes' walk from the chapel. Guests bring their own food and prepare it in the kitchen of their guesthouse. Utensils and linens are provided, and guests take care of their own cleaning. Individual men stay in the priory guesthouse; individual women stay in a separate building called Morningside. These guests take their meals with the monks.

Retreatants are expected to plan their own time. There are regular daily services at the chapel beginning at 5 or 6 A.M. morning vigils, then either two or three other prayer services, ending with Compline around 8 P.M. The contemporary orientation of the services makes them very popular. The monks are available by arrangement for informal discussions on specific topics such as community life or social justice.

The monastery is deep in the Green Mountains, offering an opportunity to explore the woodlands and follow the nature trails that the monks maintain. The monastery grounds are tended meticulously.

The Weston community has established a joint retreat effort with a community of Mexican Benedictine sisters in Cuernavaca, Mexico. Retreatants can go for ten days at a reasonable cost to experience the historical, social, and cultural context of Mexican life, under the care and direction of Mexican nuns who actively work with the poor. The Weston brothers sponsor the House of Sabbath, a retreat house in nearby Weston, to serve the poor, the homeless, and those working with them.

Weston Priory
58 Priory Hill Road
Weston, VT 05161
(802) 824-5409
(802) 824-6976 Sabbath House
www.westonpriory.org

Holy Cross Abbey
Berryville, VA

The Trappist monks came in 1950 to this 1,200-acre farm along the Shenandoah River, the site of the Battle of Cool Spring during the Civil War. Only an hour from the nation's capital, it is a welcome respite for the world-weary. As one visitor said: "You begin to care less about the destination and more about the journey." People of all faiths or none are welcome. The Benedictine tradition of welcoming guests as Christ is a major part of the monks' ministry. Visitors stay in the relatively new and quite elegant guesthouse a short distance from the monastery. There are 15 single rooms for men and women, each with private bath, bed, desk, and reading chair. Meals are served family-style in the guesthouse dining room. There is a chapel with windows looking out to the hills or guests join the monks in the main church where the community gathers six times a day for mass and sung liturgy. There are no requirements here except to be considerate of others and respect the silence. A monk is available for discussion, if requested, but otherwise visitors are on their own.

The 21 monks who live here support their community in a number of ways, and perhaps they are best known for the excellent fruitcakes they produce and sell some 24,000 each year.

It takes about 24 hours to adjust to the serenity and order of the place. There is no TV or radio, and the quiet is magnified by the occasional bells for worship and the calls of the birds. Traffic and crowds of people become a distant memory, and the sense of who you are, where you are going, and the purpose of it all begins to appear.

The prayers of monasteries throughout the world do more for peace than presidents or princes. As the saying goes, If you want a peaceful world, start with yourself. The Gospel of St. John asks: "How can you say you love God whom you do not see, if you do not love your brother whom you see?"

Holy Cross Abbey
901 Cool Spring Lane
Berryville, VA 22611
(540) 955-4383
www.hcava.org

Satchidananda Ashram–Yogaville
Buckingham, VA

One of the outstanding features of this ashram is the Light of Truth Universal Shrine or LOTUS, an ecumenical shrine which celebrates the unity behind all religious beliefs. It is constructed in the shape of the lotus flower, a symbol of enlightenment. There are 12 altars inside, each one dedicated to a major spiritual belief: Native American, African, Sikhism, Islam, Christianity, Buddhism, Taoism, Shinto, Judaism, Hinduism, Other Known Religions, and Those Still Unknown. The building is as elegant as the Taj Mahal, a breathtaking sight as one approaches through arched gates or views it from a hilltop.

This grand design of ecumenism is the guiding principle of Sri Swami Satchidananda. He teaches that practicing yoga and meditation allows a peaceful mind and an easeful body, and leads to a useful life. Born in India in 1914, he came to the west in the 1960s as a guest of devotees. His method, which is known as Integral Hatha Yoga, appealed to the New Age movement in the United States. He believes the root of all pain and suffering is the ignorance of our spiritual oneness. Through selflessness, the individual can experience inner peace and express it in all he or she does. Others learn from example and ultimately the peace and harmony established by the selfless actions of a handful of individuals can transform communities, then nations, and ultimately the world.

The ashram has 750 acres in the central Virginia countryside with all the services that a thriving community of more than 100 monastics, families, and individuals require. There are guest facilities so couples, families, and individuals can attend the regular programs. There are three daily meditation sessions, one at the Lotus Shrine. Yoga classes are held twice daily. There is a daily *satsang*. Workshops and retreats are scheduled throughout the year, as are month-long certification programs for yoga teachers.

Satchidananda has stated: "The purpose of any religion is to educate us about spiritual unity. . . . Some people make use of religion for their own benefit and literally divide humanity in the name of that which is supposed to unite us. Real unity means accepting all the various approaches and that is what ecumenism means. Ultimately we all aim for the same truth while walking different paths. Essentially we are one appearing as many. We look different but we are one in spirit. Hello Brother, Hello Sister. Care and share, love and give. Apply it in your own life."

Satchidananda Ashram-Yogaville
108 Yogaville Way
Buckingham, VA 23921
(434) 969-3121
(800) 858-9642
www.yogaville.org

Chinook Learning Center
Clinton, WA

The center is located on Whidby Island, a 20-minute car ferry ride from mainland Washington about an hour north of Seattle, or accessible from the north by the bridge at Deception Pass, named by early explorers who were deceived into thinking this was the Northwest Passage to Europe. Part of the island network of Puget Sound in the Strait of Juan de Fuca, Whidby is the largest of the eight islands that make up Island County and one of only three that are inhabited. Although it is largely rural, there are a few small villages like Clinton that provide basic services.

Chinook Learning Center, a few miles outside Clinton, is on 72 acres of meadows and evergreen trees, a remote outpost that was, in the early 1900s, a homestead of Finnish farmers. In 1972, Vivienne and Fritz Hull acquired the property for use as a place to examine the basic question of why we are here. They were inspired by the sixth-century Celtic Christian monastic school on Iona, an island off the coast of Scotland, where thousands were drawn for a special kind of education and training and then were deeply influential in Europe. Like Iona, Chinook seeks to be a center for study and teaching to create an understanding of the meaning and purpose of life, linking humanity and the earth and the concomitant spiritual values.

Chinook offers year-round courses, workshops, retreats, conferences, and training programs in religion, ecology, psychology, and cultural change. There is room for 20 people in a variety of accommodations. The reconditioned farmhouse and "Granny's," a house that was donated and moved to the property, have comfortable rooms with indoor plumbing and kitchens. Two rustic cabins, heated with wood-burning stoves, are set in the woods. There is a community bathhouse and outhouses nearby. Larger groups make use of the open meadows for camping. Private retreatants are accommodated according to space available and can use the kitchen to prepare their own food.

A small group of caretakers lives here and is aided by members of the Chinook community, who live nearby and help to keep the facility in good repair and functioning smoothly. There is a great appreciation for the land and the lifestyle demonstrated by the rustic neatness of the buildings and the well-tended flower and vegetable gardens. A number of marked trails wind through the second-growth fir and cedars.

Chinook is an Indian word meaning "warm wind blowing," describing a warm winter wind that suggests the coming of spring. The name of this remote retreat expresses its raison d'être perfectly: Like a fresh wind, it summons people to meet the challenges confronting all of us to work for a better world. "Nothing is outside the arena of what we call spiritual," Vivienne Hull writes. "Understanding that all of life is sacred changes your economics, your politics, and your relationships."

Chinook Learning Center
8898 Highway 525
Clinton, WA 98236
(360) 341-3404
www.whidbeyinstitute.org

Cloud Mountain Retreat Center
Castle Rock, WA

David and Anna Branscomb, he a carpenter and artist, she a systems analyst, were looking for a way to work with spiritual friends. Their meditation practice—Anna trained in Vipassana and David in Zen—helped them to decide to use land they had received as a gift as a place where Buddhist groups and individuals could come to meditate and study. Since 1984, the center has made the facilities available to Buddhist groups regardless of tradition or sect. In cooperation with the Northwest Dharma Association, there are regularly scheduled retreats, classes, sittings, and special events throughout the year, and private retreatants are welcome.

The charming wooden buildings are on five acres of sloping, forested land and were sited according to the earth's energy flow. There is no electricity. Light is provided by propane lamps as easy to use as striking a match; heat comes from woodstoves and propane heaters. Communal showers with hot water are in a separate building; there are a few flush toilets as well as outhouses. There are accommodations for 34 people in two buildings, some in private rooms, others dormitory-style with two to five beds per room. A large dining room in the main house offers three vegetarian meals a day. Guests help to clean up after meals. Tea and fruit are available throughout the day. Retreatants should bring bedding, pillow, towels, and a flashlight (essential).

There are two meditation halls on the property as well as a pond, garden, greenhouse, and sauna. The buildings, each in its own woodland setting, are reached by neat pathways. At night, the overhanging trees merge into the dark like an Ad Reinhardt painting. The occasional squawk of a roosting peacock lends a mysterious air. On a clear day, the snow-capped peak of Mount Rainier can be seen 50 miles north.

Cloud Mountain Retreat Center
373 Agren Road
Castle Rock, WA 98611
(360) 274-4859
www.cloudmountain.org

Holden Village
Chelan, WA

If retreats were judged on remoteness and inaccessibility, Holden Village would be at the top of the list. The adventure unfolds in stages starting from the village of Chelan at the southern tip of Lake Chelan, which lies within an 80-mile-long glacial valley near Washington's geographic center, and the ferry for the 16-mile trip to Holden's dock at Lucerne. A few miles above Chelan, both sides of the narrow lake become part of the National Forest Preserve and there are no roads—only trails for grazing deer and white-coated mountain goats that climb the high ridges. In some places the rugged shoreline is fjordlike, and the snow-capped peaks of the northern Cascade Mountains rise more than 7,000 feet in the distance. A bus from Holden Village meets the ferry and transports guests the last 12 miles up the single-lane road deep into the rugged terrain to the base of Copper Mountain.

Holden Village was built in the 1930s as a settlement for copper miners and their families with all the conveniences of small-town life. The mine ceased operation in 1957. Wes Prieb, then in Alaska, read about the closing and wrote to inquire the asking price of the property, which was $100,000. The next year he wrote again and got the same response. In 1960, while a student at the Lutheran Bible Institute in Seattle, he wrote again. This time the reply came by telephone that the mining company was donating the property to the Lutheran Bible Institute and asked that Wes be responsible for it. That summer when a group came to evaluate the property, one church official advised, "No more camps are needed by the Lutheran church"; another said, "Holden should be turned over to the

U.S. government as a center for training spies." In the fall, when Wes was living at Holden as a caretaker, he prayed one afternoon that Holden would be taken over and rebuilt, and every stone and timber there be dedicated to the honor and glory of God, that many people would come to help, and that young people would find Christ here and emerge with changed lives. In that spirit, Holden has been rebuilt and is now a thriving renewal community where 70 men, women, and children live year-round. Others come for a few months in the summer, some for a year, taking a sabbatical to evaluate where they are and where they're going. The community celebrates the wide variety of gifts and skills that people of all races, cultures, and beliefs can bring. Hospitality is a central theme, for the people of Holden Village feel that this wonderfully remote and inspiring place is not to be owned but shared.

There are plain but comfortable guest rooms. Meals are family-style in the large dining room, which is quickly transformed into a theater for an evening's festivities. Vespers are held daily, and community members with the resident chaplain take turns being responsible for the service. Aside from the busy summer schedule, there are weekend and midweek retreats throughout the year that offer a time of study and interaction around specific spiritual topics.

Holden Village
HCO Box 2
Chelan, WA 98816
www.holdenvillage.org

Indralaya
Eastsound, WA

The 76 acres of this remote retreat are on Orcas Island, at the end of a long, unpaved road where almost a mile of shorefront borders the edge of the property. The heavily wooded site has a three-acre meadow and orchard inhabited by families of wild rabbits. Facing the meadow is the community center, a large inviting structure built of unfinished wood whose kitchen/dining area and meeting room with stone fireplace make it the hub of activity. Meals are served buffet-style, taken to long tables or outside in good weather, and each person is responsible for cleanup. Hot drinks are available throughout the day. The large windows at the back of the building look out to the woods and water below.

Around the meadow, tucked beneath tall cedars and firs, are rustic cabins, each in its own setting. The cabins are furnished with bed, table, and chair, and heated with a wood-burning stove; the woodpiles are easily accessible. For those cabins without plumbing, there are separate bathhouses for men and women.

Indralaya is a Sanskrit word suggesting the home or resting place of the spiritual forces in nature. In 1927, the Theosophical Society acquired the property as a place where members and friends could come to investigate the workings of nature and man, to encourage the study of science and comparative religions. Theosophy, called the ageless wisdom or wisdom religion, is concerned with that which is hidden, not obvious. It deals with nature's unseen processes and laws that stand behind and beyond science and is concerned with living harmoniously in the world with nature and all beings. Consistent with this approach, vegetarianism and harmlessness to all life are practiced.

There is a traditional summer camp during July and August oriented to families and campers of all ages with a morning lecture and an evening campfire. During the spring, fall, and winter there are work weekends when visitors help with grounds maintenance, tree pruning, and cabin rehabilitation. There are other weekends for seminars and workshops on topics of Theosophical interest. Private retreatants who share the values espoused here can be accommodated.

A trail winds above and along the shoreline leading to benches and grassy slopes that afford secluded outlooks across the bay. Attracted by the isolation and quiet of the island, bald eagles nest in the tall trees. Loons and otters—those solitary creatures—are also frequently seen.

Indralaya
360 Indralaya Road
Eastsound, WA 98245
(360) 376-4526
www.indralaya.com

Kairos House of Prayer
Spokane, WA

This 27 acres of wooded hilltop is a sanctuary for people seeking peace and quiet. At the end of a private lane, 2,300 feet above sea level, there are splendid views to the east and west. A large house, barn, and seven hermitages are nestled among Ponderosa pines and glacier rocks.

In 1970, with the encouragement and blessing of Bishop Bernard Topel of Spokane, Sister Florence Leone established a place of contemplative experience. Following the advice of Brother David Steindl-Rast, who suggested a more experiential approach, she studied Buddhist meditation and yoga, to enlarge the traditional form of prayer. She realized that Benedictine monasticism was experiential and that centering prayer was an integral part of Catholicism centuries ago. She practiced meditative sitting and realized that "East" and "West" are only in our minds. The aim is to become aware that all things are united in the One, a realm where there is neither gentile nor Jew, servant nor free, black nor white, red nor yellow. Spiritual life is participation in the Wholeness of Be-ing. We need to cultivate the Eastern concept of letting go—with the emphasis on being rather than doing—tapping into yoga breathing techniques, postures, relaxation, awareness of a conscious presence.

Taking the Greek work *kairos*, which means "the present time, now," as a guiding directive, this contemplative community has established a rhythm of prayer, work, and study. They come together for meditation at 8:00 A.M., 11:30 A.M., and 5 P.M. There are one-day, week-long, and extended retreats; individuals can stay in the main building or in hermitages, which are very comfortable, private, and overlook the hillside.

The wind sighs through the pines and the night sky is dazzling. Vegetarian meals are served in silence. Meat may be served for dietary reasons.

People who come here are grateful for the very existence of a place where they can reconnect with their innermost selves, and explore the meaning of life. Many people return regularly, as if coming home to a welcoming spirit, a climate of love and security.

Kairos House of Prayer
1714 W. Stearns Road
Spokane, WA 99208
(509) 466-2187

St. Martin's Abbey Guesthouse
Lacey, WA

On the 350-acre campus of St. Martin's College there is a charming brick building, used as a guesthouse, at the edge of the large playing field, just a short distance from the abbey church. There are 8 double rooms, comfortably furnished with twin beds, that are available for visitors to spend time in spiritual reflection. In a separate parlor, hot drinks are always available, and meals are taken in the student dining room in the basement of Old Main nearby.

St. Martin's Abbey was founded in 1895 by Benedictine monks who came from Minnesota at the request of the bishop of Seattle to minister to German settlers. St. Martin's College was started as a grammar school, and by 1900 college-level courses were added. In 1940, the liberal arts school became fully accredited. There are now more than 500 students, and about 150 live on the south side of the campus.

Only three miles from Olympia, the state capital of Washington, the abbey setting retains a rural atmosphere, a buffer zone of tranquil open fields, surrounded by full-growth pine and fir trees. The huge cone of Mount Rainier is visible on the horizon.

The monks meet daily in the church for morning, noon, and evening sung prayer, and mass is celebrated during the week at 5 P.M., in the morning on weekends. Guests are welcome to attend all services. The fine details of the church are worth close inspection—from the intricately carved doors to the superb wooden statues and the lectern in the form of an eagle. Banners hang from the high walls behind the altar and just meet the tops of the windows—a most unusual and stunning feature. Concerts and lectures are held in the church periodically through-out the year. There are no formal retreat programs, but a monk is available for consultation. Visitors are left to their own devices to enjoy the peaceful setting and to roam the meadows and unspoiled woods.

The abbey was named after the fourth-century Italian soldier-saint who cut his cloak in half to give to a freezing beggar. The abbey and the college foster an educational attitude of creativity and originality in thinking with a strong sense of values in personal and social responsibility.

St. Martin's Abbey Guesthouse
5300 Pacific Avenue SE
Lacey, WA 98503
(360) 491-4700
www.stmartin.edu/abbey/ourmonastery

Bhavana Society
High View, WV

In 1982 Bhante Henepola Gunaratana was in a restaurant describing to a friend his desire to find a quiet place where land was cheap. Another diner overheard the conversation and brought them to this 32 acres deep in the West Virginia woods but only two hours from Washington, D.C. This remote, wooded setting fit into Gunaratana's plan to build a place to teach meditation and found a community. Born in 1927 in Sri Lanka, Gunaratana became a monk at the age of 12. During the 1950s, he worked with untouchables in India, then came to the United States in 1968. He served as Honorary General Secretary of the Buddhist Vihara Society, an urban monastery in Washington, D.C., and earned his Ph.D. in philosophy from American University where he served as Buddhist chaplain.

The first retreats were held here in 1985 and a community began to grow. Currently there are three monks and two sisters plus a cook who make it possible to hold 13 scheduled retreats a year for those interested in Theravadan Buddhist meditation, which is called Vipassana or insight meditation. The practice emphasizes a calm, centered awareness of mind and body which encourages a fresh personal perspective. This enables the individual to transcend personal conflict, confusion, and mental and physical suffering. As peace gradually develops from meditation, compassion to oneself and all beings rises naturally and anger, fear, and greed drop away.

This is a relaxed, casual, and friendly community that meditates twice a day for an hour: 5:30 to 6:30 A.M., and 7 to 8 P.M. There are two meals a day: breakfast at 7 A.M. and the main meal at 11:15 A.M. Tea is available near the woodstove that heats a side porch where one can sit and relax. There are separate dormitories for 13 men and 12 women with community washrooms. During formal retreats, a yoga session is given at 5 P.M.

"The monastic path is better for spiritual growth," Gunaratana said in a recent interview published in *Tricycle* magazine. "You have to have a place to grow, to improve your spiritual practice. That is why the Buddha said: Have few duties. The purpose of monasticism is to give people a chance to discipline themselves. It's like a laboratory. There have to be some laboratories—some sort of controlled atmosphere for a person to grow—if that person really wants to be disciplined for his or her own inner peace. Morality is no longer an important issue in some places, some societies, because people do not want to discipline themselves. They do not want to be responsible, honest, sincere. But honesty, sincerity, responsibility never become out-of-date. We want to preserve that essence."

Bhavana Society
A Forest Meditation Center
Black Creek Road
Rte. 1, Box 218-3
High View, WV 26808
(304) 856-3241
www.bhavanasociety.or

DeKoven Center
Racine, WI

When you enter the quadrangle at DeKoven Center, its seems as though you've been transported to England. The weathered stone Gothic buildings, dating from the 1800s, were built as Racine College, an Episcopal prep school for boys. The center was renamed after the Reverend James DeKoven, a revered headmaster of the college from 1859 to 1879. In 1986, the ownership of the 34-acre property was transferred to the Episcopal Diocese of Milwaukee. All of the buildings are listed on the National Register of Historic Places. This is the only 19th-century quadrangle in the United States.

The current mission of the center is to host a variety of activities including retreats and conferences, which are given in Taylor Hall. Built in 1867, the hall was originally designed for classrooms, library, and living quarters for students. It now houses retreatants in charming rooms in an old-world atmosphere. Programs include silent retreats during Advent, Lent, and the summer. Workshops focus on current issues in today's Church. All DeKoven programs have a perspective of prayer, spirituality, and theological reflection. Part of Taylor Hall is a separate living space called the Hermitage. It has four bedrooms, bathroom, living and dining rooms, and a kitchen where individuals and small groups can find space for private time and solitude.

There are walkways on the grounds where full-growth trees and well-kept lawns invite wandering to picnic tables and benches. Lake Michigan is just across the road.

The center also has a gymnasium with parquet floors for basketball and volleyball. In this same building, an indoor swimming pool has recently been renovated and the Italian mosaic tile lining the pool, walls, and deck has been restored. The pool was added to the gym in 1913 and has six-foot-high windows looking out to the grounds.

St. John's Chapel has stood at the center of the quadrangle since 1864. The high interior beamed and vaulted ceiling, stained-glass Belgian windows, and carved wooden choir pews are striking examples of good taste and an inviting space for meditation and prayer. A chapel in Taylor Hall is used for daily prayer and Eucharist celebration by the resident priest.

DeKoven Center
600 21st Street
Racine, WI 53403
(262) 633-6401
www.dekovencenter.org

Siena Center
Racine, WI

Built on the shores of Lake Michigan, this huge complex of buildings has four wings off a connecting center that serve many purposes. The center is the motherhouse of the Racine Dominicans, home to more than 150 sisters, and the site of the community's main offices. It includes St. Catherine's Infirmary, a senior companion program, an adult learning program, and a retreat center. There are 76 private bedrooms (single and double) in the retreat center with common bath facilities for guests. Meals are served cafeteria-style and taken with the community. The food is home-cooked and delicious. The dining room is especially cheerful, reflecting the ambience of the community.

The retreat ministry of the Dominican sisters is shaped by their pursuit of truth and their dedication to justice for all; their programs seek to face the issues of today's world: thematic retreats for Advent, special evenings with supper to suit busy schedules, days of prayer, retreats for men only, an annual weekend for lawyers at which they scrutinize their professional and spiritual identity, weekends for couples, weekends for single mothers, and a discerning time for individuals to explore a possible religious vocation. Directed retreats can be scheduled and private retreatants who want time alone for reflection are encouraged to inquire.

The center was built in 1960 and named after St. Catherine of Siena, a 14th-century Dominican who integrated contemplation with activity, developing a prayer life of dialogue and imagery. More than 3,000 people come annually. The goal of the director is to help participants and guests feel renewed, refreshed, and revitalized.

Those who come regularly see visiting the center as "an opportunity to get away from telephones, television, and the other distractions around the house. We are spiritually energized. We need that . . . to be drawn back into some sort of vision of sanity." A regular attendee of the lawyers' retreat said: "Really, what we're doing is recharging our batteries, looking for inspiration, and learning that other people have the same problems we do." In essence, people are looking to find direction in their lives. "Life is crazy these days," the center's director said. "If it isn't reflected on, we're missing the heart of it. We need to quiet down, let go of it all, and reflect."

Siena Center
Racine Dominican Retreat
5635 Erie Street
Racine, WI 53402
(262) 639-4100
www.racinedominicans.org

Note: Pages 256 to 305 contain historical information for reader reference. Please be aware that some of these places may have changed area codes and contact information, and some may have changed focus or closed. Check the internet, when necessary, for the latest updates.

Other Places

Alabama

Hargis Christian Retreat, 251 Hargis Dr., **Chelsea,** AL 35043. (205) 678-6512

Alabama 4-H Center, 892 4H Rd., **Columbiana,** AL 35051. (205) 669-4241

St. Bernard Retreat Center, 1600 St. Bernard Dr. SE, **Cullman,** AL 35055. (205) 734-3946

Mystic Journey Retreat, P.O. Box 1021, **Guntersville,** AL 35976. (256) 582-5745

Blessed Trinity Shrine, 107 Holy Trinity Rd., **Holy Trinity,** AL 36859. (334) 855-4474

Alaska

Holy Spirit Retreat House, 10980 Hillside Dr., **Anchorage,** AK 99516. (907) 346-2343

Khawachen Dharma Center, 1520 Orca St., **Anchorage,** AK 99501. (907) 279-0377

St. John Orthodox Cathedral, P.O. Box 771108, 18936 Monastery Dr., **Eagle River,** AK 99577. (907) 696-2002

Shrine of St. Therese, 5933 Lund St., **Juneau,** AK 99801. (907) 780-6112

Meier Lake Conference Center, H.C. 33, Box 3181, **Wasilla,** AK 99654. (907) 376-0594

Arizona

Chapel Rock, Arizona Church Conference Center, 1131 Country Club Dr., **Prescott,** AZ 86303. (520) 445-3499

Prescott Pines Baptist Camp, P.O. Box 1226, **Prescott,** AZ 86302. (520) 445-5225

Franciscan Renewal Center, 5802 E. Lincoln Dr., **Scottsdale,** AZ 85253. (480) 948-7460

Sedona Dahn Retreat Center, P.O. Box 2283, **Sedona,** AZ 86339. (520) 282-4300

Santa Rita Abbey, HC 1, Box 929, **Sonoita,** AZ 85637. (520) 455-5595

Benedictine Monastery, 800 N. Country Club Rd., **Tucson,** AZ 85716. (520) 325-8444

Picture Rocks Retreat, P.O. Box 569, **Tucson,** AZ 85652. (520) 744-3400

Arkansas

Devachan Temple, 5 Dickey St., **Eureka Springs,** AR 72632. (501) 253-6685

Little Portion Retreat, Rte. 7, Box 688, **Eureka Springs,** AR 72632. (501) 253-7718

Mount Sequoyah Conference and Retreat Center, 150 NW Skyline Dr., **Fayetteville,** AR 72701. (501) 443-4531

St. Scholastica Center, P.O. Box 3489, **Fort Smith,** AR 72913. (501) 783-1135

Holy Angels Convent, P.O. Drawer 130, **Jonesboro,** AR 72403. (870) 933-5661

Dimensions of Evolvement, Inc., Box 456, **Melbourne,** AR 72556. (870) 368-4468

The Abbey Retreat, Coury House, Subiaco Abbey, 100 College St., **Subiaco,** AR 72865. (501) 934-4411

Ozark Theosophical Camp, 104 Broadview, **Sulphur Springs,** AR 72768. (501) 298-3594

Shiloh Community, P.O. Box 97, **Sulphur Springs,** AR 72768. (501) 298-3299

California

Sacred Heart Retreat Center, 920 E. Alhambra Rd., **Alhambra,** CA 91801. (626) 289-1359

Camp Sky Meadows, 3191 Radford Rd., **Angelus Oaks,** CA 92305. (909) 866-2268

Quaker Center, P.O. Box 686, **Ben Lomond,** CA 95005. (831) 336-8333

Incarnation Monastery, 1369 La Loma, **Berkeley,** CA 94708. (510) 845-0601

Incarnation Priory, 1601 Oxford St., **Berkeley,** CA 94709. (510) 548-3406

Ruach Ha'Aretz, c/o Marty Potrop, 2519 Derby St., **Berkeley,** CA 94705. (510) 549-0441

Sacred Heart Retreat Camp, P.O. Box 1795, **Big Bear Lake,** CA 92315. (909) 866-5696

Esalen Institute, **Big Sur,** CA 93920. (408) 667-3005 (Reservations), (831) 667-3000 (General Information)

Alpine Covenant Conference Center, P.O. Box 155, **Blue Jay,** CA 92317. (909) 337-6287

Commonweal Center, P.O. Box 316, **Bolinas,** CA 94924. (415) 868-0970

Taungpulu Kaba-Aye Monastery, 18335 Big Basin Way, **Boulder Creek,** CA 95006.

Vajrapani Institute, P.O. Box 2130, **Boulder Creek,** CA 95006. (831) 338-6654

Brandeis Bardin Institute, A Jewish Educational Camp, 1101 Peppertree Ln., **Brandeis,** CA 93064. (805) 582-4450

Mercy Center, 2300 Adeline Dr., **Burlingame,** CA 94010. (650) 340-7474

Rainbow Ranch, 3975 Mountain Home Rd., **Calistoga,** CA 94515. (707) 942-5127

St. Dorothy's Rest, P.O. Box B, **Camp Meeker,** CA 95419. (707) 874-3319

Avery Ranch, P.O. Box 1186, **Columbia,** CA 95310. (209) 533-2851

Madonna of Peace Renewal Center, P.O. Box 71, **Copperopolis,** CA 95228. (209) 785-2157

Pema Osel Ling Retreat Center, 2013 Eureka Canyon Rd., **Corralitos,** CA 95076. (831) 761-6266

San Damiano Retreat House, 710 Highland Dr., P.O. Box 767, **Danville,** CA 94526. (925) 837-9141

Pyramid of Health Spa, 66563 E. Fifth St., **Desert Hot Springs,** CA 92240. (760) 329-5652

Sky Valley Retreat Center, 732 Dillon Rd., **Desert Hot Springs,** CA 92240. (760) 329-6994

Madre Grande Monastery of the Paracelsian Order, 18372 Hwy. 94, **Dulzura,** CA 91917. (619) 468-3810, (619) 468-3006

Holy Spirit Retreat Center, 4316 Lanai Rd., **Encino,** CA 91436. (818) 784-4515

Christ the Victor Lutheran Retreat, 2626 Sir Francis Drake Blvd., **Fairfax,** CA 94930. (415) 454-6365

Our Lady of Trust Spirituality Center, 205 S. Pine Dr., **Fullerton,** CA 92633. (714) 956-1020

Heartwood Institute, 220 Harmony Ln., **Garberville,** CA 95440. (707) 923-2021

Isis Oasis, 20889 Geyserville Ave., **Geyserville,** CA 95441. (707) 857-3524

Star Foundation, P.O. Box 516, **Geyserville,** CA 95441. 1-888-857-STAR

Sivananda Ashram, Vrindavan Yoga Farm, 14651 Ballantree Ln., **Grass Valley,** CA 95949. (916) 272-9322, (800) 4MY-YOGA

Silver Spring Mountain Retreat, P.O. Box 1331, **Hayfork,** CA 96041. (530) 628-5489

El Rancho del Obispo (The Bishop's Ranch), 5297 Westside Rd., **Healdsburg,** CA 95448. (707) 433-2440

Riverrun Retreat Hermitage, c/o Simon Jeremiah, 1569 Fitch Mountain, **Healdsburg,** CA 95448. (707) 433-6754

St. Columba Retreat House, Box 430, **Inverness,** CA 94937. (415) 669-1039

Astral Mountain Retreat, Box 1881, Dept. YJ, **Julian,** CA 92036. (619) 765-1225

Rigzin Ling, P.O. Box 279, **Junction City,** CA 96048. (916) 623-2714

Far Horizons, Inc., P.O. Box 857, **Kings Canyon National Park,** CA 93633. (209) 565-3692

Villa Maria House of Prayer, 1252 N. Citrus, **La Habra,** CA 90631. (562) 691-5838

Double D Ranch, 3212 E. 8th St., **Long Beach,** CA 98084. (562) 434-3453

Jesuit Retreat House, 300 Manresa Way, **Los Altos,** CA 94022. (650) 948-4491

Claretian Renewal Center, 1119 Westchester Pl., **Los Angeles,** CA 90019. (213) 737-8464

Metivta, A Center for Jewish Wisdom, 2001 South Barrington Ave., #106, **Los Angeles,** CA 90025. (310) 477-5370

Jikoji, 12100 Skyline Blvd., **Los Gatos,** CA 95030. (408) 741-9562

Presentation Center, 19480 Bear Creek Rd., **Los Gatos,** CA 95030. (408) 354-2346

Serra Retreat, P.O. Box 127, **Malibu,** CA 90265. (562) 456-6631

Four Springs, 14598 Sheveland Rd., **Middletown,** CA 95461. (888) 428-5189 toll-free

Harbin Hot Springs, P.O. Box 782, **Middletown,** CA 95461. (707) 987-2477

Ralston L. White Retreat, 2 El Capitan Ave., **Mill Valley,** CA 94941. (415) 388-0858

DePaul Center, 1105 Bluff Rd., **Montebello,** CA 90640. (213) 723-7343

Mount Baldy Zen Center, P.O. Box 429, **Mount Baldy,** CA 91759. (909) 985-6410

Zen Mountain Center, P.O. Box 43, **Mountain Center,** CA 92361. (909) 659-5272

Las Brisas Retreat Center, 43500 Camino de Las Brisas, **Murrieta,** CA 92562. (909) 677-4544

Ananda Seclusion Retreat, 14618 Tyler Foote Rd., **Nevada City,** CA 95959. (800) 346-5350

California Vipassana Center, P.O. Box 1167, **North Fork,** CA 93643. (209) 877-4386

Episcopal Conference Center, 43803 Hwy. 41, **Oakhurst,** CA 93644. (209) 683-8162

Holy Redeemer Center, 8945 Golf Links Rd., P.O. Box 5427, **Oakland,** CA 94605. (510) 635-6341

Carmelite House of Prayer, Oakville Grade Rd., **Oakville,** CA 94562. (707) 944-2454

Chagdud Gonpa Foundation Inc., P.O. Box 90, **Oakville,** CA 94562. (707) 944-1907

Krotona Institute of Theosophy, 2 Krotona Hill, **Ojai,** CA 93023. (805) 646-2653

The Ojai Foundation, P.O. Box 1620, **Ojai,** CA 93023. (805) 646-8343

Center for Spiritual Development, 434 S. Batavia, **Orange,** CA 92668. (714) 744-3175

House of Prayer for Priests, 7734 Santiago Canyon Rd., **Orange,** CA 92669. (714) 639-9740

Asilomar Conference Center, P.O. Box 537, **Pacific Grove,** CA 93950. (831) 372-8016

Aldersgate Retreat Center, 925 Haverford Ave., **Pacific Palisades,** CA 90272. (310) 454-6699

Aldersgate Retreat Center, P.O. Box 6006, **Pasadena,** CA 91102. (626) 872-4300

Silver Penny Farm, 5215 Old Lakeville Rd. #1, **Petaluma,** CA 94954. (707) 762-1498

Walker Creek Ranch, 1700 Marshall/Petaluma Rd., **Petaluma,** CA 94952. (707) 491-6600

Shenoa Retreat Center, P.O. Box 43, **Philo,** CA 95466. (707) 895-3156

Wellspring Renewal Center, P.O. Box 332, **Philo,** CA 95466. (707) 895-3893

Mary and Joseph Retreat Center, 5300 Crest Rd., **Rancho Palos Verdes,** CA 90274. (310) 377-4867

El Carmelo Retreat House, 926 E. Highland Ave., **Redlands,** CA 92373. (909) 792-1047

Mount Alverno Conference Center, P.O. Box 1028, 3910 Bret Harte Dr., **Redwood City,** CA 94064. (650) 369-0798

Christian Brothers Retreat House, 2233 Sulphur Springs Ave., **St. Helena,** CA 94574. (707) 963-1411

Spiritual Ministry Center, 4822 Del Mar Ave., **San Diego,** CA 92107. (858) 224-9444

Zen Center, 300 Page Street, **San Francisco,** CA 94102. (415) 863-3136

Mission San Luis Rey Retreat, P.O. Box 409, **San Luis Rey,** CA 92068. (760) 757-3659

United Camps, Conferences, & Retreats, 199 Greenfield, **San Rafael,** CA 94901. (415) 456-5102

St. Mary's Retreat House, 505 E. Los Olivos, **Santa Barbara,** CA 93105. (661) 682-4117

White Lotus Foundation, 2500 San Marcos Pass, **Santa Barbara,** CA 93105. (661) 964-1944

Angela Center, 535 Angela Dr., **Santa Rosa,** CA 95401. (707) 528-8578

San Lorenzo Friary, P.O. Box 247, 1802 Sky Dr., **Santa Ynez,** CA 93460. (805) 688-1993

Westerbeke Ranch & Conference Center, 2300 Grove St., **Sonoma,** CA 95476. (707) 996-7546

Villa Maria Retreat Center, 159 Sky Meadow Dr., **Stamford,** CT 06903. (203) 322-0107

Emmaus-Diocesan Spiritual Life Center, 24 Maple Ave., **Uncasville,** CT 06382. (860) 848-3427

Holy Family Retreat House, 303 Tunxis Rd., **West Hartford,** CT 06107. (860) 521-0440

Benedictine Grange, Dorethy Rd., **West Redding,** CT 06896. (203) 938-3689

Immaculata Retreat House, Windham Rd., **Willimantic,** CT 06226. (860) 423-8484

Delaware

Virden Retreat Center, University of Delaware, 700 Pilottown Rd., **Lewes,** DE 19958. (302) 645-4100

St. Francis Renewal Center, 1901 Prior Rd., **Wilmington,** DE 19809. (302) 798-1454

District of Columbia

Monastery of the Holy Cross, 1302 Quincy St. NE, **Washington,** D.C. 20017. (202) 832-8519

St. Anselm's Abbey, 4501 S. Dakota Ave. NE, **Washington,** D.C. 20017. (202) 269-2300

Tibetan Meditation Center, 5603 16th St. NW, **Washington,** D.C. 20011. (202) 829-0005

Washington Retreat House, 4000 Harewood Rd. NE, **Washington,** D.C. 20017. (202) 529-1111

Florida

Mother of God House of Prayer, 17800 Cypress Creek Rd., **Alva,** FL 33920. (941) 728-3614

Zacchaeus House, 2704 33rd Ave. W., **Bradenton,** FL 34205. (941) 755-5812

The Pines Retreat Center, 7029 Cedar Ln., **Brooksville,** FL 34601. (352) 796-4457

Shady Grove ECO-Ranch, 8151 NW 77th Pl., **Chiefland,** FL 32626. (352) 490-8349

Our Lady of Divine Providence House of Prayer, 702 Bayview Ave., **Clearwater,** FL 34619. (727) 797-7412

Living Waters, 11450 SW 16th St., **Davie,** FL 33325. (954) 476-7466

Duncan Conference Center, 15820 S. Military Trail, **Delray Beach,** FL 33484. (561) 496-4130

Dayspring Episcopal Conference Center, P.O. Box 661, **Ellenton,** FL 34222. (941) 776-1018

Gainesville Zen Circle, 562 NE 2nd Ave., **Gainesville,** FL 32601. (352) 373-7567

Church of the Brethren, P.O. Box 74, **Gotha,** FL 34734. (407) 293-3481

Loretto House of Prayer, 4118 Loretto Rd., **Jacksonville,** FL 32223

Marywood, 1714-5 St. Rd. 13, **Jacksonville,** FL 32259. (904) 287-2525

Cenacle Spiritual Life Center, 1400 S. Dixie Hwy., **Lantana,** FL 33462. (561) 582-2534

Vision Farms, P.O. Box 154, **McIntosh,** FL 32664. AA meditation center. (352) 591-4791

Dominican Retreat House, 7275 SW 124th St., **Miami,** FL 33156. (305) 238-2711

John Paul II Retreat House, 720 NE 27th St., **Miami,** FL 33137. (305) 576-2748

Our Lady of Florida Spiritual Center, 1300 U.S. Hwy. 1, **North Palm Beach,** FL 33408. (561) 626-1300

Dunklin Memorial Camp, 3342 SW Hosannah Ln., **Okeechobee,** FL 34974. (863) 597-2841

Canterbury Retreat & Conference Center, 1601 Alfaya Trail, **Oviedo,** FL 32765. (407) 365-5571

St. Leo Abbey, P.O. Box 2369, **St. Leo,** FL 33574. (352) 588-2000

Buddha Sasana Vihara, 1085 Plaza Comercio Dr. NE, **St. Petersburg,** FL 33702. (727) 576-9209

Montgomery Conference Center, Rte. 3, Box 1102, **Starke,** FL 32091. (904) 473-4516

Cypress Tree Zen Center, P.O. Box 1856, **Tallahassee,** FL 32302.

St. John Neumann Center, 685 Miccosukee Rd., **Tallahassee,** FL 32308. (850) 224-2971

Tampa Karma Triyana Dharmachakra (KTC), 820 S. MacDill, **Tampa,** FL 33609. (813) 870-2904

Our Lady of Perpetual Help Spirituality Center, 1000 Pinebrook Rd., **Venice,** FL 34292. (941) 484-9543

San Pedro Spiritual Center, 2400 Dike Rd., **Winter Park,** FL 32792. (321) 671-6322

Georgia

Green Bough House of Prayer, Rte. 1, Box 65A, **Adrian,** GA 31002. (478) 668-4758

Koinonia Partners, 1324 Georgia Hwy. 49S., **Americus,** GA 31709. (229) 924-0391

Ignatius House, 6700 Riverside Dr. NW, **Atlanta,** GA 30328. (404) 255-0503

God's Country Farm, Hwy. 325, **Blairsville,** GA 30512. May–Oct. (706) 745-1560

Monastery of Our Lady of the Holy Spirit, 2625 Hwy. 212, **Conyers,** GA 30208. (770) 760-0959.

Cohutta Springs Conference Center, 1175 Cohutta Springs Rd., **Crandall,** GA 30711. (706) 695-9093

Calvin Camp and Conference Center, 13550 Woolsey Rd., **Hampton,** GA 30228. (770) 946-4276

Center for Spiritual Awareness, **Lakemont,** GA 30552. May–Sept. (706) 782-4723

Simpsonwood Conference and Retreat Center, 4511 Jonesbridge Cir. NW, **Norcross,** GA 30092. (770) 441-1111

Epworth by the Sea, P.O. Box 20407, **St. Simons Island,** GA 31522. (912) 638-8688

Covecrest, Rte. 1, Box 3117, **Tiger,** GA 30576. (706) 782-5961

Four Winds Village, Gt. Spirit Retreat, P.O. Box 112, **Tiger,** GA 30576. (706) 782-6939

Mikell Camp & Conference Center, Rte. 3, Box 343, **Toccoa,** GA 30577. (706) 886-7515

Georgia Episcopal Camp and Conference Center, "Honey Creek," RR 1, Box 94, **Waverly,** GA 31565. (912) 265-9218

Hawaii

Soto Mission of Aiea, P.O. Box 926, **Aiea,** HI 96701. (808) 488-6794

Hawaii International Conference Center, 1208 Laukahi St., **Honolulu,** HI 96821

Honolulu Diamond Sangha, 2747 Waiomao Rd., **Honolulu,** HI 96816. (808) 735-1347

Mantra Meditation of Hawaii, 169 S. Kukui St., **Honolulu,** HI 96813. (808) 533-0277

Nichiren Mission of Hawaii, 33 Pulelehua Way, **Honolulu,** HI 96817. (808) 595-3517

Spiritual Life Center, 2717 Pamoa Rd., **Honolulu,** HI 96822. (808) 988-7800

Vipassana Hawaii, 380 Portlock Rd., **Honolulu,** HI 96825. (808) 395-5301

Kalani Honua, P.O. Box 4500, **Kalapana,** HI 96778. (808) 965-7828

Spiritual Life Center, 6401 Pal Hwy., **Kaneohe,** HI 96744. (808) 263-8844

Kahuna Retreats, Aloha International, P.O. Box 599, **Kapaa,** HI 96746. (808) 822-9272

Kalani Honua Conference and Retreat Center, RR 2 Box 4500, **Kehena Beach,** HI 96778. (800) 800-6886, (808) 965-7828

Manulani, 515 S. Kihei Rd. #C-105, **Kihei,** HI 96753. (800) 772-1899 ext. 65644

Kai Mana, P.O. Box 612, **Kilauea,** HI 96754. (800) 837-1782

Hui Ho'olana, P.O. Box 99, **Kualapuu,** HI 96757. (808) 567-6430

St. Isaac Hermitage, P.O. Box 731, **Mountain View,** HI 96771. Nearest phone 7 miles. Rustic.

Nechung Dorje Drayang Ling, Wood Valley Retreat Center, P.O. Box 250, **Pahala,** HI 96777. (808) 928-8539

Hale Mauli Ola Hou, aka Re-Creation Center, P.O. Box 1653, **Pahoa,** HI 96778. (808) 965-9880

Karma Rimary Osal Ling, P.O. Box 1029, **Paia,** HI 96779. (808) 579-8076

Idaho

Nazareth Retreat Center, 4450 N. 5 Mile Rd., **Boise,** ID 83704. (208) 375-2932

Monastery of St. Gertrude, HC 3, Box 121, **Cottonwood,** ID 83522. (208) 962-3224

Ascension Priory and Ministry Center, 541 E. 100th S., **Jerome,** ID 83338. (208) 324-2377

Marymount Hermitage, 2150 Hermitage Ln., **Mesa,** ID 83643. (208) 256-4354

Illinois

United Charities Camp Algonquin, 1889 Cary Rd., **Algonquin,** IL 60102. (847) 658-8212

Bellarmine Hall, P.O. Box 268, **Barrington,** IL 60010. (847) 381-1261

St. Benedict Abbey, 7561 W. Lancaster Rd., **Bartonville,** IL 61607. (309) 633-0057

King's House Retreat and Renewal Center, 700 N. 66th St., **Belleville,** IL 62223. (618) 397-0584

National Shrine of Our Lady of the Snows, Missionary Oblates of Mary Immaculate, 9500 W. State Rte. 15, **Belleville,** IL 62223. (618) 397-6700

Emani House, 1340 E. 72nd St., **Chicago,** IL 60619. (773) 643-0359

Convent of St. Anne, 1125 N. La Salle, **Chicago,** IL 60610. (312) 642-3638

Our House of Prayer, 8718 Pauline St., **Chicago,** IL 60620. (773) 233-5609

Priory of Christ the King, 4334 N. Hazel St., #110, **Chicago,** IL 60613. (773) 404-2767

Resurrection Retreats, 7432 W. Talcott Ave., **Chicago,** IL 60631. (773) 792-6363

Vivekananda Vedanta Society, 5423 S. Hyde Park Blvd., **Chicago,** IL 60615. (773) 363-0027

Wat Dhammaram, 7059 W. 75th St., **Chicago,** IL 60638. (773) 594-8100

Toddhall Retreat & Conference Center, 350 Todd Center Dr., **Columbia,** IL 62236. (618) 281-8180, (618) 281-7569

Aylesford Carmelite Spiritual Center, 8433 Bailey Rd., **Darien,** IL 60561. (708) 969-4141

Cabrini Retreat Center, 9430 Golf Rd., **Des Plaines,** IL 60016, (847) 297-6530

St. Joseph Retreat Center, 353 N. River Rd., **Des Plaines,** IL 60016. (847) 298-4070

Siloam Retreat, 18 N. 600 W. Hill Rd., **Dundee,** IL 60118. (847) 428-6949

Burmese Buddhist Association, 15 W. 110 Forest Ln., **Elmhurst,** IL 60126. (630) 941-7608

Chicago Zen Center, 2029 Ridge, **Evanston,** IL 60201. (847) 475-3015

Portiuncula Center for Prayer, 9263 W. St. Francis Rd., **Frankfort,** IL 60423. (815) 469-4880

La Salette Retreat Center, RR 1, Box 403, **Georgetown (Olivet),** IL 61846. (217) 662-6671

Villa Redeemer Redemptorist Center, 1111 N. Milwaukee Ave., **Glenview,** IL 60025. (847) 724-7804

King's House of Retreats, P.O. Box 165, **Henry,** IL 61537. (309) 364-3084

Buddha Dharma Meditation Center, 8910 S. Kingerly Hwy., **Hinsdale,** IL 60521. (630) 789-8866

St. Mary's Retreat House, 1400 Main St., Box 608, **Lemont,** IL 60439. (630) 257-5102

Marytown-Kolbe Shrine, 1600 W. Park Ave., **Libertyville,** IL 60048. (847) 367-7800

Cardinal Stritch Retreat House, P.O. Box 455, **Mundelein,** IL 60060. (847) 566-6060

Center for Development in Ministry, University of St. Mary of the Lake, **Mundelein,** IL 60060. (847) 566-8290

Christian Brothers LaSalle Manor, 12480 Galena Rd., **Plano,** IL 60545. (630) 552-3224

Oasis Place of Prayer, 17175 Galena Rd., **Plano,** IL 60545. (630) 552-8201

Dominican Conference Center, 7200 W. Division St., **River Forest,** IL 60305. (708) 771-3030

Dominican Renewal Center-Benincasa, 7th and Adams, P.O. Box 679, **Riverton,** IL 62561. (217) 629-8469

Bishop Lane Retreat Center, 7708 E. McGregor Rd., **Rockford,** IL 61102. (815) 965-5011

Sacred Heart House of Prayer, 2810 Fifth Ave., **Rock Island,** IL 61201. (309) 786-6785

Sacred Heart Seminary, 3800 W. Division St., **Stone Park,** IL 60165. (708) 345-8270

Divine Word International, 2001 Waukegan Rd., P.O. Box 176, **Techny,** IL 60082. (847) 272-1100

Plow Creek Fellowship, Rte. 2, Box 2A, **Tiskilwa,** IL 61368. (815) 640-4730. Retreat cabin.

Cenacle Retreat House, P.O. Box 797, **Warrenville,** IL 60555. (630) 393-1231

Resurrection Center, 2710 S. Country Club Rd., **Woodstock,** IL 60098. (815) 338-1032

Indiana

Benedict Inn and Conference Center, 1402 Southern Ave., **Beech Grove,** IN 46107. (317) 788-7581

Lindenwood, PHJC Ministry Center, **Donaldson,** IN 46513. (219) 935-1780

Open Spaces, 115 W. Cleveland Ave., **Elkhart,** IN 46516. (219) 522-5350

Sarto Retreat House, P.O. Box 4169, **Evansville,** IN 47724. (812) 424-5536

Kordes Enrichment Center, 841 E. 14th St., **Ferdinand,** IN 47532. (800) 880-2777

Monastery Immaculate Conception, 802 E. 10th St., **Ferdinand,** IN 47532. (812) 367-1411

Pope John XXIII Center, 407 W. McDonald St., **Hartford City,** IN 47348. (317) 348-4008

Fatima Retreat House, 5353 E. 56th St., **Indianapolis,** IN 46226. (317) 545-7681

American Camping Association, 5000 State Rd. 67 N., **Martinsville,** IN 46151. (765) 342-8456 ext. 312

Mount St. Francis Retreat Center and St. Mary of the Angels Hermitage, 101 Anthony Dr., **Mount St. Francis,** IN 47146. (812) 923-8817

Epworth Forest Conference Center, P.O. Box 16, **N. Webster,** IN 46555. (219) 834-2212

Fatima Retreat Center, P.O. Box 929, **Notre Dame,** IN 46556. (219) 631-8288

Mary's Solitude, St. Mary's, **Notre Dame,** IN 46556. (219) 284-5599

Sisters of St. Francis Convent, Main St., **Olsenburg,** IN 47063. (812) 934-2475

Quaker Hill Conference Center, 10 Quaker Hill Dr., **Richmond,** IN 47374. (765) 962-5741

Geneva Center, 5282 N. Old U.S. 31, **Rochester,** IN 46975. (219) 223-69⁚5

Handmaids of the Most Holy Trinity, Monastery-Hermitage, 23089 Adams Rd., **S. Bend,** IN 46628. Groups only. (219) 272-9425 (before 7:45 P.M. E.T.)

Little Noddfa, RR 3, P.O. Box 291A, **Tipton,** IN 46072. (765) 675-3950

Iowa

Beacon House Ministries, 915 N. 3rd St., **Burlington,** IA 52601. (319) 752-2121

American Martyrs Retreat House, P.O. Box 605, **Cedar Falls,** IA 50613. (319) 266-3543

Shalom Retreat House, 1001 Davis Ave., **Dubuque,** IA 52001. (319) 582-3592

Creighton University Retreat Center, 16493 Contrail Ave., **Griswold,** IA 51535. (712) 278-2466

Wakonda House of Prayer, Box 370, **Griswold,** IA 51535. (712) 778-4325

Camp Wesley Woods, 1086 Nixon St., **Indianola,** IA 50125. (515) 961-4523

Christian Conference Center, Rte. 3, Box 70, **Newton,** IA 50208. (515) 792-1266

Kansas

The Mount Conference Center, 801 South 8th St., **Atchison,** KS 66002. (913) 367-6110

St. Benedict's Abbey, 1020 N. 2nd St., **Atchison,** KS 66002. (913) 367-7853

Sophia Center, 801 S. 8th St., **Atchison,** KS 66002. (913) 367-6110

Hollis Renewal Center, P.O. Box 402, **Bonner Springs,** KS 66012. (913) 441-0451

Manna House of Prayer, P.O. Box 675, 323 E. 5th St., **Concordia,** KS 66901. (785) 243-4428

Shantivanam, 22019 Meagher Rd., **Easton,** KS 66020. (913) 773-8255

Rock Springs 4-H Center, 5405 W. Hwy. K-157, **Junction City,** KS 66441. (785) 257-3221

Kansas Zen Center, 1115 Ohio, **Lawrence,** KS 66044. (785) 842-8909

Tall Oaks Conference Center, 12797 189th St., P.O. Box 116, **Linwood,** KS 66052. (913) 723-3307, (913) 723-3213

Ursuline Retreat Center, 901 East Miami, **Paola,** KS 66071. (913) 294-2349

Acuto Center, 1165 Southwest Blvd., **Wichita,** KS 67213. (316) 945-2542

Spiritual Life Center, 7100 East 45th St. N., **Wichita,** KS 67226. (316) 744-0167

Kentucky

Furnace Mountain, P.O. Box 545, **Clay City,** KY 40312. (606) 438-3066

Foxhollow, 8909 Hwy. 329, **Crestwood,** KY 40014. (502) 241-5423

Kavanaugh Life Enrichment Center, 7505 Kavanaugh Rd., **Crestwood,** KY 40014. (502) 241-1279, (502) 241-9091

Marydale Retreat Center, 945 Donaldson Hwy., **Erlanger,** KY 41018. (800) 995-4863

Kentucky Leadership Center, HC 66, Box 4075, **Faubush,** KY 42532. (502) 866-4215

The Close, P.O. Box 610, **Lexington,** KY 40586. (606) 252-6527

Lexington Zen Center, 345 Jesselin Dr., **Lexington,** KY 40503. (606) 277-2438

St. Agnes House, 635 Maxwelton Ct., **Lexington,** KY 40508. (606) 254-1241

Flaget Center, 1935 Lewiston Pl., **Louisville,** KY 40216. (502) 448-8581

Mount St. Joseph Center, 8001 Cummings Rd., **Maple Mount,** KY 42356. (502) 229-4103

The Dwelling Place, 150 Mt. Tabor Rd., **Martin,** KY 41649. (606) 886-9624

Moye Spiritual Life Center, St. Anne Convent, **Melbourne,** KY 41059. (606) 441-0679

Cleftrock Retreat Center, Rte. 1, Box 397, **Mt. Vernon,** KY 40456. (606) 256-2336

Catherine Spalding Center, P.O. Box 24, **Nazareth,** KY 40048. (502) 348-1546

Knobs Haven, Loretto Motherhouse, **Nerinx,** KY 40049. (502) 865-2621

Bethany Spring, 115 Dee Head Rd., **New Haven,** KY 40051. (502) 549-8277

St. Walburg Monastery, 2500 Amsterdam Rd., **Villa Hills,** KY 41017. (606) 331-6324

Louisiana

Manresa Retreat House, P.O. Box 89, **Convent,** LA 70723. (504) 562-3596, (800) 782-9431

Regina Coeli Retreat Center, 17225 Regina Coeli Rd., **Covington,** LA 70433. (504) 892-4110

Jesuit Spirituality Center, St. Charles College, P.O. Box C, **Grand Coteau,** LA 70541. (337) 662-5251

Our Lady of the Oaks Retreat House, P.O. Box D, **Grand Coteau,** LA 70541. (318) 662-5410

Calcasieu Center for Catholic Studies, 920 Seventh St., **Lake Charles,** LA 70601. (318) 439-7432

Ave Maria Retreat House, RR 1, Box 0368, **Marrero,** LA 70072. (504) 689-3837

Maryhill Renewal Center, 600 Maryhill Rd., **Pineville,** LA 71360. (318) 640-1378

Magnificat Center of the Holy Spirit, Lee's Landing Rd., Hwy. 445, **Ponchatoula,** LA 70454. (504) 529-1636

Rosaryville Spirit Life Center, Star Rte., 39003 Rosaryville Rd., **Ponchatoula,** LA 70454. (504) 294-5039, (504) 466-1476, (800) 627-9183

The Episcopal Conference Center, P.O. Box 779, **Robert,** LA 70455. (504) 748-6634

Lumen Christi Retreat Center, 100 Lumen Christi Ln., **Schriever,** LA 70395. (504) 868-1523

Maine

Notre Dame Spiritual Center, **Alfred,** ME 04002. (207) 324-6160, (207) 324-6612 (Monday–Friday, 9 A.M.–4 P.M. E.T.)

St. Paul's Retreat House and Cursillo Center, 136 State St., **Augusta,** ME 04330. (207) 622-6235

China Lake Conference Center, Rte. 3, Box 149, **China,** ME 04926. (207) 968-2101

Rockcraft Retreat Center, P.O. Box 198, **East Sebago,** ME 04029. Groups only. (207) 787-2876

St. Benedict's House, Rte. 105, **Hope,** ME 04847. (207) 763-4020

Franciscan Guest House, P.O. Box 980, **Kennebunkport,** ME 04046. (207) 967-2011

Oceanwood, P.O. Box 338, **Ocean Park,** ME 04063. (207) 934-9655

Mother of the Good Shepherd Monastery by the Sea, 235 Pleasant Ave., **Peaks Island,** ME 04108. (207) 766-2717

Northern Pines, 599 Rte. 85, **Raymond,** ME 04071. (207) 655-7624

Bay View Villa Guest and Retreat House by the Sea, Rte. 9/187 Bay View Rd., **Saco,** ME 04072. (207) 283-3636

Ferry Beach Park Association, 5 Morris Ave., **Saco,** ME 04072. (207) 282-4489

Hersey Retreat, P.O. Box 1183, **Stockton Springs,** ME 04982. (207) 567-3420. Winter: P.O. Box 810, **Brooks,** ME 04921. (207) 722-3405

Goose Cove Lodge, Deer Isle, **Sunset,** ME 04683. (207) 348-2508. Winter: (207) 767-3003

Morgan Bay Zendo, P.O. Box 188, **Surry,** ME 04684. (207) 667-5428, (207) 677-7170

Hermitage Arts, RR1, Box 398, **Thorndike,** ME 04986. (207) 568-3731. One hermitage.

Sky-Hy Conference and Retreat Center, RR 2, Box 85A Meadow Rd., **Topsham,** ME 04086. (207) 725-7577

Maryland

Christian Brothers Spiritual Center, P.O. Box 29, **Adamstown,** MD 21710. (301) 874-5180

Annunciation Monastery, P.O. Box 21238, **Catonsville,** MD (410) 747-6140

Our Lady's Center, 3301 Rodgers Ave., **Ellicott City,** MD 21043. (301) 461-5066

Seton Retreat Center, 333 S. Seton Ave., **Emmitsburg,** MD 21727. (301) 447-6021

Loyola Retreat House, P.O. Box 9, Popes Creek Rd., **Faulkner,** MD 20632. (301) 934-8862

American Zen College, 16815 Germantown Rd., **Germantown,** MD 20784. (301) 428-0665

Dayspring, 11301 Neelsville Church Rd., **Germantown,** MD 20876. (301) 428-9348

Camp Maria, RFD 1, Box 59-1, **Leonardtown,** MD 20650. (301) 475-8330

Retreat Center Sisters of Bon Secours, 1525 Marriottsville Rd., **Marriottsville,** MD 21104. (410) 442-1320

New Windsor Conference Center, 500 Main St., P.O. Box 188, **New Windsor,** MD 21776. (410) 635-8715

Charter Hall Church Center, 499 Charter Hall Rd., **Perryville,** MD 21903. (301) 642-2500

Kunzang Palyul Chöling, 18400 River Rd., **Poolesville,** MD 20837. Day visits (301) 428-8116

Chesapeake Center, 50 Happy Valley Rd., **Port Deposit,** MD 21904. (410) 378-2267

Berg Center, St. Gertrude's Monastery, 14259 Benedictine Lane, **Ridgely,** MD 21660. (410) 634-2497

Raven Rock Lutheran Camp, 17912 Harbaugh Valley Rd., Box 136, **Sabillasville,** MD 21780. (717) 794-2667

Shepherd's Spring, P.O. Box 369, **Sharpsburg,** MD 21782. (301) 223-8193

Cambodian Buddhist Society Inc., 13800 New Hampshire Ave., **Silver Spring,** MD 20902. (301) 622-6544

CYO Retreat House, 15523 York Rd., **Sparks,** MD 21152. (301) 472-2400

Theravada Buddhist Meditation, IMC-USA, 438 Bankard Rd., **Westminster,** MD 21158. (410) 346-7889

Drayton Retreat Center, 12651 Coopers Ln., **Worton,** MD 21678. (410) 778-2869

Massachusetts

The Kindling Point, 80 Concord St., **Ashland,** MA 01721. Workshops and intentional visits. (508) 881-4984

La Salette Center for Christian Living, 947 Park St., P.O. Box 2965, **Attleboro,** MA 02703. (508) 222-8530

Becket-Chimney Corners YMCA Camps, 748 Hamilton Rd., **Becket,** MA 01223. (413) 623-8991

Cenacle Retreat House, 200 Lake St., **Brighton,** MA 02135. (617) 254-3150

Adelynrood, 46 Elm St., **Byfield,** MA 01922. (508) 462-6721

Society of St. John the Evangelist, Monastery of SS. Mary and John, 980 Memorial Dr., **Cambridge,** MA 02138. (617) 876-3037

Pioneer Valley Zendo, 263 Warnerhill Rd., **Charlemont,** MA 01339. (413) 339-4000

Bement Camp and Conference Center, Drawer F, **Charlton Depot,** MA 01509. (508) 248-7811

Sisters of St. Joseph Retreat Center, 339 Jerusalem Rd., **Cohasset,** MA 02025. (781) 383-6029

Craigville Conference Center, **Craigville,** MA 02636. (508) 775-1265

St. Stephen Priory Spiritual Life Center, 20 Glen St., Box 370, **Dover,** MA 02030. (508) 785-0124 (Mon.–Fri., 9:30 A.M.–4:30 P.M. E.T.)

Miramar Retreat Center, P.O. Box M, **Duxbury,** MA 02331. (617) 585-2460

St. Margaret's Convent, 71 Washington St., Box C, **Duxbury,** MA 02331. (617) 934-5696

St. Marina's Guest House and Bertram Conference Center, Harden Hill Rd., **Duxbury,** MA (617) 445-8961

The Marist House, 518 Pleasant St., **Framingham,** MA 01701. (508) 879-1620

United Church of Christ Conference Center, Salem End and Badger Rds., Box 2246, **Framingham,** MA 01701. (508) 875-5233

Grotonwood, 167 Prescott St., **Groton,** MA 01450. (508) 448-5763

Mount Marie Conference Center, Lower Westfield Rd., **Holyoke,** MA 01040. (413) 536-0853

National Shrine of Our Lady of La Salette, 315 Topsfield Rd., **Ipswich,** MA 01938. (978) 356-3266

Sacred Heart Retreat House, Route 1A, Box 567, **Ipswich,** MA 01938. (978) 356-3838

Order of St. Anne, 18 Cambridge Turnpike, **Lincoln,** MA 01773. (617) 259-9800

New England Keswick Youth Camp, Adult Conference and Retreat Center, Chestnut Hill Rd., P.O. Box 156, **Monterey,** MA 01245. (413) 528-3604

Briarwood Conference Center, Shore Rd., P.O. Box 315, **Monument Beach,** MA 02532. (508) 759-3476

Rolling Ridge Conference Center, 660 Great Pond Rd., **North Andover,** MA 01845. (978) 682-8815

Stevens Estate at Osgood Hill, **North Andover,** MA 01845. (978) 682-7072

St. Joseph's Convent, 27 Mount Pleasant St. N., **North Brookfield,** MA 01535. (508) 867-6811

Holy Cross Fathers Retreat, 824 Tucker Rd., **North Dartmouth,** MA 02747. (508) 993-2238

St. Joseph's Hall, 800 Tucker Rd., **North Dartmouth,** MA 02747. Retirement center for priests. (508) 996-2413

Holy Cross Fathers Retreat House, 409 Washington St., **North Easton,** MA 02356. (508) 238-2051

Foyer of Charity, 74 Hollett St., **North Scituate,** MA 02060. (617) 545-1080

The Community of Jesus, Inc., 5 Bay View Dr., Box 1094, **Orleans,** MA 02653. (508) 255-1094

Most Holy Trinity Monastery Guesthouse, 67 Dugway Rd., **Petersham,** MA 01366 (978) 724-3347

St. Scholastica Priory, P.O. Box 606, **Petersham,** MA 01366. (978) 724-3227

St. Margaret's Convent, 17 Highland Park St., **Roxbury,** MA 02119. (617) 445-3895

Rowe Camp and Conference Center, Kings Highway Rd., **Rowe,** MA 01367. (413) 339-4216

Salvation Army, Hillcrest Conference Center, 10 Capen Hill Rd., **Sharon,** MA 02067. (781) 784-8924

Vipassana Meditation Center, P.O. Box 24, **Shelburne Falls,** MA 01370. (413) 625-2160

Calvary Retreat Center, 59 South St., **Shrewsbury,** MA 01545. (508) 842-8821

Sirius, 72 Baker Rd., **Shutesbury,** MA 01072. (413) 259-1251

Temenos, 65 Mount Mineral Rd., **Shutesbury,** MA 01072. (413) 367-9779

Blairhaven Retreat Center, P.O. Box 1414, **South Duxbury,** MA 02332. (617) 837-6144. Mailing address: Massachusetts New Church Union, 175 Newbury St., **Boston,** MA 02116.

Mary House, P.O. Box 20, **Spencer,** MA 01562. (508) 885-5450

St. Benedict Priory, 252 Still River Rd., Box 67, **Still River,** MA 01467. (508) 456-3221

Packard Manse, 583 Plain St., **Stoughton,** MA 02072. (781) 344-9634

Espousal Retreat and Conference Center, 554 Lexington St., **Waltham,** MA 02154. (781) 893-3465

Genesis Spiritual Life Center, 53 Mill St., **Westfield,** MA 01085. (413) 562-3627

Stump Sprouts Lodge, West Hill Rd., **West Hawley,** MA 01339. (413) 339-4265

Campion Renewal Center, 319 Concord Rd., **Weston,** MA 02493. (781) 788-6810

Mount Carmel Retreat House, Oblong Rd., Box 613, **Williamstown,** MA 01267. (413) 458-3164

Esther House of Spiritual Renewal, 1015 Pleasant St., **Worcester,** MA 01602. One room available. (508) 757-6053

Michigan

Weber Center, 1257 E. Siena Heights Dr., **Adrian,** MI 49221. (517) 263-7088

Heart Center KTC, 315 Marion Ave., **Big Rapids,** MI 49307. (616) 796-2398

Manresa Retreat House, 1390 Quarton Rd., **Bloomfield Hills,** MI 48304. (248) 564-6455

Emrich Conference Center, 7380 Teahen Rd., **Brighton,** MI 48116. (810) 231-1060

Camp Friedenswald, Rte. 3, **Cassopolis,** MI 49130. (616) 476-2426

Colombiere Center, 9075 Big Lake Rd., **Clarkston,** MI 48348. (248) 620-2534

Augustine Center, The Sacramentine Monastery, P.O. Box 84, **Conway,** MI 49722. (616) 347-3657

Mariannhill Retreat Center, 23715 Ann Arbor Trail, **Dearborn Heights,** MI 48127. (313) 278-9461

St. Paul of the Cross Retreat Center, 23333 Schoolcraft, **Detroit,** MI 48223. (313) 535-9563

St. Francis Retreat Center, 703 E. Main, P.O. Box 250, **DeWitt,** MI 48820. (517) 669-8321

Marygrove Retreat Center, P.O. Box 38, 1000 State St., **Garden,** MI 49835. (906) 644-2771

Camp Concordia, Rte. 1, Pinewood Rd., **Gowen,** MI 49326. (616) 754-3785

Dominican Center at Marywood, 2025 E. Fulton St., **Grand Rapids,** MI 49503. (616) 454-1241

Michindoh Conference Center, 4545 E. Bacon Rd., **Hillsdale,** MI 49242. (517) 523-3616

Maryville Youth Center, 18307 Taylor Lake Rd., **Holly,** MI 48442. (313) 634-5566

Kennedy Center, 1875 Eager Rd., **Howell,** MI 48843. (517) 546-4440

St. Joseph Home Retreat Center, 1000 E. Porter, **Jackson,** MI 49202. (517) 787-3320

Cedar Bend Farm, 1021 Doerr Rd., **Mancelona,** MI 49659. (616) 587-8126

St. Mary Conference Center, 502 W. Elm Ave., **Monroe,** MI 48161. (313) 241-3990 ext. 13

Visitation, 529 Stewart Rd., **Monroe,** MI 48161. (313) 242-5520

Transformations, Sisters of St. Joseph Life Center, 3427 Gull Rd., **Nazareth,** MI 49074. (616) 381-6290

Camp Holiday, 669 Grange Hall Rd., **Ortonville,** MI 48462. (313) 627-2558

St. Benedict Monastery, 2711 E. Drahner Rd., **Oxford,** MI 48370. (248) 628-2249

St. Mary's Retreat House, 775 W. Drahner Rd., Box 167, **Oxford,** MI 48371. (810) 628-3894

Full Circle House of Prayer, 2532 S. Blvd., **Port Huron,** MI 48060. (810) 364-3326

Camp Chickagami, Lake Esau, **Presque Isle,** MI 49777. (517) 595-6752

Dormition of the Mother of God Orthodox Monastery, 3389 Rives Eaton Rd., **Rives Junction,** MI 49277. (517) 569-2873

Ralph A. Macmullan Conference Center, 104 Conservation Dr., **Roscommon,** MI 48653. (517) 821-6200

Diocesan Ministries Institute, 705 Hoyt, **Saginaw,** MI 48607. (517) 799-7917

Queen of Angels Retreat, 3400 S. Washington St. Box 2026, **Saginaw,** MI 48605. (517) 755-2149

Detroit Conference of the United Methodist Church, 21700 Northwestern Hwy. #1200, **Southfield,** MI 48075. (248) 559-7000 ext. 62

St. Lazare Retreat House, 18600 W. Spring Lake Rd., **Spring Lake,** MI 49456. (616) 842-3370

Kettunen Center, 2859 Camp Kett Rd., **Tustin,** MI 49688. (616) 829-3421

The Song of the Morning Ranch, 9607 E. Sturgeon Valley Rd., **Vanderbilt,** MI 49795. (517) 983-4107

Emmaus Community, 7001 E. Tamarack, **Vesterberg,** MI 48891. (517) 268-5494

Capuchin Retreat, 62460 Mount Vernon Rd. Box 188, **Washington,** MI 48094 (313) 651-4826

Minnesota

Luther Crest Bible Camp, 8231 County Rd. 11 NE, **Alexandria,** MN 56308. (320) 846-2431

Angle Outpost Resort, Lake of the Woods, **Angle Inlet,** MN 56711. For religious clergy. (218) 223-8101

Clare's Well, 13537 47th St. NW, **Annandale,** MN 55302. (320) 274-3512

Faith Haven Youth Lodge, **Battle Lake,** MN 56515. (218) 864-5303

Center for Spiritual Development, P.O. Box 538, 211 Tenth St., **Bird Island,** MN 55310. (320) 365-3644

Christ the King Retreat Center, 621 S. First Ave., **Buffalo,** MN 55313. (612) 682-3453

Center for Spiritual Growth, 35197 Wakenen Dr. NE, **Cambridge,** MN 55008. (612) 689-5502

Hazelden Renewal Center, P.O. Box 11, **Center City,** MN 55012. (612) 257-4010

Hospitality House, 18 E. Golden Lake Rd., **Circle Pines,** MN 55104. (612) 784-5177

House of Prayer, P.O. Box 5888, **Collegeville,** MN 56321. (320) 363-3293

Mount St. Benedict Center, 620 E. Summit Ave., **Crookston,** MN 56716. (218) 281-3441

McCabe Renewal Center, 2125 Abbotsford Ave., **Duluth,** MN 55803. (218) 724-5266

St. Scholastica Monastery, 1200 Kenwood Ave., **Duluth,** MN 55811. (218) 723-6763

Mount Olivet Retreat Center, 7984 257th St. W., **Farmington,** MN 55024. (612) 469-2175

Villa Maria Center, 29847 County Rd. 2 Blvd., **Frontenac,** MN 55026. (612) 345-4582

Wilderness Canoe Base, Center for Life Education, 940 Gunflint Trail, **Grand Marais,** MN 55604. (218) 388-2241

Lutheran Island Camp, RR1, **Henning,** MN 56551. (218) 583-2905

Space for Spirit, RR 2 Box 23B, **Laporte,** MN 56461. (218) 224-2408

St. Francis Center, 116 8th Ave. SE, **Little Falls,** MN 56345. (320) 632-0695 or (612) 632-2981

Cathedral of the Pines, **Lutsen,** MN 55612. (218) 663-7255

Good Counsel Education Center, 150 Good Counsel Dr., **Mankato,** MN 56001. (507) 389-4287

St. Paul's Priory, 2675 E. Larpenteur Ave., **Maplewood,** MN 55109. (612) 777-7251

Dunrovin, 15525 St. Croix Trail N., **Marine on St. Croix,** MN 55047. (612) 433-2486

Wilder Forest, 14189 Ostlund Trail N., **Marine on St. Croix,** MN 55047. (612) 433-5198

The Dwelling in the Woods, HCR 2, Box 54, **McGrath,** MN 56350. (320) 592-3708

Hudson House, 3201 First Ave. S., **Minneapolis,** MN 55408. (612) 825-2993

Minnesota Zen Meditation Center, 3343 E. Calhoun Pkwy., **Minneapolis,** MN 55408. (612) 822-5313

Skete of St. Seraphim, 1201 Hathaway Ln., **Minneapolis,** MN 55432. (612) 574-1001

St. Andrew Village, **New London,** MN 56273. (320) 354-2240

Nazareth House, 1225 Hallmark Ct. N., **Oakdale,** MN 55128. (612) 730-6197

Northern Pines United Methodist Assembly Grounds, HC 06, Box 46A, **Park Rapids,** MN 56470. (218) 732-4713

Franciscan Retreat Center, 16385 St. Francis Lane, **Prior Lake,** MN 55372. (612) 447-2182

Assisi Community Center, 1001 14th St. NW, Box 4900, **Rochester,** MN 55903. (507) 289-0821

Pacem in Terris, P.O. Box 418, **St. Francis,** MN 55070. (612) 444-6408

Spirituality Center, Sisters of St. Benedict, 104 Chapel Lane, **St. Joseph,** MN 56374. (320) 363-7114

Carondelet Center, 1890 Randolph Ave., **St. Paul,** MN 55105. (612) 696-2750

Maryhill Retreat House, 260 Summit Ave., **St. Paul,** MN 55102. (612) 224-3615, (612) 224-8566

St. Paul's Priory, Benedictine Center, 2675 E. Larpenteur Ave., **St. Paul,** MN 55109. (612) 777-7251

The Dwelling Place, 216 Third Ave. S., **Sauk Rapids,** MN 56379. (320) 253-3656

Shetek Lutheran Bible Camp, Keeley Island 1, Rte. 2, **Slayton,** MN 56172. (507) 763-3567

Koinonia Retreat Center, 7768 Pilger Ave. NW, **South Haven,** MN 55382. (320) 236-7746

Green Lake Bible Camp, 9916 Lake Ave. S., **Spicer,** MN 56288. (320) 796-5461

ARC Ecumenical Retreat Community, RR 2, Box 354, **Stanchfield,** MN 55080. (320) 689-3540

Camp Omega, Rte. 2, Box 117B, **Waterville,** MN 56096. (507) 685-4266

Cenacle Retreat House, 1221 Wayzata Blvd., **Wayzata,** MN 55391. (612) 473-7308

Tau Center, 511 Hilbert St., **Winona,** MN 55987. (507) 454-2993

Mississippi

St. Augustine Retreat Center, 199 Seminary Dr., **Bay St. Louis,** MS 39520 (601) 467-9837

Seashore United Methodist Assembly, 1410 Leggett Dr., **Biloxi,** MS 39530 (601) 436-6767

Blue Mountain College, 201 West Main St., **Blue Mountain,** MS 38610. (601) 685-4771

The Dwelling Place, HC 01, Box 126, **Brooksville,** MS 39739. (601) 738-5348

St. Mary of the Pines, P.O. Box 38, **Chatawa,** MS 39632. (601) 783-3494

Camp Garaywa, Box 1014, **Clinton,** MS 39056. (607) 924-7034, (601) 968-3800 ext. 3920

Renewal Center Diocese of Jackson, 2225 Boling St., **Jackson,** MS 39213. (601) 366-4452

Gulfshore Baptist Assembly, 100 First St., **Pass Christian,** MS 39571. (601) 452-7261

Henry S. Jacobs Camp, P.O. Drawer C, **Utica,** MS 39175. (601) 362-6357

Missouri

Fresh Renewal Center, P.O. Box 219, **Augusta,** MO 63332. (314) 228-4548

Assumption Abbey, Rte. 5 Box 1056, **Ava,** MO 65608. (417) 683-5110

Benedictine Monastery, RR1, Box 101, **Clyde,** MO 64432. (816) 944-2221

Our Lady of Peace Monastery, 3710 W. Broadway, **Columbia,** MO 65203. (573) 446-2300

Retreat and Conference Center, Conception Abbey, P.O. Box 501, **Conception,** MO 64433. (816) 944-2218

Il Ritiro, The Little Retreat, P.O. Box 38 Eime Rd., **Dittmer,** MO 63023. (314) 285-3759

RES Forest Monastery, 3704 Hwy. 13, **Dunnegan,** MO 65640. (417) 754-2562

Marianist Retreat & Conference Center, 4000 Hwy. 109, Box 718, **Eureka,** MO 63025. (314) 938-5390

Pallottine Renewal Center, 15270 Old Halls Ferry Rd., **Florissant,** MO 63034. (314) 837-7100

Shining Waters Ashram, Rte. 3, Box 560, **Fredericktown,** MO 63645. (573) 783-6715

Franciscan Prayer Center, 2100 N. Noland Rd., **Independence,** MO 64050. (816) 252-1673

The Rickman Center, P.O. Box 104298, **Jefferson City,** MO 65110. (573) 635-0848

Camp Gaea, P.O. Box 10442, **Kansas City,** MO 64117. (660) 756-0719

Rockhurst College, 1100 Rockhurst Rd., **Kansas City,** MO 64110. (660) 926-4000

St. John's Diocesan Center, 2015 E. 72nd St., **Kansas City,** MO 64132. (660) 363-3585

Queen of Heaven Solitude, Rte. 1, Box 107A, **Marionville,** MO 65705. (417) 744-2011

Vision of Peace Hermitages, P.O. Box 69, Abbey Ln., **Pevely,** MO 63070. (314) 475-3697

YMCA of the Ozarks/Trout Lodge Family and Conference Center, RR 2, **Potosi,** MO 63664. (573) 438-2154

Cliff Springs Camp and Conference Center, County Rd. T.269, P.O. Box 751, **Richland,** MO 65556. (417) 286-3688

Caroline Conference & Retreat Center, 320 E. Ripa Ave., **St. Louis,** MO 63125. (314) 544-4756

Kenrick Pastoral Center, 7800 Kenrick Rd., **St. Louis,** MO 63119. (314) 961-4320

Mercy Center, 2039 N. Geyer Rd., **St. Louis,** MO 63131. (314) 966-4686

St. Charles Lwanga Center, 5021 Northland Ave., **St. Louis,** MO 63113. (314) 367-7929

St. Louis Abbey, 500 S. Mason Rd., **St. Louis,** MO 63141. (314) 434-2557

Seton Center, 7800 Natural Bridge, **St. Louis,** MO 63121. (314) 382-2800

Thompson Center, 12145 Ladue Rd., **St. Louis,** MO 63141. (314) 434-3633

White House Retreat, 7400 Christopher Dr., **St. Louis,** MO 63129. (314) 533-8903, (314) 846-2575

Unity Village Retreats, 1901 NW Blue Pkwy., **Unity Village,** MO 64065. (816) 251-3535

Ozark Retreat Center, RR 2, Box 45, **Willow Springs,** MO 65793. (417) 469-2439

Montana

Sacred Heart Renewal Center, 26 Wyoming Ave., P.O. Box 20795, **Billings,** MT 59104. (406) 252-0322

Ursuline Retreat Center, 2300 Central Ave., **Great Falls,** MT 59401. (406) 452-8585

Feathered Pipe Ranch, Box 1682, **Helena,** MT 59624. (406) 442-8196

The Sycamore Tree, Contemplative Prayer Center, **Swan Lake,** MT 59911 (406) 754-2429

Nebraska

The Leadership Center, 1609 E. Hwy. 34, **Aurora,** NE 68818. (402) 694-3934

House of Transfiguration, Box 217, **Bayard,** NE 69334. (308) 586-1845

Crosier Renewal Center, 223 E. 14th St., Box 789, **Hastings,** NE 68901. (402) 463-3188

Niobrara Valley House of Renewal, P.O. Box 117, **Lynch,** NE 68746. (402) 569-3433

Nebraska Zen Center, 816 S. 67th St., **Omaha,** NE 68106. (402) 551-4063

Notre Dame Center, 3501 State St., **Omaha,** NE 68112. (402) 455-4083

Columban Retreat Center, **St. Columbans,** NE 68056. (402) 291-1920

Christ the King Priory, P.O. Box 528, **Schuyler,** NE 68661. (402) 352-8819

Good Counsel Retreat House, Rte. 1, Box 110, **Waverly,** NE 68462. (402) 786-2705

Benedictine Mission House, P.O. Box 528, RR1, **Schuyler,** NE 68661. (402) 352-2177

Nevada

Wellspring Retreat House, P.O. Box 60818, 701 Park Pl., **Boulder City,** NV 89006. (702) 293-4988

Sierra Spirit Ranch, 3000 Pinenut Rd., **Gardenville,** NV 89410. (702) 782-7011

Joy Lake Mountain Seminar Center, P.O. Box 1328, **Reno,** NV 89504. (702) 323-0378

New Hampshire

Geneva Point Center, HCR 62, P.O. Box 469, **Center Harbor,** NH 03226. (603) 253-4366

Wilmot Camp and Conference Center, P.O. Box 158, N. Wilmot Rd., **Danbury,** NH 03230. (603) 768-3350

Deering Conference Center, RFD 1, P.O. Box 138, Rte. 149, **Deering,** NH 03244. (603) 529-2311

La Salette Shrine and Conference Center, P.O. Box 420, **Enfield,** NH 03748 (603) 632-4301

Oblate Retreat House, 200 Lowell Rd., **Hudson,** NH 03051. (603) 882-8141

Joseph House, 279 Cartier St., **Manchester,** NH 03102. (603) 627-9493

Monastery of the Precious Blood, 700 Bridge St., **Manchester,** NH 03104. (603) 623-4264

Our Lady of Hope House of Prayer, 400 Temple Rd., **New Ipswich,** NH 03071. (603) 878-2346

Star Island, P.O. Box 178, Isle of Shoals, **Portsmouth,** NH 03802. (603) 964-7252. Winter: 10 Arlington St., **Boston,** MA 02116. (617) 426-7988

New Jersey

The Inn at the Shore, 301 4th Ave., **Belmar,** NJ 07719. (732) 681-3762

St. Pius X House, P.O. Box 214, **Blackwood,** NJ 08080. (856) 227-1436

The Marianist, P.O. Box D-2, **Cape May Point,** NJ 08212. (609) 884-3829

Jizo'an (A Christian Zen Center), 1603 Highland Ave., **Cinnaminson,** NJ 08077. (609) 786-4150

Xavier Conference and Retreat Center, P.O. Box 211, **Convent Station,** NJ 07961. (973) 292-6488

Stella Maris Retreat House, 981 Ocean Ave., **Elberon,** NJ 07740. (908) 229-0602

St. Walburga Monastery, 851 N. Broad St., **Elizabeth,** NJ 07208. (908) 352-4278

Cenacle Retreat House, 411 River Rd., **Highland Park,** NJ 08904. (732) 249-8100

San Alfonso Retreat House, 755 Ocean Ave., **Long Branch,** NJ 07740. (732) 222-2731

Villa Pauline, Hilltop Rd., **Mendham,** NJ 07945. (973) 543-9058

Loyola House of Retreats, 161 James St., **Morristown,** NJ 07960. (973) 539-0740

Francis House of Prayer, Box 1111, Springside Rd., **Mount Holly,** NJ 08060. (609) 871-1999

John Woolman Memorial House, 99 Branch St., **Mount Holly,** NJ 08060. (609) 267-3226

The Upper Room Spiritual Center, West Bangs Ave., Rte. 33, P.O. Box 1104, **Neptune,** NJ 07753. (732) 922-0550

St. Paul's Abbey, Queen of Peace Retreat House, **Newton,** NJ 07860. (973) 383-2470 (Monastery), (973) 383-0660 (Retreat house)

Emmaus Retreat House, 101 Center St., **Perth Amboy,** NJ 08861. (732) 442-7688

Mount St. Francis Retreat Center, 474 Sloatsburg Rd., **Ringwood,** NJ 07456. (973) 962-9778

St. Joseph by the Sea, 400 Rte. 35 North, **South Mantoloking,** NJ 08738. (973) 892-8494

Trinity Center, 1292 Long Hill Rd., P.O. Box 205, **Stirling,** NJ 07080. (908) 647-7112

Villa Maria by the Sea Retreat House, **Stone Harbor,** NJ 08247. (609) 368-3621

Aldersgate Center, P.O. Box 122, **Swartswood,** NJ 07877. (973) 383-5978

Morning Star House of Prayer, 312 West Upper Ferry Rd., **Trenton,** NJ 08628. (609) 882-2766

Mount Eden Retreat, 56 Millpond Rd., P.O. Box 287, **Washington,** NJ 07882. March–October. (908) 689-8345

Tibetan Buddhist Learning Center, 93 Angen Rd., **Washington,** NJ 07882. Monthly seminars only on 2nd and 4th Sundays. (908) 689-6080

Mount St. Mary House of Prayer, 1651 US Hwy. 22, **Watchung,** NJ 07060. (908) 753-2091

New Mexico

Dominican Retreat House, 5825 Coors Rd., SW, **Albuquerque,** NM 87121. (505) 877-4211

Madonna Retreat Center, 4000 St. Joseph's Pl. NW, **Albuquerque,** NM 87120. (505) 831-8100

Tres Rios Christian Center, 1159 Black River Village Rd., **Carlsbad,** NM 88220. (505) 785-2361

The Mandala Center, P.O. Box 158, **Des Moines,** NM 88418. (505) 278-3002

Sacred Heart Retreat, P.O. Box 1989, **Gallup,** NM 87301. (505) 722-6755

Glorieta Baptist Conference Center, P.O. Box 8, **Glorieta,** NM 87535. (505) 757-6161

Bodhi Manda Zen Center, P.O. Box 8, **Jemez Springs,** NM 87025. (505) 829-3854

Rose Mountain Retreat Center, P.O. Box 355, **Las Vegas,** NM 87701. (505) 425-5728

Lord and Precious Retreat House, P.O. Box 627, **Magdalena,** NM 87825. (505) 854-2837

Holy Cross Retreat Center, P.O. Box 158, **Mesilla Park,** NM 88047. (505) 524-3688

Ocamora Foundation, P.O. Box 43, **Ocate,** NM 87734. (505) 666-2389

Takoja Retreats, 656 N. Star Rte., **Questa,** NM 87556. (505) 586-1086

Heart Seed Retreat Center, P.O. Box 6019, **Santa Fe,** NM 87502. (505) 471-7026

Immaculate Heart of Mary Conference Center, Mount Carmel Rd., **Santa Fe,** NM 87501. 3-month sabbaticals only for sisters and priests. (505) 983-3494

Plaza Resolana en Santa Fe, 401 Old Taos Hwy., **Santa Fe,** NM 87501. (505) 982-8539

Sangre de Cristo Center, Rte. 4, **Santa Fe,** NM 87501. (505) 983-7291

UpaYaH Conference Center, 935 Alto St., **Santa Fe,** NM 87501. Buddhist study and retreat center. (505) 982-5049

Mable Dodge Luhan B&B and Conference Center, P.O. Box 558, **Taos,** NM 87571. (505) 751-9686

Vallecitos Mountain Refuge, P.O. Box 1507, **Taos,** NM 87571. (505) 751-0351

New York

Abba House of Prayer, 647 Western Ave., **Albany,** NY 12203. (518) 438-8320

Ruach, 230 Davis Ave., **Albany,** NY 12208. 1 spring weekend a year of Jewish renewal. (518) 489-3983

Alfred University Conference Center, 26 N. Main St., **Alfred,** NY 14802. (607) 871-2183

Franciscan Ritiro, 115 E. Main St., **Allegany,** NY 14706. (716) 372-0195

Camp Pioneer (Lutheran), 9324 Lakeshore Rd., **Angola,** NY 14006. (716) 549-1420

Jesuit Retreat House, **Auriesville,** NY 12016. (518) 853-4496

Camp Ma-He-Tu, **Bear Mountain,** NY 10911 (914) 351-4508. Mailing address: 231 Madison Ave., **New York,** NY 10016. (212) 696-6771

Crystal Spring House, 49 Burnham Hollow Rd., **Big Indian,** NY 12410. (914) 254-5738

St. Ursula Center, Middle Rd., **Blue Point,** NY 11715. (631) 363-2422

Barry House, Rte. 8, **Brant Lake,** NY 12815. (518) 494-3314

St. Joseph's Convent, College Bldg., **Brentwood,** NY 11717. (631) 273-4531

Cursillos Center, 118 Congress St., **Brooklyn,** NY 11201. (718) 624-5670

Discovery Jewish Heritage Seminars, 1388 Coney Island Ave., **Brooklyn,** NY 11230. For retreats in New York and other states. (718) 377-8819

Neshama, 1049 E. 13th St., **Brooklyn,** NY 11230. Jewish retreat. (718) 338-8442

Karuna Tendai Dharma, Center & Bodhi Tree Inn, P.O. Box 323, **Canaan,** NY 12029. (518) 392-7963

Notre Dame Retreat House, P.O. Box 342, Foster Rd., **Canandaigua,** NY 14424. (716) 394-5700

Lily Dale Metaphysical Assembly, 5 Melrose Park, **Cassadaga,** NY 14752. (716) 595-8721

Thornfield Conference Center of the Episcopal Diocese of CNY, 4668 West Lake Rd., **Cazenovia,** NY 13035. (315) 655-3123

St. Mary's Mission Center, 28 Oak St., **Champlain,** NY 12919. (518) 298-3503

Bellinger Hall, Chautauqua Institution, **Chautauqua,** NY 14722. (716) 357-6250

The Priory, P.O. Box 336, **Chestertown,** NY 12817. (518) 494-3733

North Central New York Conference of the United Methodist Church, 8422 N. Main St., P.O. Box 1515, **Cicero,** NY 13039. (315) 699-8715

Frost Valley YMCA, 2000 Frost Valley Rd., **Claryville,** NY 12725. (845) 985-2291

Vanderkamp, Martin Road, **Cleveland,** NY 13042. (315) 675-3651

Anawim House of Prayer, 122 E. First St., **Corning,** NY 14830. (607) 936-4965

Pumpkin Hollow Farm, RR 1, P.O. Box 135, **Craryville,** NY 12521. (518) 325-3583

St. Columban Center, 6892 Lake Shore Rd., P.O. Box 816, **Derby,** NY 14047. (716) 947-4708

New York City Mission Society, 300 Dover Furnace Rd., **Dover Plains,** NY 12522. (845) 832-6151

Karuna Tendai Dharma Center, 1525 Rte. 295, **East Chatham,** NY 12060. (518) 392-7963

Dechen Chöling, Box 549, **East Meredith,** NY 13757. (607) 278-5144

Our Lady of the Adirondacks House of Prayer, 7270 Star Rd., Rte. 190, **Ellenburg Center,** NY 12934. (518) 594-3253

Monastery of Mary the Queen, 1310 W. Church St., **Elmira,** NY 14905. (607) 734-9506

Marist Brothers Retreat House, P.O. Box 197, **Esopus,** NY 12429. Group retreats for high school students. (845) 384-6620

Mount St. Alphonsus Retreat Center, Rte. 9W, **Esopus,** NY 12429. (845) 384-6550

Kanatsiohareke, 4934 State Hwy. 5, **Fonda,** NY 12068. Native American retreat center. (518) 673-5092. Mohawk B&B.

St. Francis Retreat House, Fonda Kateri Shrine, P.O. Box 627, **Fonda,** NY 12068. (518) 853-3646

Graymoor Spiritual Life Center, Rte. 9, **Garrison,** NY 10524. (845) 424-3300

Emmanuel Christian Church Retreat House, 31 Retreat House Rd., **Glenmont,** NY 12077. (518) 463-1296

Wellsprings, 93 Maple St., **Glens Falls,** NY 12801. (518) 792-3183

Orgyen Chö Dzong, Rte. 81, P.O. Box 570, **Greenville,** NY 12083. (518) 966-5149

St. Joseph's Retreat House, 81 Lynn Ave., **Hampton Bays,** NY 11946. (516) 731-5244. Evenings (groups).

Camp Epworth, 8 Epworth Ln., **High Falls,** NY 12440. (845) 687-0215

Bethany Retreat House, County Rd. 105, Box 1003, **Highland Mills,** NY 10930. (845) 928-2213

Presbyterian Center at Holmes, 183 Denton Lake Road, **Holmes,** NY 12531. (845) 878-6383

Wilbur Herrlich Retreat Center, P.O. Box 59, RFD, **Holmes,** NY 12531. (845) 878-6662. Mailing address: 585 Townline Rd., **Hauppauge,** NY 11787. (631) 265-1183

Holy Trinity Community, 7200 Tobes Hill Rd., **Hornell,** NY 14843. (607) 324-7624

Greenkill Conference Center, P.O. Box B, **Huguenot,** NY 12746. (845) 856-4382

Bishop Molloy Passionist Retreat House, 86–45 178th St., **Jamaica Estates,** NY 11432. (718) 739-1229

Cenacle Retreat House, Center for Spiritual Renewal, 310 Cenacle Rd., **Lake Ronkonkoma,** NY 11779. (631) 588-8366

Trinity Retreat, 1 Pryer Manor Rd., **Larchmont,** NY 10538. (914) 235-6839

Monastery of Bethlehem, Grooville Rd., **Livingston Manor,** NY 12758. (845) 439-4300

Beaver Camp, Star Rte., Box 221, **Lowville,** NY 13367. (315) 376-2640

Unirondack, Inc., Star Rte. 4, **Lowville,** NY 13367. (315) 376-6888. Mailing address: 220 South Winton Rd., **Rochester,** NY 14610. (716) 473-3301

St. Ignatius Retreat House, Searingtown Rd., **Manhasset,** NY 11030. (516) 621-8300

Ananda Ashram, RD 3, P.O. Box 141, **Monroe,** NY 10950. (845) 782-5575

Casowasco Conference Center, RD 4, Box 110, **Moravia,** NY 13118. (315) 364-8756

House of Holy Innocents, 771 Mount Sinai Corem Rd., **Mount Sinai,** NY 11766. (631) 331-1745

Little Portion Friary, P.O. Box 399, **Mount Sinai,** NY 11766. (631) 473-0553

Matagiri, 1218 Wittenberg Rd., **Mount Tremper,** NY 12457. (845) 679-8322

Our Lady of Hope Center, 434 River Rd., **Newburgh,** NY 12550. (845) 561-0685

St. Margaret's House, Jordan Rd., **New Hartford,** NY 13413. (315) 724-2324

Hadassah Jewish Education Dept., 50 W. 58th St., **New York,** NY 10019. For study retreats in New York and other states. (212) 303-8167

House of the Redeemer, 7 E. 95th St., **New York,** NY 10128. (212) 289-0399

JACS (Jewish Alcoholics and Chemically Dependent Persons and Significant Others), 426 W. 58th St., **New York,** NY 10019. (800) 398-2630, (845) 626-0157

The Jewish Retreat Center, 50 W. 17th St., 7th fl., **New York,** NY 10011. Finds retreat settings and helps plan. (212) 242-5985

The Leo House, 332 W. 23rd St., **New York,** NY 10011. (212) 929-1010

St. Hilda's House, 621 W. 113th St., **New York,** NY 10025. (212) 932-8098 ext. 305

St. Joseph's Cursillo Center, 523 W. 142nd St., **New York,** NY 10031. (212) 926-7433

Sivananda Yoga Vedanta Center, 243 W. 24th St., **New York,** NY 10011. (212) 255-4560

Union Theological Seminary, 3041 Broadway, **New York,** NY 10027. (212) 280-1313

Powell House, 524 Pitt Hall Rd., **Old Chatham,** NY 12136. (518) 794-8811

Crystal Spring House, **Oliverea,** NY. Mailing address: Susan Wadler, Star Rte., Box 198, **Phoenicia,** NY 12464. (845) 688-7211

Mariandale Retreat Center, 299 N. Highland Ave., **Ossining,** NY 10562. (914) 941-4455

Holy Myrrhbearers Monastery, 144 Bert Washburn Rd., **Otego,** NY 13825. (607) 432-3179

Watson Homestead Conference and Retreat Center, 9620 Dry Run Rd., **Painted Post,** NY 14870. (607) 962-0541, (800) 962-8040

G.R.O.W. II, 548 Cooley Rd., **Parksville,** NY 12768. (845) 295-0655

Holiday Hills Conference Center, 2 Lakeside Dr., **Pawling,** NY 12564. (845) 855-9535

St. Mary's Convent and Retreat House, John St., **Peekskill,** NY 10566. (914) 737-0113

Menla Mountain Retreat, P.O. Box 70 (375 Pantherkill Rd.), **Phoenicia,** NY 12464. Contact Tibet House (212) 807-0563

Phoenicia Pathwork Center, P.O. Box 66, **Phoenicia,** NY 12464. (845) 688-2211

Regina Maria Retreat House, 77 Brinkerhoff St., **Plattsburgh,** NY 12901. Groups only. (518) 561-3421

Linwood Spiritual Center, 139 South Mill Rd., **Rhinebeck,** NY 12572. (845) 876-4178

Cardinal Spellman Retreat House, 5801 Palisade Ave., **Riverdale,** NY 10471 (718) 549-6500

Mercy Prayer Center, 65 Highland Ave., **Rochester,** NY 14620. (716) 473-6893

Rochester Zen Center, 7 Arndo Park, **Rochester,** NY 14607. (716) 473-9180

Holy Family House of Prayer, 980 North Village Ave., **Rockville Centre,** NY 11570. (516) 766-2044

Yoga Asana Retreat Center (Dharma Mittra), **Roscoe,** NY. Mailing address: 297 Third Ave., New York, NY 10010. (212) 889-8160.

Wainwright House, 260 Stuyvesant Ave., **Rye,** NY 10580. (914) 967-6080

Arrowwood, Anderson Hill Rd., **Rye Brook,** NY 10573. (914) 939-5500

Maycroft, **Sag Harbor,** NY 11963. (631) 725-1181

Resurrection House, 20 River St., **Saranac Lake,** NY 12983. (518) 891-1182

Spiritearth, 43 Spaulding Ln., **Saugerties,** NY 12477. (845) 247-0816

Dominican Retreat House, 1945 Union St., **Schenectady,** NY 12309. (518) 393-4169

St. Gabriel's Retreat House, 64 Burns Rd., P.O. Box P, **Shelter Island,** NY 11965. (631) 749-0850

Silver Bay YMCA Christian Conference Center, **Silver Bay,** NY 12874. (518) 543-8833

Stella Maris Retreat Center, 130 East Genesee St., **Skaneateles,** NY 13152. (315) 685-6836

St. Mary's Villa, 50 Table Rock Rd., **Sloatsburg,** NY 10974. (845) 753-5100

SYDA Foundation, P.O. Box 600, **South Fallsburg,** NY 12779. (845) 434-2000

Jerusalem House of Prayer, Rte. 340, **Sparkill,** NY 10976. (845) 359-8671

Rune Hill, Box 416, **Spencer,** NY 14883. (607) 589-6392

Beaver Cross Camp, P.O. Box 218, **Springfield Center,** NY 13468. (607) 549-9489

Mount Manresa, 239 Fingerboard Rd., **Staten Island,** NY 10305. (718) 727-3844

Center of Renewal, 4421 Lower River Rd., **Stella Niagara,** NY 14144. (716) 754-7376

Vivekananda Retreat, P.O. Box 321, **Stone Ridge,** NY 12484. (845) 687-4574

Stony Point Center, Crickettown Rd., **Stony Point,** NY 10980. (845) 786-3734

Bethany House, 806 Court St., **Syracuse,** NY 13208. (315) 472-4638

Christ the King Retreat House, 500 Brookford Rd., **Syracuse,** NY 13224. (315) 446-2680

Convent of St. Helena, P.O. Box 426, **Vails Gate,** NY 12584. (845) 562-0592

St. Joseph Spiritual Life Center, RD 5, Box 113, **Valatie,** NY 12184. (518) 784-9481

Camp De Wolfe, Northside Rd., **Wading River,** NY 11792. (631) 929-4325. Mailing address: 36 Cathedral Ave., Garden City, NY 11530

St. Andrew's Retreat House, 257 St. Andrew's Rd., **Walden,** NY 12586. (845) 778-2102

Deer Hill Conference and Retreat Center, Wheeler Hill Rd., RD 1, **Wappingers Falls,** NY 12590. (845) 297-2323

Kagyu Thubten Chöling, 127 Sheafe Rd., **Wappingers Falls,** NY 12590. (845) 297-2500

Mount Alvernia Retreat House, P.O. Box 858, **Wappingers Falls,** NY 12590. (914) 297-5707

Skye Farm Camps, Schroon River Rd., **Warrensburg,** NY 12885. (518) 494-2137

Mount Alverno Center, 20 Grand St., **Warwick,** NY 10990. (845) 986-2267

Union of American Hebrew Congregations, Kutz Camp, P.O. Box 443, Bowen Rd., **Warwick,** NY 10990. (845) 987-6300

Warwick Conference Center, Inc., P.O. Box 349, **Warwick,** NY 10990. (845) 986-1164

Marian Shrine, Filors Ln., **West Haverstraw,** NY 10993. (845) 947-2200

Sivananda Ashram Yoga Ranch, P.O. Box 195, **Woodbourne,** NY 12788. (845) 434-9242

Karma Triyana Dharmachakra, 352 Meads Mountain Rd., **Woodstock,** NY 12498. (845) 679-5906

Wise Woman Center, P.O. Box 64, **Woodstock,** NY 12498. (845) 246-8081

Beaver Conference Farm, Underhill Ave., RD 3, **Yorktown Heights,** NY 10598. (914) 962-6033

Inn of the Spirit, Washington Lake Rd., **Yulan,** NY 12792. Groups only. (845) 557-8145

North Carolina

Lutheridge, P.O. Box 685, **Arden,** NC 28704. (828) 684-2361

Journey into Wholeness, P.O. Box 169, **Balsam Grove,** NC 28708. (828) 877-4809

YMCA Blue Ridge Assembly, 84 Blue Ridge Cir., **Black Mountain,** NC 28711. (828) 669-8422

The Summit, An Episcopal Center, 339 Conference Center Dr., P.O. Box 660, **Brown Summit,** NC 27214. (919) 342-6163

Catholic Conference Center, P.O. Box 36776, **Charlotte,** NC 28236. (828) 327-7441

Kanuga Conferences, Inc., P.O. Drawer 250, **Hendersonville,** NC 28793. (828) 692-9136

The Mountain, Highlands Camp and Conference Center, Inc., P.O. Box 1299, 841 Hwy. 106, **Highalnds,** NC 28741. (828) 526-5838

Jesuit House of Prayer, P.O. Box 7, **Hot Springs,** NC 28743. (828) 622-7366

Sunny Bank Retreat, Inn at Hot Springs, **Hot Springs,** NC 28743. (828) 622-7206

Living Waters, 1420 Soco Rd., **Maggie Valley,** NC 28751. (828) 926-3833

Montreat Conference Center/Mountain Retreat Association, P.O. Box 969, **Montreat,** NC 28757. (828) 669-2911

Trinity Center, P.O. Box 380, **Salter Path,** NC 28575. (919) 247-5600

The Snail's Pace, P.O. Box 593, **Saluda,** NC 28773. (828) 749-3851

Short Journey Youth/Adult Center, 2323 Cleveland Rd., **Smithfield,** NC 27577. (919) 934-7463

Valle Crucis Conference Center, P.O. Box 654, **Valle Crucis,** NC 28691. (828) 963-4453

North Dakota

Presentation Prayer Center, 1101 32nd Ave. S., **Fargo,** ND 58103. (701) 237-4857

Queen of Peace Retreat Center, 1310 N. Broadway, **Fargo,** ND 58102. (701) 293-9286

Koinonia Ecumenical Center, 2801 Olson Dr., **Grand Forks,** ND 58201. (701) 772-4607

Sacred Heart Monastery, P.O. Box 364, **Richardton,** ND 58652. (701) 974-2121

Ohio

Franciscan Renewal Center, 320 W. St., **Carey,** OH 43316. (419) 396-7635

Our Lady of Consolation Basilica & National Shrine, 315 Clay St., **Carey,** OH 43316. (419) 396-7107, (419) 396-3355

Convent of the Transfiguration, 495 Albion Ave., **Cincinnati,** OH 45246. (513) 771-5291

Friarhurst Retreat House, 8136 Wooster Pike, **Cincinnati,** OH 45227. (513) 561-2270

St. Francis Center for Peace & Renewal, 10290 Mill Rd., **Cincinnati,** OH 45231. (513) 825-9300

St. Andrew Svorad Abbey, 10510 Buckeye Rd., **Cleveland,** OH 44104. (216) 721-5300

St. Joseph Christian Life Center, 18485 Lake Shore Blvd., **Cleveland,** OH 44119. (216) 531-7370

Loyola of the Lake Jesuit Retreat House, 700 Killinger Rd., **Clinton,** OH 44216. (330) 896-2315

St. Mary of the Springs Conference Center, 2320 Airport Dr., **Columbus,** OH 43219. (614) 252-0380

St. Therese's Retreat Center, 5277 E. Broad St., **Columbus,** OH 43213. (614) 866-1611

Bergamo Center for Lifelong Learning, 4400 Shakertown Rd., **Dayton,** OH 45430. (937) 426-2363

Tri-State Yokefellow House, RR 2D, **Defiance,** OH 43512. (419) 428-2891

Community of the Transfiguration, 495 Albion Ave., **Glendale,** OH 45246. (513) 771-5338

Yankee Ingenuity Programs, 623 Grant St., **Kent,** OH 44240. (330) 673-1875

Grailville, 932 O'Bannonville Rd., **Loveland,** OH 45140. (513) 683-2340

Maria Stein Center, 2365 St. John's Rd., P.O. Box 95, **Maria Stein,** OH 45860. (419) 925-7625

Milford Spiritual Center, 5361 S. Milford Rd., **Milford,** OH 45150. (513) 248-3500

Spirituality Center/Sisters of Charity, 5900 Delhi Rd., **Mount St. Joseph,** OH 45051. (513) 347-5453

Woodland Altars, 33200 State Rte. 41, **Peebles,** OH 45660. (513) 588-4411

Ursulines of Brown County, 20900 State Rte. 251, **St. Martin,** OH 45118. (513) 875-2054

Trinity House of Prayer, 6832 Convent Blvd., **Sylvania,** OH 43560. (419) 882-4617

St. Joseph Renewal Center, 200 St. Francis Ave., **Tiffin,** OH 44883. (419) 443-1485

Queen of Heaven Monastery, 8640 Squires Ln. NE, **Warren,** OH 44484. (330) 856-1813

Yellow Springs Dharma Center, 502 Livermore St., **Yellow Springs,** OH 45387. (937) 767-9919

Oklahoma

Central Christian Camp and Conference Center, 1 Twin Cedar Ln., **Guthrie,** OK 73044. (405) 282-2811, (800) 299-2811

Red Plains Monastery, 728 Richland Rd. SW. **Piedmont,** OK 73078. (405) 373-4565

St. Gregory's Abbey, 1900 W. MacArthur Dr., **Shawnee,** OK 74801. (405) 878-5490

Oregon

Monastery of Our Lady of Consolation, 23300 Walker Ln., **Amity,** OR 97101. (503) 835-8080

Our Lady of Peace Retreat, 3600 SW 170th Ave., **Beaverton,** OR 97006. (503) 649-7127

Cerro Gordo, P.O. Box 569, **Cottage Grove,** OR 97424. (541) 942-7720

Chagdud Gonpa, 198 N. River Rd., **Cottage Grove,** OR 97424. (541) 942-8619

Alton L. Collins Retreat Center, 32867 SE Hwy. 211, **Eagle Creek,** OR 97022. (503) 637-6411

Shalom Prayer Center, Queen of Angels Monastery, 840 S. Main St., **Mount Angel,** OR 97362. (503) 845-6773

Nestucca Sanctuary, **Pacific City,** OR 97135

Franciscan Renewal Center, 0858 SW Palatine Hill Rd., **Portland,** OR 97219. (503) 287-3774

Loyola Retreat House, 3220 SE 43rd Ave., **Portland,** OR 97206. (503) 777-2225

Harbor Villa Retreat Center (a ministry of Twin Rocks Friends Camp and Conference Center), P.O. Box 6, **Rockaway Beach,** OR 97136. (503) 355-2284

Taucross Farm, 41211 Oupor Rd., **Scio,** OR 97374. (503) 394-3901

Christian Renewal Center, 22444 N. Fork Rd. SE, **Silverton,** OR 97381. (503) 873-6743

Aesculapia Wilderness Retreat, P.O. Box 301, **Wilderville,** OR 97543. (541) 476-0492

Namasté Retreat Center, 29500 SW Grahams Ferry Rd., **Wilsonville,** OR 97070. (800) 893-1000

Oregon House, 94288 Highway 101, **Yachats,** OR 97498. (541) 547-3329

Pennsylvania

Community of Celebration, P.O. Box 309, **Aliquippa,** PA 15001. (724) 375-1510

Kirkridge Retreat and Study Center, 2495 Fox Gap Rd., **Bangor,** PA 18013. (610) 588-1793

Greene Hills Methodist Camp, Box 3, **Barree,** PA 16611. (570) 669-4212. Mailing address: 900 South Arlington Ave., Room 112, **Harrisburg,** PA 17109

St. Mary's House of Greater Solitude, Rte. 1, P.O. Box 276, **Bedford,** PA 15522. (814) 623-1796

Bethel Holy Ghost Animation Center, 6230 Brush Run Rd., **Bethel Park,** PA 15102. (412) 835-3510

St. Francis Center for Renewal, 395 Bridle Path Rd., **Bethlehem,** PA 18017. (610) 866-5030

Glendorn Executive Retreat and Conference Center, 1032 W. Corydon St., **Bradford,** PA 16701. (814) 362-6511

Transfiguration House, 295 W. Jefferson Rd., **Butler,** PA 16001. (724) 352-1354

Trinity Spiritual Center, 3609 Simpson Ferry Road, **Camp Hill,** PA 17011. (717) 761-7355

Spruce Lake Retreat, RD 1, P.O. Box 605, **Canadensis,** PA 18325. (570) 595-7505

St. Gabriel's Retreat House, 631 Griffim Pond Rd., **Clarks Summit,** PA 18411. (570) 586-4957

Precious Blood Spirituality Center, St. Joseph Convent, **Columbia,** PA 17512. (717) 285-4536

Our Lady of the Sacred Heart Convent, 1500 Woodcrest Ave., **Coraopolis,** PA 15108. (412) 264-5140

Mercy Consultation Center, Box 370, Lake St., **Dallas,** PA 18612. (570) 675-2131

Fatima Renewal Center, 1000 Seminary Rd., **Dalton,** PA 18414. (570) 563-8500

Regina Mundi Priory, Waterloo and Fairfield rds., **Devon,** PA 19333. (610) 688-5130

St. Francis Friary Retreat House, 3918 Chipman Rd., **Easton,** PA 18042. (610) 258-3053

Sisters of St. Ann, Mount St. Ann Retreat House, P.O. Box 328, **Ebensburg,** PA 15931. (814) 472-9354

Dominican Retreat House, 750 Ashbourne Rd., **Elkins Park,** PA 19117. (215) 782-8520, (215) 224-0945

Orthodox Monastery of the Transfiguration, RD 1, P.O. Box 184X, **Ellwood City,** PA 16117. (724) 758-4002

Mount St. Benedict Monastery, 6101 East Lake Rd., **Erie,** PA 16511. (814) 899-0614

Deer Valley YMCA, RD 1, Box 180, **Fort Hill,** PA 15540. (814) 662-4005

Cardinal Wright Vocation and Prayer Center, Babcock Blvd., P.O. Box 252, RD 4, **Gibsonia,** PA 15044. (412) 961-6884

Ecclesia Center, 9109 Ridge Rd., **Girard,** PA 16417. (814) 774-9691

Deaconess Community Center, 801 Merion Square Rd., **Gladwyne,** PA 19035. (610) 642-8838

St. Emma Retreat House, 1001 Harvey Ave., **Greensburg,** PA 15601. (724) 834-3060

Agape Ministries Bible Camp, RD 1, P.O. Box 64, **Hickory,** PA 15340. (315) 356-2268

The Himalayan Institute, RR 1, P.O. Box 400, **Honesdale,** PA 13431. (315) 253-5551

Sequanota Lutheran Conference Center, P.O. Box 245, **Jennerstown,** PA 15547. (814) 629-6627

St. Vincent Summer Retreat House, 300 Fraser Purchase Rd., **Latrobe,** PA 15650 (412) 539-9761

Mount Assisi Monastery, St. Francis Laymen's Retreat League, P.O. Box 38, **Loretto,** PA 15940. (814) 472-5324

Olmsted Manor Adult Retreat Renewal Center, P.O. Box 8, **Ludlow,** PA 16333. (814) 945-6512

St. Joseph's-in-the-Hills Retreat House, 315 S. Warren Ave., **Malvern,** PA 19355. (610) 644-0400

Bethany House of Prayer, 515 Montgomery Ave., **Merion Station,** PA 19066. (610) 667-3066

Laurelville Mennonite Church Center, Rte. 5, P.O. Box 145, **Mount Pleasant,** PA 15666. (412) 423-2056

Villa of Our Lady Retreat House, HCR 1, P.O. Box 41, **Mount Pocono,** PA 18344. (370) 839-7217

Kirby Episcopal House, 381 Sunset Rd., **Mountaintop,** PA 18707. (570) 474-5800

White Cloud, RR 1, Box 215, **Newfoundland,** PA 18445. (717) 676-3162

Mount Asbury Methodist Center, 1310 Centerville Rd., **Newville,** PA 17241. (717) 486-3827. Mailing address: 900 South Arlington Ave., Room 112, Harrisburg, PA 47109

St. Barnabas House Retreat and Conference Center, 12430 East Lake, **North East,** PA 16428. (814) 725-4850

Fatima House, Rolling Hills Rd., **Ottsville,** PA 18942. (610) 795-2947

National Havurah Committee, 7318 Germantown Ave., **Philadelphia,** PA 19119. Holds Jewish summer institute and regional retreats. (215) 248-9760

Peace Hermitage, Medical Mission Sisters, 8400 Pine Rd., **Philadelphia,** PA 19111. (610) 342-0961

St. Anna's Convent, 2016 Race St., **Philadelphia,** PA 19103. (215) 567-2943

St. Margaret's House, 5419 Germantown Ave., **Philadelphia,** PA 19144. (215) 844-9410

Carlow College Campus Ministry, 3333 Fifth Ave., **Pittsburgh,** PA 15213. (412) 578-6065

St. Paul of the Cross Retreat Center, 148 Monastery Ave., **Pittsburgh,** PA 15203. (412) 381-7676

Fellowship Farm, 2488 Sanatoga Rd., **Pottstown,** PA 19464. (610) 326-3008

Black Rock Retreat, 1345 Kirkwood Pike, **Quarryville,** PA 17566. (610) 786-1266

Maria Wald Retreat House, c/o Missionary Sisters of the Precious Blood, P.O. Box 97, **Reading,** PA 19607. (610) 777-1624

Cornelia Connelly Center, 1359 Montgomery Ave., **Rosemont,** PA 19333. (610) 527-2428

Holy Shankaracharya Center, RD 8, Box 8116, **Stroudsburg,** PA 18360. (570) 629-0481

Camp Penn, P.O. Box 511, **Waynesboro,** PA 17268. (717) 762-2693. Mailing address: Commission on Outdoor Christian Education and Retreats, Council Office, 900 S. Arlington Ave., Rm. 112, Harrisburg, PA 17109

Wesley Forest Methodist Camp, **Weikert,** PA 17885. (717) 922-1348. Mailing address: Commission on Outdoor Christian Education and Retreats, Council Office, 900 S. Arlington Ave., Rm. 112, Harrisburg, PA 17109

Jesuit Center for Spiritual Growth, 501 N. Church Rd., **Wernersville,** PA 19565. (610) 670-3640

Temenos at Broad Run, 685 Broad Run Rd., **West Chester,** PA 19382. (610) 696-8145

Rhode Island
Mercy Lodge, P.O. Box 7651, **Cumberland,** RI 02864. (401) 333-2801

Our Lady of Peace Spiritual Life Center, Box 507, Ocean Rd., **Narragansett,** RI 02882. (401) 783-2871, (401) 884-7676

Nazareth Center, 12 Cliff Terrace, **Newport,** RI 02840. (401) 847-1654

St. Dominic Savio Youth Center, 211A Broadrock Rd., **Peacedale,** RI 02883. (401) 783-4055

Father Marot CYO Center, 53 Federal St., **Woonsocket,** RI 02895. (401) 762-3252

South Carolina
Rose Hill, P.O. Box 3126, **Aiken,** SC 29802. (803) 641-1614

Center of Spirituality, 424 Fort Johnson Rd., Box 12410, **Charleston,** SC 29412. (803) 795-6851

Clemson University Outdoor Laboratory, PRTM Dept., 263 Lehotsky Hall,
Clemson Univ., **Clemson,** SC 29634. (864) 646-7502

Sea of Peace House of Prayer, 59 Palmetto Pointe, **Edisto Island,** SC 29438.
(843) 869-0513

Emmanuel House, Monastery of St. Clare, 1916 N. Pleasantburg Dr.,
Greenville, SC 29609. For women and priests. (864) 244-4514

Meher Center, 10200 Hwy. 17N, **Myrtle Beach,** SC 29572. (843) 272-5777

The Oratory Center for Spirituality, P.O. Box 11586, **Rock Hill,** SC 29731.
(803) 327-2097

South Dakota

Blue Cloud Abbey Retreat Center, P.O. Box 98, **Marvin,** SD 57251. (605) 432-
5528

Benedictine Monastery of St. Martin, 2110C St. Martin's Drive, **Rapid City,**
SD 57702. (605) 343-8011

Manna Retreat Center, 27213 473rd Ave., **Sioux Falls,** SD 57106. (605) 743-2228

Mother of God Monastery, **Watertown,** SD 57201. (605) 886-6799

Sacred Heart Monastery, 1005 W. 8th St., **Yankton,** SD 57078. (605) 668-1011

Tennessee

Penuel Ridge Retreat Center, 1440 Sam's Creek Rd., **Ashland City,** TN
37015. (615) 792-3734

House of the Lord, 1306 Dellwood, **Memphis,** TN 38127. (901) 357-7398

Iona House Retreat Center, 4577 Billy Maher Rd., **Memphis,** TN 38135.
(901) 377-9284

Stritch Conference Center, 2455 Avery Ave., **Memphis,** TN 38112. (901) 722-
0243

Dubose Conference Center, P.O. Box 339, **Monteagle,** TN 37356. (615) 924-
2353

Nashville Zen Group, c/o Steven Warren, 3925 Estes Rd., **Nashville,** TN
37215. (615) 298-3754

Scarritt-Bennett Center, 1008 19th Ave. S., **Nashville,** TN 37212 (615) 340-
7500

United Methodist Church, P.O. Box 840, **Nashville,** TN 37202. (615) 340-
7177

The Farm, 34, The Farm, **Summertown,** TN 38483. (931) 964-3574

Texas

Bishop Defalco Retreat Center, 2100 N. Spring, **Amarillo,** TX 79107. (806)
383-1811

Bishop Quartermain Conference Center, 232 E. Cottonwood, **Amarillo,** TX
79108. (806) 383-6878

Holy Family Retreat Center, 9920 N. Major Dr., **Beaumont,** TX 77713. (409) 899-5617

Cedarbrake Renewal Center, P.O. Box 58, **Belton,** TX 76513. (254) 780-2436

Christ of the Hills Monastery, New Sarov, **Blanco,** TX 78606. (830) 833-5363

Convent of Holy Pasha and Blessed Pelagia, Russian Orthodox Nuns, Rte. 103, New Sarov, **Blanco,** TX 78606. (830) 833-5860

Guadalupe River Ranch, P.O. Box 877, **Boerne,** TX 78006. (830) 537-4837

Omega Retreat Center, 216 W. Highland, **Boerne,** TX 78006. (830) 249-3894

Texas 4-H Center, RR 1, Box 527, **Brownwood,** TX 76801. (915) 784-5482

Moye Renewal Center, 600 London St., **Castroville,** TX 78009. (830) 931-2227

Bishop Thomas J. Drury Retreat House, 1200 Lantana, **Corpus Christi,** TX 78407. (512) 289-6501

Mount Tabor Retreat House, 12940 Up River Rd., **Corpus Christi,** TX 78410. (512) 241-1955

Mount Carmel Center, 4600 W. Davis St., **Dallas,** TX 75211. (214) 331-6224

Christian Renewal Center, 1515 Hughes Rd., Box 635, **Dickinson,** TX 77539. (281) 337-1312

Bishop Mason Retreat & Conference Center, 4700 Wichita Trail, **Flower Mound,** TX 75028. (972) 539-9715

Catholic Renewal Center of North Texas, 4503 Bridge St., **Fort Worth,** TX 76103. (817) 429-2920

Glen Lake United Methodist Camp & Retreat Center, P.O. Box 928, **Glen Rose,** TX 76043. (251) 897-2247

Cenacle Retreat House, 420 N. Kirkwood, **Houston,** TX 77079. (713) 497-3131

Holy Name Retreat Center, 430 Bunker Hill Rd., **Houston,** TX 77024. (713) 464-0211

Monastery of the Four Evangelists, 3011 Roe Dr., **Houston,** TX 77087. (713) 645-0843

Mount Carmel House of Prayer, 9600 Deer Trail Dr., **Houston,** TX 77038. (713) 445-8830

Presbyterian Mo-Ranch Assembly, HCI Box 158, **Hunt,** TX 78024. (830) 238-4455

Laity Lodge, P.O. Box 670, **Kerrville,** TX 78029. (830) 896-2505

Mount Wesley Conference Center, 610 Methodist Encampment Rd., **Kerrville,** TX 78028. (830) 895-5700

Holy Spirit Retreat Center, 501 Century Dr. S., **Laredo,** TX 78046. (956) 726-4352

Camp Allen Camps and Conference Center, Rte. 1, Box 426, **Navasota,** TX 77868. (936) 825-7175

First United Methodist Church, 422 S. Magnolia, **Palestine,** TX 75801

Christ the King Retreat Center, 802 Ford St., **San Angelo,** TX 76905. (915) 685-3900

Oblate Renewal Center, 285 Oblate Renewal Center, **San Antonio,** TX 78216. (210) 349-4173

Benedictine Retreat Center, Corpus Christi Abbey, HCR 2, Box 6300, **Sandia,** TX 78383. (210) 547-3257

Whispering Pines, 114 Pine Grove Rd., **Scroggins,** TX 75280. (903) 860-3326

Our Lady of Mercy Catholic Center, 1225 W. Division St., P.O. Box 744, **Slaton,** TX 79364. (806) 828-6428

Spiritual Renewal Center, Rte. 3, Box 238, **Victoria,** TX 77901. (512) 572-0836

Utah

Last Resort, P.O. Box 707, **Cedar City,** UT 84721. (435) 682-2289

Desert Light, 2775 Nuevo, **Moab,** UT 84532. (801) 259-6056

Mount Benedict Priory, 5462 S. 200 E., **Ogden,** UT 84405. (801) 479-8107

Our Lady of the Mountain, 1794 Lake St., **Ogden,** UT 84401. (801) 392-9231

Kanzeon Zen Center Utah, 1274 E. South Temple, **Salt Lake City,** UT 84102. (801) 328-8414

Vermont

Charterhouse of the Transfiguration, RD 2, Box 2411, **Arlington,** VT 05250. (802) 362-1115

Milarepa Center, Barnet Mountain, **Barnet,** VT 05821. (802) 633-4136

Bishop Booth Conference Center, 20 Rock Point Cir., **Burlington,** VT 05401. (802) 658-6233

Mount St. Mary Convent, 100 Mansfield Ave., **Burlington,** VT 05401. (802) 863-6835

Mandala Buddhist Center, Quaker St., **Lincoln,** VT 05467. (802) 453-5038

Self-Realization Fellowship, Rte. 1, Box 519, **Shaftesbury,** VT 05257. (802) 442-4311

Monastery of the Immaculate Heart of Mary, HCR 13, Box 11, **Westfield,** VT 05874. (802) 744-6525. Women only.

Maple Forest Monastery, P.O. Box 60, **Woodstock,** VT 05091. (802) 457-2255

Virginia

Virginia United Methodist Assembly Center, 707 4th St., **Blackstone,** VA 23824. (804) 292-5308

St. Benedict Monastery, 9535 Linton Hall Rd., **Bristow,** VA 20136. (703) 361-0106

Phoebe Needles Retreat Center, Rte. 1, Box 440, **Callaway,** VA 24067. (540) 483-3381

Openway, RR 10, Box 205, **Charlottesville,** VA 22903. (804) 293-3245

Mountain Light Retreat Center, Rte. 2, Box 419, **Crozet,** VA 22932. (804) 978-7770

Our Lady of the Angels Monastery, Rte. 2, Box 288A, **Crozet,** VA 22932. (804) 823-1452

Blue Ridge Zen Group, 4460 Advance Mills Rd., **Earlysville,** VA 22936. (804) 793-5435

Nazareth House of Prayer, Rte. 2, Box 277, **Gate City,** VA 24251. (540) 386-7428

Eagle Eyrie Baptist Conference Center, Rte. 4, Box 213, **Lynchburg,** VA 24503. (804) 384-2211

Seven Oaks Pathwork Center, Rte. 1, Box 86, **Madison,** VA 22727. (540) 948-6544

Highroad Camp and Retreat Center, 21164 Steptoe Hill Rd., **Middleburg,** VA 22117. (540) 689-1215

Shrine Mont, General Delivery, **Orkney Springs,** VA 22845. (540) 856-2141

Mary Mother of the Church Abbey, 12617 River Rd., **Richmond,** VA 23233. (757) 784-3508

The Well Retreat Center, 18047 Quiet Way, **Smithfield,** VA 23430. (757) 255-2366

Chanco Camp and Conference Center, 394 Floods Dr., P.O. Box 378, **Surry,** VA 23883. (757) 294-3126

Association for Research and Enlightenment, 67th St. and Atlantic Ave., P.O. Box 595, **Virginia Beach,** VA 23451. (757) 428-3588

Washington and British Columbia

Washington

Encouragement Lodge, 28709 115th Ave. NE, **Arlington,** WA 98223. (360) 403-0335

Washington Buddhavanaram, 4401 S. 360th St., **Auburn,** WA 98001. (253) 927-5408

Christ Lutheran Retreat Center, NE 3701 N. Shore Rd., **Belfair,** WA 98528. (360) 275-5403

St. Thomas Center, 14500 Juanita Dr. NE, **Bothell,** WA 98011. (425) 823-1300

Camp Don Bosco, 1401 327th Ave. NE, **Carnation,** WA 98014. (425) 382-4562

Bethlehem Farm, 508 Coal Creek Rd., **Chehalis,** WA 98532. (360) 748-1236

St. Peter the Apostle Retreat Center, 15880 Summit View Rd., **Cowiche,** WA 98923. (509) 678-4935

Soli-time Retreats, 3531 108th St. SE, **Everett,** WA 98208

Huston Camp and Conference Center, P.O. Box 140, **Gold Bar,** WA 98251. (360) 793-0441

Loma Center for Renewal, 3607 228th Ave. SE, **Issaquah,** WA 98027. (425) 392-1871

Lutheran Bible Institute Conference Center, 4221 228th Ave., **Issaquah,** WA 98027. (425) 392-0400

Priory Spirituality Center, 500 College St. NE, **Lacey,** WA 98516. (360) 438-2595

Meditative Retreat Cottage, Whidbey Island, P.O. Box 624, **Langley,** WA 98260. (360) 730-9488

Camp Field Retreat Center, P.O. Box 128, **Leavenworth,** WA 98826. (509) 548-7933

Camp Brotherhood, 2301 Legge Rd., **Mount Vernon,** WA 98273. (360) 445-5061

Rainbow Lodge, P.O. Box 963, **North Bend,** WA 98045. (425) 888-4181

Doe Bay Village Resort, Star Rte. 86, **Olga,** WA 98279. (360) 376-2291

Northwest Vipassana Association, 3022 Simmons Rd. NW, **Olympia,** WA 98502. (360) 866-8176

Pilgrim Firs Conference Center, 3318 SW Lake Flora Rd., **Port Orchard,** WA 98366. (360) 876-2031

Seabeck Christian Conference Center, P.O. Box 117, **Seabeck,** WA 98380. (360) 830-5010

Camp Don Bosco, 910 Manson St., **Seattle,** WA 98104. (206) 382-4562

Our Lady of the Rock Priory, OSB, P.O. Box 425, **Shaw Island,** WA 98286. (360) 468-2321. Limited facilities.

Immaculate Heart Retreat House, South 6910 Ben Burr Rd., **Spokane,** WA 99223. (509) 448-1224

Padma Amrita, West 1014 7th Ave., **Spokane,** WA 99204. (509) 747-1559

St. Mary's Conference and Retreat Center, 107 Spencer Rd., **Toledo,** WA 98591. (360) 864-6464

Harmony Hill, East 7362 Hwy. 106, **Union,** WA 98592 (360) 898-2363

St. Andrew's House, 87550 Hwy. 106, **Union,** WA 98592. (360) 898-2362

Burton Camp and Conference Center, 9326 SW Bayview Dr., **Vashon Island,** WA 98070. (206) 622-3935

British Columbia

Kagyu Kunkhyab Chuling, 4939 Sidley St., **Burnaby,** BC V5J 1T6, Canada. (604) 434-4920

Prince of Peace Priory, 2904 Josephine St., Box 960, **Chemainus,** BC V0R 1K0, Canada. (250) 246-9578

Hollyhock, Box 127, Manson's Landing, **Cortes Island,** BC V0P 1K0, Canada. (250) 935-6465

Fairburn Farm, 3310 Jackson Rd., RR 7, **Duncan,** BC V9L 4W4, Canada. (250) 746-4637

Mount St. Nicholas Priory, 4655 Westside Rd., **Kamloops,** BC V2C 1Z3, Canada. (250) 579-9150

Seton House of Prayer, RR 4 Site 20 Box 9, **Kelowna,** BC V1Y 7R3, Canada. (250) 764-4333

Yasodhara Ashram, P.O. Box 9A, **Kootenay Bay,** BC V0B 1X0, Canada. (250) 227-9224

Westminster Abbey, 34224 Dewdney Trunk Rd., **Mission,** BC V2V 4J2, Canada. (604) 826-8975

Anawim House of Prayer, Bealby Point, **Nelson,** BC V1L 1T4, Canada. (250) 352-2930

The Salt Spring Centre, 355 Blackburn Rd., **Salt Spring Island.** Mailing address: Box 1133, Ganges, BC V0S 1E0, Canada. (250) 537-2326

Sorrento Centre, Box 99, **Sorrento,** BC V0E 2W0, Canada. (250) 675-2421

Queenswood, 2494 Arbutus Rd., **Victoria,** BC V8N 1V8, Canada. (250) 477-3822

West Virginia

John XXIII Pastoral Center, 100 Hodges Rd., **Charleston,** WV 25314. (304) 342-0507

The Claymont Soc., Rte. 1, Box 279, **Charlestown,** WV 25414. (304) 725-4437

Priestfield, Box 133, Rte. 51, **Kearneysville,** WV 25430. (304) 725-1435

Good Counsel Friary, Rte. 7, Box 183, **Morgantown,** WV 26505. (304) 594-1714

Lightstone Foundation, HC 63, Box 73, **Moyers,** WV 26813. (304) 249-5271

Peterkin Conference Center, P.O. Box 853, **Romney,** WV 26757. (304) 822-4519

Jackson's Mill State 4-H Conference Center, P.O. Box 670, **Weston,** WV 26452. (304) 269-5100

Mount St. Joseph, Pogue Run Rd., **Wheeling,** WV 26003. (304) 232-8160

Wisconsin

Monte Alverno Retreat Center, 1000 N. Ballard Rd., **Appleton,** WI 54911. (920) 733-8526

St. Joseph Retreat Center, 3035 O'Brien Rd., **Baileys Harbor,** WI 54202. (920) 839-2391

St. Isaac of Syria Russian Orthodox Skete, Rte. 1, Box 168, **Boscobel,** WI 53805. (608) 375-5500; 1-800-81-ICONS for icon orders.

Byron Center, Rte. 1, Box 78, **Brownsville,** WI 53006. (920) 583-3633

St. Francis Retreat Center, 503 S. Browns Lake Dr., **Burlington,** WI 53105. (262) 763-3600

The Convent House, Rte. 1, Box 161, **Cashton,** WI 54619. (608) 823-7992, (608) 823-7906

St. Clare Center for Spirituality, 7381 Church St. (Polonia), **Custer,** WI 54423. (715) 592-4680

House in the Wood, 3300-1 Bay Rd., **Delavan,** WI 53115. (262) 728-2752

The Bridge Between Retreat Center, 4471 Flaherty Dr., **Denmark,** WI 54208. (920) 864-7230

Ministry and Life Center, St. Norbert Abbey, 1016 N. Broadway, **DePere,** WI 54115. (920) 337-4315

St. Bede Retreat & Conference Center, 1190 Priory Rd., P.O. Box 66, **Eau Claire,** WI 54702. (715) 834-3176

St. Vincent Pallotti Center, N6409 Bowers Rd., **Elkhorn,** WI 54121. (715) 723-2108

The Clearing, P.O. Box 65, **Ellison,** WI 54210. May–Oct. (920) 854-4033

Convent of the Holy Nativity, 101 E. Division St., **Fond du Lac,** WI 54935. (920) 921-2560

Marynook Conference and Retreat Center, 500 S. 12th St., Box 9, **Galesville,** WI 54630. (608) 582-2789, (608) 526-9550

Holy Name Retreat House, P.O. Box 23825, 1825 Riverside Dr., **Green Bay,** WI 54305. (920) 437-7531 (Green Bay), (920) 735-1112 (Fox Valley)

Green Lake Conference Center, American Baptist Assembly, W. 2511 State Hwy. 23, **Green Lake,** WI 54941. (920) 294-3323

Holy Hill National Shrine of Mary, 1525 Carmel Rd., **Hubertus,** WI 53033. (262) 628-1838

Dillman's Sand Lake Lodge, Box 98, **Lac du Flambeau,** WI 54532. (800) 359-2511, (715) 588-3143

Geneva Bay Centre (Covenant Harbor), 1724 Main St., **Lake Geneva,** WI 53147. (262) 248-3600

St. Benedict Center, P.O. Box 5070, **Madison,** WI 53705. (608) 836-1631

St. Anthony Retreat Center, 300 E. 4th St., **Marathon,** WI 54448. (715) 443-2236

LaSalle Spiritual Formation Center, 522 Second St., **Menasha,** WI 54952. (920) 722-8918

Sisters/St. Benedict, 4200 County Hwy. M, **Middleton,** WI 53562. (608) 836-1631

Archdiocesan Retreat Center, 3501 S. Lake Dr., **Milwaukee,** WI 53207. (414) 769-3491

Cardoner Retreat Center, 1501 S. Layton Blvd., **Milwaukee,** WI 53215. (414) 384-2120, 384-3491

Lucerne Camp and Retreat Center, Rte. 1, Box 3150, **Neshkoro,** WI 54960. (920) 293-4488

Perpetual Help Retreat Center, 1800 N. Timber Trail Ln., **Oconomowoc,** WI 53066. (262) 567-6900

Jesuit Retreat House, 4800 Fahrnwald Rd., **Oshkosh,** WI 54901. (920) 231-9060

The Tyme Out Youth Center, N45 W25338 Lindsay Rd., **Pewaukee,** WI 53072. (262) 691-5780

Silver Springs, N4683 Silver Springs Ln., **Plymouth,** WI 53073. (920) 893-0969

Hunt Hill Audubon Sanctuary, Rte. 1, Box 285, Audubon Rd., **Sarona,** WI 54870. (715) 635-6543

Dominican Education Center, **Sinsinawa,** WI 53824. (608) 748-4411

Schoenstatt Center, W. 284 N. 698 Cherry Ln., **Waukesha,** WI 53188. (262) 547-7733

Camp Webb, Rte. 2, Box 705, **Wautoma,** WI 54982. (414) 787-3812, (920) 259-9322

Cedar Valley Retreat Center, 5349 Hwy. D, **West Bend,** WI 53095. (262) 334-9487

Christine Center for Unitive Planetary Spirituality, West 8291 Mann Rd., **Willard,** WI 54493. (715) 267-7507

George Williams College/Lake Geneva Campus, P.O. Box 210, **Williams Bay,** WI 53191. (262) 245-5531

Wyoming

Alta Retreat Center, P.O. Box 407, **Alta,** WY 83422. (307) 353-8100

Wyoming Catholic Lay Ministry Retreat, 623 S. Wolcott, **Casper,** WY 82601. (307) 237-2723

Thomas the Apostle Center, 45 Rd. 3CXS, **Cody,** WY 82414. (307) 587-4400

San Benito Monastery, P.O. Box 520, **Dayton,** WY 82836. (307) 655-9013

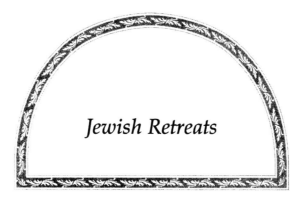

Jewish Retreats

A recent flyer from the New York Open Center speaks of the flowering of a Jewish renewal movement: "Many who had left the tradition seeking spiritual shelter elsewhere are returning, bringing new practices and a renewed passion. Jewish Renewal has, at its core, the idea of *tikkun*, which means to heal, repair, and transform. The twin concerns—*tikkun nefesh*, to heal the spirit, and *tikkun olam*, to heal the universe—challenge and support us as we work for both inner and outer, personal and social change."

Although retreats in the formal sense have not been a part of the overall Jewish tradition, this list is included as a reference to help those looking for Jewish rest and renewal in various forms and a variety of places. Not all of them offer accommodation but each provides a real opportunity for further exploration.

ALEPH: Alliance for Jewish Renewal, 7318 Germantown Ave., Philadelphia, PA 19119. (215) 247-9700. ALEPH is headquarters for a number of interesting organizations, including P'nai Or/The Shalom Center where Rabbi Zalman Schachter-Shalomi is active. ALEPH holds a biannual "Kallah," a gathering of the Jewish Renewal Movement, (970) 221-0327.

The Bibliodrama Training Institute with Peter Pitzele, 441 W. Carpenter Ln., Philadelphia, PA 19119. (215) 438-6108. Rivkah Walton, director.

Brandeis Bardin Institute, A Jewish Educational Camp, 1101 Peppertree Ln., Brandeis, CA 93064. (805) 582-4450

Camp Isabella Freedman, 116 Johnson Rd., Falls Village, CT 06031. (860) 824-5991. Summer camp owned by United Jewish Appeal Federation for seniors.

Conference on Judaism in Rural New England, P.O. Box 659, Montpelier, VT 05601. (802) 223-2962

Congregation B'nai Jeshurun, 270 W. 89th St., New York, NY 10024. (212) 787-7600. Led by Rabbi Rolando Matalon, this is a very active and dynamic congregation.

Elat Chayyim, A Center for Healing and Renewal, 99 Mill Hook Rd., Accord, NY 12404. (800) 398-2630, (914) 626-0157. A full program of adult and children's retreats (see page 166 for more details).

Hadassah, Jewish Education Dept., 50 W. 58th St., New York, NY 10019. (212) 303-8167. *Kallot* (study weekends) for members of Hadassah.

Hebrew Union College, the Center for Liberal Jewish Study, 1 W. 4th St., New York, NY 10012. (212) 674-5300. Rabbi Joshua Salzman.

Henry S. Jacobs Camp, P.O. Drawer C, Utica, MS 39175. (601) 362-6357

JACS (Jewish Alcoholics and Chemically Dependent Persons and Significant Others), 426 W. 58th St., New York, NY 10019. (800) 398-2630, (845) 626-0157

Jewish Renewal Life Center, 7318 Germantown Ave., Philadelphia, PA 19119. (215) 843-4345. Rabbi Julie Greenberg, director.

The Jewish Retreat Center, 50 W. 17th St., 7th fl., New York, NY 10011. (212) 242-5985. Finds settings for retreats and will help with planning. Rachel Brodie, founder and director.

The Jewish Theological Seminary of America, 3080 Broadway, New York, NY 10027. (212) 678-8000. Rabbi Steven Shaw is a good contact for information on activities there.

Living Waters, 11450 S.W. 16th St., Davie, FL 33325. (954) 476-7466. A spiritual health spa based on kabbalistic teachings.

Metivta, a Center for Jewish Wisdom, 2001 South Barrington Ave., #106, Los Angeles, CA 90025. (310) 477-5370. Holds a yearly conference/ retreat. Rabbi Jonathan Omer-Man.

Mount Eden Retreat, 56 Millpond Rd., P.O. Box 287, Washington, NJ 07882. (908) 689-8345. March–October. Healing center that holds some Jewish retreats in the summer.

National Havurah Committee, 7318 Germantown Ave., Philadelphia, PA 19119. (215) 248-9760. Holds an annual summer institute and regional retreats.

National Jewish Healing Center, 9 E. 69th St., New York, NY 10021. (212) 969-0030

Neshama, 1049 E. 13th St., Brooklyn, NY 11230. (718) 338-8442. Rabbi Meyer Fund.

Rose Mountain Retreat Center, P.O. Box 355, Las Vegas, NM 87701. (505) 425-5728. Andy Gold and Rabbi Shefa Gold.

Ruach, 230 Davis Ave., Albany, NY 12208. (518) 489-3983. Holds a 3-day renewal weekend each year.

Ruach Ha'Aretz, c/o Marty Potrop, 2519 Derby St., Berkeley, CA 94705. (510) 549-0441. Jewish exploration and renewal in Northern California.

Union of American Hebrew Congregations, Kutz Camp, P.O. Box 443, Bowen Rd., Warwick, NY 10990. (845) 987-6300.

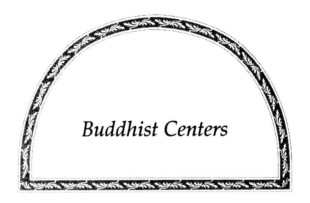

Buddhist Centers

For more complete listings of Buddhist centers, both residential and nonresidential, consult:

Inquiring Mind
A Semi-annual Journal of the Vipassana Community
P.O. Box 9999
N. Berkeley Station
Berkeley, CA 94709

Insight
Insight Meditation Society Newsletter
1230 Pleasant St.
Barre, MA 01005
(978) 355-4378

Shambhala Sun
1585 Barrington St., Ste. 300
Halifax, NS, B3J 1Z8 Canada
(902) 422-8404

Tricycle, The Buddhist Review
92 Vandam St.
New York, NY 10013
(212) 645-1143

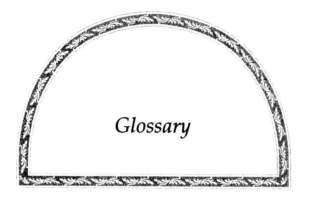

Glossary

Ango (Japanese word meaning "peaceful dwelling") An intensive 90-day training period in the Zen Buddhist tradition.

Ashram A place of simple lifestyle and intense spiritual exercises, generally in the Hindu or Vedanta traditions.

Canonical hours The liturgy of the hours is the official daily prayer cycle of the Catholic Church, an adaptation of the liturgy of the synagogue which has evolved over the centuries. The "hours" consist of Vigils, Lauds, Terce, Sext, None, Vespers, and Compline. "Seven times a day do I praise thee . . ." (Psalm 119:164)

Centering prayer Meditative prayer, using a sacred word to focus attention internally. Father Thomas Keating's book *Open Mind, Open Heart* describes this in detail.

Charismatic retreat Christian healing retreat involving praying in tongues and prophecy.

Cursillo An uplifting weekend retreat for Christian groups to experience their religion from a new perspective.

Dana (Sanskrit word meaning "generosity") Used to describe a donation.

Deacon Someone who has taken holy minor orders—a step on the way to priesthood.

Dharma Used in both Hindu and Buddhist traditions to represent the law, the truth, or spiritual teaching.

Directed retreat Usually a six- to eight-day period of silent prayer which includes a daily meeting with a spiritual director.

Diurnum (Latin, meaning "daily") A short noon office.

Divine office Official, formal, liturgical prayer of the church.

Dojo (Japanese, meaning "hall of the way") Hall or room in which one of the Japanese "ways" are practiced. Used as a synonym for zendo.

Engaged encounter Weekend retreats sponsored by the church for engaged couples (or marriage encounters for married couples) to explore and clarify their belief systems and values.

Enneagram An ancient circular diagram with nine points which can be used to bring insight into the divine activity within each person.

Foundation A branch of the main monastery.

Guided retreat Retreat which includes meeting with a spiritual director from time to time, but not on a daily basis.

Hermitage A secluded residence.

Icon A representation in painting or enamel of a sacred personage.

Kuti Another word for hermitage, or cabin.

Mantra A word or group of words originally in Sanskrit whose repetition is conducive to quieting the mind, often used during meditation.

Oblate A layperson affiliated with a particular order who adopts a modified vow—a way of deepening lay spirituality. Each order confers certain special privileges on oblates; for example, the Carmelites allow their oblates to be buried in the Carmelite habit.

Poustinia (Greek, meaning "silence of God") A designated period or place where a complete retreat, silence, fasting, and separation from normal activities takes place.

Private retreat A time of solitude without guidance or direction.

Refectory Monastery dining hall.

Satsang (Sanskrit) A spiritual gathering.

Sesshin (Japanese) A period of concentrated Zen practice and teaching.

Shambhala *The Sacred Path of the Warrior* by Chögyam Trungpa describes Shambhala practice, which is founded on the gentleness of the Tibetan Buddhist tradition and directly cultivates who and what we are as human beings. A secular rather than a religious outlook for anyone seeking a genuine and fearless existence.

Soto Zen One of two active schools of Zen Buddhism in Japan. Stresses meditation practice as a path to enlightenment. It relies on heart-to-heart transmission to stay alive, since it has no scripture.

Spiritual director A guide or advisor who helps put your spiritual journey into perspective and connects it to your "daily life."

Sufism An eclectic school of mysticism with roots in Islam that has grown to encompass many traditions, and that includes an elaborate symbolism much used by poets. There is scholarly disagreement on the exact origins of the name and practice, some saying it comes from a Persian word meaning "wisdom," others that it comes from the Persian word *sūf* ("wool") because of the coarse robes early Sufi ascetics and renunciates wore.

T'ai chi chuan Chinese "meditation in motion," a series of flowing, gentle movements or exercises intended to quiet the mind and body.

Taizé A small ecumenical monastery in southern France where one of the brothers developed a particular form of chant that has become popular throughout the world.

Vipassana meditation Insight meditation practiced by nuns, monks, and laypeople in Southeast Asia, and used to attain a quality of mindfulness and understanding by looking at mind and body directly. A belief that loving kindness, compassion, and a spirit of generosity can be cultivated consciously.

Yurt A circular tent of felt or skins on a framework of poles used by nomads in Mongolia, which has been adapted as a dwelling, made of various materials, by others.

With thanks to Chimney Sweep Religious Bookstore in Santa Cruz, CA, for their help on many definitions.

Index of Featured Places

About the Authors

Jack and Marcia Kelly are writers who live in New York. Over the years they have chosen monasteries and retreats as stopping places in their travels. Their first book, *Sanctuaries: The Northeast*, was published in 1991. *Sanctuaries: The West Coast and Southwest* followed in 1993. They have also edited *One Hundred Graces*, a collection of mealtime blessings gathered along the way.

Lightning Source UK Ltd.
Milton Keynes UK
UKOW03f1249060514

231182UK00001B/236/P